Race, Religion, and Politics

Toward Human Rights in the United States

Stephanie Y. Mitchem
University of South Carolina

ROWMAN & LITTLEFIELD
Lanham • Boulder • New York • London

Executive Editor: Rolf Janke
Editorial Assistant: Courtney Packard
Marketing Manager: Kim Lyons

Credits and acknowledgments for material borrowed from other sources, and reproduced
with permission, appear on the appropriate page within the text.

Published by Rowman & Littlefield
An imprint of The Rowman & Littlefield Publishing Group, Inc.
4501 Forbes Boulevard, Suite 200, Lanham, Maryland 20706
https://rowman.com

Unit A, Whitacre Mews, 26-34 Stannary Street, London SE11 4AB,
United Kingdom

British Library Cataloguing in Publication Information Available

Library of Congress Cataloging-in-Publication Data Available
ISBN 978-1-5381-0794-2 (cloth : alk. paper)
ISBN 978-1-5381-0795-9 (pbk. : alk. paper)
ISBN 978-1-5381-0796-6 (electronic)

♾ ™ The paper used in this publication meets the minimum requirements of American
National Standard for Information Sciences Permanence of Paper for Printed Library
Materials, ANSI/NISO Z39.48-1992.

Printed in the United States of America

Contents

Acknowledgments

Crossing the sacred terrains of multiple races and ethnicities in the United States is a journey inspired by the times in which we live but informed by many across the country. With gratitude, I thank the many conversation partners who listened to my ideas, challenged my perceptions, and shared their wisdom with me: Andrea Smith, Brett Esaki, Christie Otter, Ernie Otter, Barbra Fitzgerald, Miguel De La Torre, Stephen Criswell, Ifáṣèyí Bamgbàlà, Christopher Judge, Brent Burgin, and Adam Biggs. I also thank the editors, especially Kwok Pui-Lan and Sarah Stanton, for their clear-eyed vision.

Introduction

NAMING THE RACE, POLITICS, AND RELIGION INTERSECTION

The 2016 presidential election, and the months following, exposed the fantasy that the United States is postracial. As a report from the Southern Poverty Law Center stated: "Right-wing populism, driven in part by . . . conspiracy theories and bigoted thinking, . . . has become the answer for many Americans. . . . Populism is the idea . . . that 'pits a virtuous and homogenous people against a set of elites and dangerous "others" who are depicted as depriving the sovereign people' of their prosperity and rights."[1]

The election further verified for me the inability of many churches to promote justice, particularly in the face of popularly held beliefs about "religion." This election cycle confirmed my simmering belief that race, politics, and religion form an intersection, an interwoven, embedded power matrix. That intersection—race, politics, and religion—is the first focus of this book. The second is that of human rights in the United States, and I will return to that shortly.

The election and its ongoing aftermath are instructive and will be analyzed repeatedly over the next years. Identifying and analyzing the nexus of race, politics, and religion expand beyond an early twenty-first-century political season. The rise of white nationalism and all forms of nativism give evidence of this expansion. Whether through quarrels about affirmative action or voting suppression, through acts of domestic terrorism or the persistence of macroaggressions, white racism seems to be infused into our twenty-first-century political system. I will argue that such events are not unconnected but fit in the frame of a larger, social, intersectional construction that supports and maintains oppressions.

As I write, the image that keeps coming to me is kudzu, also known as "the plant that ate the South." Kudzu was brought to the United States in the late nineteenth century from Japan. Despite the good agricultural intentions for its import, the South does not have a severe enough winter to kill off kudzu. So, the plant has spread, becoming an invasive pest that can destroy crops and forests. Like kudzu, concepts of race, imported with and fed by British and European colonizers, invaded the religion and politics of the growing nation's consciousness. The resultant racism has become a home-grown invasion that gets exported to other countries by the United States.

I will occasionally draw examples from contemporary American experiences, but seek a broader perspective throughout this book. Analyzing how the systemic construction of the race-religion-politics intersection works will be complex: the normalizing of oppression is itself a way to obfuscate the issues, to redirect attention, blame victims, and step into plausible deniability.

I view the intertwined practices and concepts of race, politics, and religion as a nexus, creating an intersectional construction. The importance of understanding this as a construction is to be able to name the power it wields in society. How might a religion justify unjust treatment of one group of people? Or does a religious group ignore injustice, pretending it does not exist? How do religions utilize lobbying groups in the United States to define legislative agendas and resultant policies? Does naming its location begin to unravel the interwoven race-politics-religion intersection? Why is race a constant in our communal conflicts?

There are parallel constructions for understanding race, politics, and religion operating as intersectional systems. In the 1970s and 1980s, some American legal scholars who identified as critical race theorists "concerned themselves with the marginality of racial analysis within judicial opinions and legal doctrine."[2] In doing so, the idea of objective, impartial American justice is set aside in order to more fully understand actual operations of legal systems. It could be said that the current Black Lives Matter movement is a continuation of such analysis, brought into a lay or public frame wherein the encounters of black people with the law enforcement side of the legal system are highlighted.

Around the same time period as the development of critical race theory, black women began to bring a new frame of analysis to bear on the ideas of feminism. Not just gender, but also race and social class needed to be understood as operating in American social systems. Angela Y. Davis fine-tuned the discussion with her 1981 text, *Women, Race and Class*. Hers was just one of several books by African American women capturing race with gender with class as constructive, interconnected concepts.[3] Through efforts such as critical race theory and black feminism, intersectionality has become a major analytical frame for feminist studies. Both conceptual frameworks have developed over the years, with new dimensions added to each.

In the twenty-first century, as indicated by the 2016 election cycle, it has become clear that the interweaving among religion, politics, and race is just as powerful a system in the United States as the connections among race, class, and gender. Critical race theory and race-class-gender intersectionality provide models to enter the race, politics, and religion intersection. Both analytical frames shine a light on myriad systemic interconnections that work to privilege those in power in distinctly American ways. Yet, parsing the interconnections to identify where individual components enter may be difficult because the intersections do not work mechanistically. The major work of this book is to point to how and where the race-politics-religion intersection operates and how components fall together. The aim of such exploration here is not just to study, but also to rethink how we in the United States do— or do not—promote human rights.

Mixed in all the intersecting categories of race, politics, and religion is human rights, the second focus of this book. Americans too often congratulate ourselves that we exemplify success in constructing human rights. Yet we are one of the most violent societies in the industrialized world. No, the violence is not the result of predatory black and brown people running through the streets, although these too often become the presumed guilty parties in the minds of the public, the police, and the press. Individual states continue the practice of executions, even when companies no longer sell state governments the drugs to commit the acts, leaving the United States as the last of the industrialized countries to do so. Policing methods, with their state-sponsored violence, alienate community members. In the interests of supporting the Second Amendment of the Constitution of the United States, guns are available to all, including the mentally ill. Fears of black and brown people become rationales for concealed- and open-carry permits in many states. The prison population of the United States is the highest in the world. Private prisons, once on the decline, are increasing again, especially as immigrant detention, particularly of brown people, is more viciously enforced. Refugees fleeing from untenable living situations are met with cold rejection at the U.S. borders. Environmental disasters are ignored in the name of profit. Ferguson, Missouri; Charleston, South Carolina; Flint, Michigan; Charlottesville, VA; the southern borders of the United States; and the island of Puerto Rico, have been scenes of American violence, racial hatred, and environmental tragedy in the first part of the twenty-first century.

Actualizing human rights in the United States is more than addressing each of these instances piecemeal. I am aiming to pinpoint the common threads, often overlooked, not always visible. It is not just racism, not simply poor political action, and not an absence of religious life. It is the combination, the intersection, of the three that plays one off the other, builds back on the previous thing, in order to weave a web of power that benefits few but uses all. Therefore, this book takes a whole systems view. Whole system theories were developed from social work and insist that it is not just the child acting out who is in need of therapy but also the entire family. In other words, don't treat symptoms without understanding causes. Racism, religion, or politics cannot be treated singly and the issue of human rights is indicative of the needs of whole systems. A deeper discussion of the components of the intersection is needed for clarity.

INTERSECTIONAL POWER IN PLACES[4]

Systems

To define locations where, and the means by which, intersectional power functions begins with thinking about systemic constructions. To be clear, *systemic* does not mean *mechanistic*; that is, point A will not automatically trigger point B. Systems lay a grid of power in a society: the normalized customs and embedded beliefs contribute to laws, practices, living conditions, businesses, and governmental or nongovernmental structures. These power lines shift and twist and, sometimes, are not easily seen. As a result, one good person or one corrective law will not take a system apart no more than pulling one kudzu plant from the ground will end its invasion. To achieve restructuring of unjust systems into places that promote human rights requires analysis of the encompassing, interlocking parts.

In South Carolina, many can understand systems when thinking about education in the state. The educational inequities in the "Corridor of Shame" are glaring. This Corridor is composed of mostly black, rural students in locations that cut through the center of the state. When students arrive in college classrooms, the inequities become evident through written papers, classroom comportment, and ability to build networks. In November 2015, the South Carolina Supreme Court ruled in *Abbeville County School District v. State of South Carolina* that the state had failed to meet educational standards for poorer, blacker school districts. Of course, the state now has a committee to study the problems. The committee chair, House legislator Rita Allison, has been clear: "'What this is, is creating a blueprint for what we have to do once we've identified the specific problems,' said Allison, who added that nothing would be gained by simply 'throwing money at the problem.'"[5] Little has been done to eradicate the problem. Both the problems that students encounter and the insufficient legislative responses comprise and undergird a system, and one good teacher, alone, will not make the Corridor any less shameful.

While educational inequities may look like those in South Carolina, the racial and economic segregation of American schools has grown, not lessened, as white parents found ways out of public school and integrated systems. Such decisions have impacts. "Since 2000, judges have released hundreds of school districts, from Mississippi to Virginia, from court-enforced integration. . . . Black children across the South now attend majority-black schools. . . . Nationally, the achievement gap between black and white students, which greatly narrowed during the era in which schools grew more integrated, widened as they became less so."6

Race is clearly a concern here, even as the concept of race is difficult.to pin down in the United States. That leads to an initial discussion of race.

Race

Is race biological or social, nature or nurture? Scientifically, race is insignificant in defining differences among humanity. Socially, however, race has become a predominant way that humans in the United States are subdivided—among themselves, by the census, in communities, in our interactions. Citizens of the United States often believe that they can "read" bodies, looking at a person to determine race, intention, or character. Yet, we are seldom successful at determining a person's race with unambiguous accuracy. A young woman I know refers to herself a Latina in public settings, especially if someone should ask. She is of Middle Eastern origin and she often feels threatened. She expects that no one will ask follow-up questions to find out if she is Christian or American (she is both) but will assume that she is Muslim and of ill intent.

Purported body reading adds one level to blur understanding race. American language about race also distorts understanding because a black-white binary becomes the assumed definitional framework. Discussions of "race" begin and veer into the binary. Some have attempted to use the term "colored" to show they mean more than just black people; yet the term "colored" is inadequate as all raced experiences cannot be reduced to one category and the term can become a pseudonym for "black." Our language for conversations about race is imprecise and often awkward.

Bringing more confusion to these discussions, Americans popularly tend to call all ethnic groups "races." People from Mexico, Mesoamerica (Central America), and South America might consider themselves various ethnic groups—but, here, in the United States, each group can be lumped into a single race. Alexander Weheliye's definitions of raced terms demonstrate the breadth of our usage. He defines performances of "race, racialization, and racial identities" in terms of interconnected "political relations that require, through constant perpetuation via institutions, discourses, practices, desires, infrastructures, languages, technologies, sciences, economies, dreams, and cultural artifacts, the barring of nonwhite subjects from the category of the human."7

The Understanding Race Project of the American Anthropological Association's definition of race, as we know it today, is placed in the context of history and is "a recent idea created by western Europeans following exploration across the world to account for differences among people." The idea of race was sometimes random, and seldom scientific, even with biology as a reference. Their constructions of race were used to "justify colonization, conquest, enslavement, and social hierarchy among humans."[8] In other words, race is socially constructed, and biological markers, such as skin color or eye shape, are "perceived." Here is seen a primary example of politics in action, impacting people's lives for centuries.

Further, the politically determined biological markers are too often culturally interpreted as a sign of something else, so meaning is layered onto bodies, and how someone looks or speaks can result in arrest or unemployment or non-service at a sales counter. The people who are so judged may then seek to change their appearances in order to remove a physical shape that is seen in a negative light. As one author pointed out: "Such beliefs and attitudes, continually propagated and strengthened by the relations of power and economic advantages among the world's people, create an ideal arena for aesthetic surgery, with its promise to help people 'pass' as whoever they wish to be."[9] For those who cannot afford cosmetic surgery, there is an array of products available for do-it-yourself body alterations, including skin lighteners, buttock fillers, perms and colors for hair, padded bras, hair removal or addition, and so on.

The Problem of Culture

Like a bass line pulsing beneath race is culture. Culture can be considered a product of human and community interaction in a given time and place. Culture may refer to class expectations for groups at different economic levels. Culture also becomes part of given religions or races. But culture is immensely more complicated today. We are cyborgs, connected to each other by new relationships born of social media. We are global by travel, relocation, work, or purchases, even as we might attempt to remain tied to a locality. We are more easily able to import or appropriate other cultures' products such as dress or music.

The idea of cultural identity is important for American groups despite the myth of a melting pot that crafts an "American" identity. Groups of people have lost or are losing their own cultures through accommodation to imagined white American cultural frames. Other people are finding their identities through rediscovery of past cultural links. As Ada Maria Isasi-Diaz stated, the necessity of claiming their own culture for Hispanic women:

Survival for us is not only a matter of economics but it is also cultural: "the cultural struggle is a struggle for life." It has to do with questions of self-definition and self-determination. Survival for middle-class Hispanic women is related to the difficult task of living in a culture that is not our own; it comes down repeatedly to choosing between faithfulness to self or, at the risk of losing cultural values and identity, adopting the values and behavior of the dominant culture in order to maintain our status, to survive. [10]

Culture is often woven into discussions of race. Which part of our American expressions are tied to race? Which to culture? When one racially identified group picks up the music, hairstyles, dance steps, speech patterns, and so on of another racial group, who can then claim it? In the adoption or appropriation, is race erased? Culture is porous, especially as social media expands our world. Speaking with people across the globe or the continent is possible. New ways of making connections and building communal links are possible. At this time, we have an incredible access to information about other cultures. We do not need to travel to learn how to cook Moroccan food or celebrate the Chinese New Year. Even learning to speak a language "like a native" is the advertised claim of some companies.

But the line between appreciation and misappropriation of cultures can be easily crossed. At what point does the adoption of the dress, language, or mannerisms of another culture become abusive? Commercializing and profiting from "authentic" music or art from a culture can become a problem, especially when the contexts are removed. Sociologist Cheryl Townsend Gilkes stated:

A critical approach to culture involves identifying the stresses, strains, contradictions, and antagonisms that constrain and motivate the participants, particularly in a situation of inequity and oppression. Such a critical perspective seeks to identify the forces within and without a culture that may, particularly in situations of colonial oppression, deform or assault certain aspects of social organization, such as kinship, economics, religion, and politics, and that may prevent the meeting of basic social and individual needs. [11]

Religions also have cultures. Christianity, for example, is not one group, but comprised of widely divergent cultures. Different dress codes, food consumption, music, food, art may be required even though Christians claim the same sacred texts or traditions. These cultures shape ways of life for their members.

Sometimes other types of cultures result when religion crosses politics, thereby demanding religion or party members' allegiance. Therefore, the American political cultures may be defined in multiple ways, whether through a political party or a focus area such as environmentalism or abortion. Both religious and political cultures may demand that members conform to behavior that negates a race-derived cultural point of view. Culture becomes an important thread in the race-politics-religion webbing.

Racism

Racial and cultural identities influence constructions of racism. Racism is systemic yet it also baffles some Americans because the effects may impact a group but intention is not clear. That the Corridor of Shame's educational shortfalls impact mostly African American students is not surprising because racism today works in seemingly accidental ways: it just happened that way. Further, in popular culture, accusations of *who* is racist fly through social media. Rejection of affirmative action, for some, springs from accusations of racism against white people. (This statement will become clearer in chapter 1.) A definition of racism from the American Anthropological Association provides greater specificity: Racism uses "race to establish and justify a social hierarchy and system of power that privileges, preferences or advances certain individuals or groups of people usually at the expense of others. Racism is perpetuated through both interpersonal and institutional practices."[12]

Racism is a system that, in the United States, revolves around the power and racial constructions of white people. Even when it seems that a town or area is heavily populated by another race, when the broadest sociopolitical structures are taken into account, power can be arrayed against people of color. For instance, in 2017, federal immigration law enforcement was employed heavily against Mexicans illegally in the United States. To be clear, Mexicans are not the only immigrants residing in the United States illegally, but they were targeted as dangerous, taking "American" jobs, or transporting drugs. As reported by CNN, "Across the United States, some unauthorized immigrants are keeping their children home from school. Others have suspended after-school visits to the public library. They have given up coffee shop trips and weekend restaurant dinners with family. Some don't answer knocks on their doors. They're taping bedsheets over windows and staying off social media. Nervous parents and their children constantly exchange text messages and phone calls."[13]

In the United States, racism is a system that can result in a public determination that any white person is authoritative or good. There is a commercial for insurance where a white man has different people in his office to give them investment advice. Each potential client discovers that the trustworthy, authoritative man in business attire before him or her is a cleaned-up disc jockey. The commercial would have ended much differently if the man had been brown and spoken with a heavy Spanish accent: even if he had the credentials to give investment advice, he would not have been viewed as trustworthy. A quote on the Understanding Race website states, "Racism is not about how you look, it is about how people assign meaning to how you look."[14]

For many white Americans, the belief that racism has ended confounds discussions. "Why are you talking about race? Just get over it!" The charge of identity politics is used as a cudgel against any person who brings up race. Any person who expresses dismay or anger over remarks against color or ethnicity are silenced with charges of political correctness. Both are effective ways to end discussions. Neither resolves underlying tensions; ignoring social problems will not make them disappear. Angela Davis asked, "The question is, why there has not been up until now a serious effort to understand the impact of racism on institutions and on individual attitudes?"[15]

As a system, racism operates on a spectrum—from cumulative acts of everyday racism to extreme acts of hatred. Racism may be expressed in awkward statements at a gathering, such as white people not "seeing" color or having one black friend, complicit in rather than innocent of racist acts. Racism may be structured into laws, judicial systems, or police practices. But these ideations that have power over other peoples' lives can also take the shape of white nationalism, disenfranchising the votes of black people, claiming the God-granted rights of whites to rule, or calling for exclusion of all people of color from the United States. People of color experience different degrees of violence when they encounter these hateful attitudes or actions. For such reasons, racism would seem to be the area on which human rights should focus. But the additives of religions and politics makes a simple focus on "end racism!" inadequate. The structuring of racist beliefs becomes embedded into laws and religious institutions, thus returning to the importance of understanding the systemic effects. As parts of American institutional life, racism shows up in churches too.

Religion

Religion is not an antidote to injustice, but adds more layers of complexity to this discussion of race and politics. American institutions include religions. These religions are uniquely positioned institutions because they are able to sanction or challenge political, embedded sociocultural beliefs. Yet this ability to challenge may be hampered by the constructions of institutions and the actors within.

Religion is often placed, consciously or not, in a private sphere, differentiated from a public sphere, rendering it innocuous for social injustice in many Americans' eyes. Churches are believed to be separate from our profane search for daily bread. More information on thinking about and studying religion is needed.

Religion is not always recognized as a social science, especially when theological content is given more weight by the general public. Further, religion is popularly understood as only personal, about *me* and *my* belief. While there are many religions, the particularity of a given religion becomes a self-sustaining boundary that defines *us* from *them*. Yet, a feminist slogan from the 1960s—"the personal is political"—firmly places religion into the public sphere. Throughout this book, I am treating religion more from a social science perspective. Personal belief does not erase the political dimensions that religions enter. The political issues remind us that religions should be understood as lived institutions, not as sacrosanct theories. Religion includes, but is beyond, personal or communal faith; a person can believe many things but never follow through with action. One's faith and faith community may serve as a grounding; then action becomes commitment. The theories of faith are often found in religions' holy books, but authentic beliefs are exposed through practices. Actions and practices are as much areas of research in social science as are belief and scripture.

Since the late twentieth century, contemporary analyses of religions and religious thought have moved into an academic framework. Russell McCutcheon challenged misleading notions of "'religion' . . . construed as an independent variable occupying the untainted realm of pure and private moral insight that is opposed to, and the salvation of, the messy public worlds of politics and economics."[16] McCutcheon is not advocating an end to all religion or a rejection of belief; he instead broadened the scope of research to include "messy" public worlds.

Many of the seventeenth- and eighteenth-century European colonists came to the New World seeking religious freedom. Such a history was embedded in the idea of religion in the developing nation. The question today, rooted in the same developmental process, is this: "freedom for whom and for which religions?" Theory often collides with practice, no matter how well-meaning the intentions. Fear of and inability to recognize the validity of others' religious views have given the United States a poor showing in building religious bridges. To underscore such a broad view, the authors Douglas Jacobsen and Rhonda Hustedt Jacobsen laid out "six sites of engagement" within academic studies of religion as a framework for more fruitful discussions. They identify the two areas of (1) ideas, and (2) practices in three categories: historic, public, and personal religion.[17] We see the realities of such connections each day through multiple political issues in American contexts, from demonization of all Muslims (i.e., not Christian) as terrorists to attempts to declare the entire United States as a Christian theocracy. Ideas and practices of historic, public, and personal religion need greater analyses. Baldly stated by the two authors cited above, "America is one of the most highly religious nations in the world, and perhaps paradoxically, Americans are also, as a whole, remarkably illiterate about religion."[18] Without opportunities to recognize religions as components of the public realm, we continue to act as if each religion is a private enterprise, and we have no need to learn others' religions.

Attempts to change lack of knowledge about religions in the past often fell short despite good will. Some interfaith groups tend to include only Abrahamic faiths of Muslim, Jew, and Christian, often without intra-faith distinctions. Other people argue for tolerance of other religions, but this can quickly slide into relativism. Others look to identify "universal" themes or connections between different religions, but these approaches do not provide realistic dialogues as they ignore differences. This is particularly true when humanists or atheists are part of conversations. Or when difference does show up, often in cultural or racial divides, one side can easily condemn the other as not really "one of us." Ultimately, ignorance about others' religions continues to benefit powerful persons who can pit one group against another and thereby retain power.

Politics

Politics weaves through all these facets of the intersection—race, religion, culture—in complex and systemic ways. Because the public versions of politics are often nasty and brutish, many Americans shy away from any form of it. Yet politics, at its core, is relationships, not simply legislative processes. Anyone who thinks politics is limited to government has not experienced familial politics: who sits where in the funeral car; who will sit by cranky Grandma during dinner; or how to provide diplomatic briefings to the children before *those* relatives show up and proceed to say *those* things.

When politics moves to the public stage, it becomes a means for management of the larger society. In this management, some forms of politics drive religion and race together to protect power. One such form of politics is called *transactional*, focused only on winning the next election. In this structure, politics becomes victimized by its own success in guarding the status quo. For instance, some legislative structures can provide cover for racism, through practices such as gerrymandering or the ongoing "study" of resolving inequities of the Corridor of Shame. Problems occur when results of gerrymandering or a never-ending study strain credulity

Education, as the Corridor of Shame schools demonstrate, is often driven by politics, especially when history is rewritten. While I was teaching one course, three students from three different southern school systems responded with surprise to a discussion about the Ku Klux Klan—"The KKK? We were taught that they were just a gentlemen's club where a few members went bad." In another state, a middle school social studies textbook misstated the reason for wars between white settlers and Native Americans: the Indians did not want to share. Ultimately, whether through the story of misunderstood KKK clubs or misunderstood white settlers, violence is done to students who are given misinformation, and this can be particularly harmful in our American political lives.

For example, there has been a tree planted to the memory of Robert E. Lee on the University of South Carolina Columbia campus near the Visitor Center. The plaque beneath the tree states that it was presented by the Columbia chapter of the United Daughters of the Confederacy in May 1954. The plaque was presented nearly a hundred years after the end of the Civil War but the same year that the Supreme Court decided *Brown v. Board of Education*, which ended state-sanctioned segregation of public schools, such as University of South Carolina. But even misinformation will not last forever. A larger marker was erected in December 2017, not far from the confederacy memento. This new one states that the original university buildings were built in 1801 and "its buildings and historic wall were substantially constructed by slave labor made and built of slave-made brick. . . . The University of South Carolina recognizes the vital contributions made by enslaved people."[19] The old plaque was not removed and the new one will not make systemic problems disappear. But it is a start. Contexts make social meanings tri-dimensional.

Still, the intersection of race, politics, and religion helps build and informs a system of power by maintaining Americans' misunderstandings of the KKK or of Native Americans. The intersection generates its own power as well as ideas that play off each other in order to distract or to offer dysfunction as solutions. So, some people will insist that Americans should just stop talking about race and stop counting different races in education or the census; the implication is that related problems will disappear. Others will charge that discussions of race only cause confusion and divisions among Americans; therefore, a group like Black Lives Matter, some charge, is promoting racism. To that end, an August 2017 FBI report accuses that something called Black Identity Extremism (BIE) and "perceptions of police brutality against African Americans spurred an increase in premeditated, retaliatory lethal violence against law enforcement and will very likely serve as justification for such violence."[20] In other words, those who suffer state-sanctioned violence are not permitted to protest their abuses. I believe that we should approach human rights with a whole-systems approach, as I have stated before. We should begin with the idea that these rights cannot be reduced to legal definitions and arguments. To limit the meaning of "rights" to the strength or weakness of one or another political party is to invalidate any of them. For example, to say that the immigration laws of the United States need reform can be a statement garnering widespread agreement. But to use that argument in a way that denies entrance or to eject all immigrants sets up human rights offenses, violating the dignity of persons. We need the lens of race-politics-religion to assist our analyses of human rights in given contexts.

OVERVIEW OF THE BOOK

Like other intersectional constructions, the flow between components of race, politics, and religion in the United States does not operate in some automatic, step-by-step connection but represents fluid and porous interconnections, one taking the lead over another at any given time. So, the religious may be implied, covered in seemingly ethical content about "them" and prescribing related policies. At other times the religious content may be obvious but racial meanings are masked. Throughout each point, questions of human rights as lived and needed in the United States will be raised.

These concepts—race, politics, and religion—formed into a nexus and continue to function as a fluid system that informs American national consciousness. I will consider the continuing impact of the race-politics-religion system on different groups of people. Thinking through these issues will point to lingering questions and future directions for human rights—especially at local levels. The election cycle of 2016 brought the current state of race, politics, and religion into the forefront, no longer hidden, but splashed across the nation's news and social media. The months following the election have seen shifts and exacerbation but no termination to the strength of the intersection. Exploring the multiple levels of contemporary twenty-first-century situations, with some reference to their historical roots, shapes the flow of this book.

Chapter 1 delves into the history of human rights and connections to religions in the United States. What has happened to the understandings of and actions for human rights in the United States? Why do we feel so distant from the work of the United Nations? These questions begin a longer discussion of human rights as concepts and, most importantly, as political realities. Yet another question needs to be asked: cannot religions resolve any unresolved human rights issues? I explore some of the profound changes in twenty-first-century popular and academic understandings of religion in the United States in conjunction with its seeming intimacy with the idea of human rights.

Chapter 2 begins a series of focused analyses of different American racial/ethnic/religious groups. The white race and related national politics and religious thought establish a bottom line for understanding the race, politics, and religious nexus. Historical roots of white racism did not end with the Emancipation Proclamation, but were endlessly re-created for birthing in new times. The development and promotion of whiteness comprise the original identity politics of America. The current, visible political resurgence of white nationalism is a continuation of very old religious and racial ideologies, dressed in suits and ties instead of sheets. This chapter provides the context for understanding who benefits from the race-politics-religion intersection.

Native Americans, the focus of chapter 3, encountered the first constructions of white racism with results that devastated their populations. In some ways, these encounters became the first practice run by white colonists in Othering a people. There were attempts to enslave the natives, but the efforts were not successful. Yet, domination occurred through systemic colonization under names like "Manifest Destiny," accompanied by the constructions of negative views of "the warrior" or "the squaw." Today one source for political strength is the spirituality of Native peoples. This strength can be viewed in the ongoing crisis with construction of a North Dakota pipeline through Native lands.

Chapter 4 turns to black Americans and encounters with white political power. Groups of people from different lands were renamed "slave, nigra, colored" and so on. Science was used to construct a sharply distinctive Otherness: from white arguments about the humanity of black people; to eugenicist plans to sterilize black people; to claims of the intellectual inferiority of black people. A colonialist attitude was bred into the faith-talk of white colonizers: we're doing them a favor and will humanize them. White theology was used to construct black people as necessarily depraved and godless. These historic views linger and are given some weight today by white racists as well as by black people caught in self-hatred. The thoroughness by which black Americans were Othered in the white imagination, in American political life, and across social practice became a model that was replicated. Meanwhile, some black people used religious thought to analyze and discredit racial and political oppression even while they called for America to live into its promises of life, liberty, and justice. The contemporary work of the black evangelical Repairers of the Breach in North Carolina provides an excellent example of working to undo the race-politics-religion intersection by reclaiming religion.

Other groupings that get caught in the intersection are raced in the white imagination according to the boilerplate developed to craft the category of black people. In chapter 5, many ethnicities of Spanish- or Portuguese-speaking peoples are dropped into a group called "Hispanic." This grouping has not been not considered a race in census designations, but designated as ethnicities. However, with the generally slippery language of "minorities" and the current raft of politicians' nativist calls for building walls and rejecting refugees, "Hispanic" has become a race in the popular imagination: brown people. White nativists have misnamed immigrants and refugees as threats: rapists, murderers, drug couriers, or gang members. Puerto Ricans, who are already American citizens; Cubans with sets of complicated relationships with and within the United States; and French-speaking Haitians are among the peoples who have suffered the continued American colonialist attitude of "doing them a favor." The underlying fear is that the growing numbers of brown people will lessen the white majority and its political power. There is another dimension in migrant work as some Christian churches have programs and statements, setting themselves as sanctuaries for refugees, providing food, education, worship, and other services in the language of the people. As a result, some churches have become targets of the nativists' wrath, another way the race-politics-religion intersectionality operates. These churches are sometimes demonstrating a non-colonialist view, because they are doing the one thing that has not happened through too much of the relationship between white people of faith and all those who have been Othered. They are speaking *with* them and building communities, rather than making determinations *for* them and lecturing.

Chapter 6 turns to Eastern groupings, often called Asian, who have been considered a race on the census. From 1870, the census groupings at one time or another over the centuries, included Chinese, Japanese, Filipino, Korean, Asian Indian, Vietnamese, other Asian Pacific Islanders, and brief appearances from the categories of "part Hawaiian" and "Hindu." The term Orientalism has been used to define the construction of groups of people from the East into exoticized Others.[21] Today, we generally hear all these groups called "Asian," a designation that ignores intragroup distinctions, perhaps a subtler form of Orientalism. That crafting is often achieved with a sly congratulatory note, by considering Asians in the United States as model minorities, which opens a host of problems. One question to explore is if the religious diversity of those called Asian aids in maintenance of their own cultural or ethnic identities, even as traditional Chinese, Japanese, and Indian religious beliefs are co-opted into American New Age beliefs.

Chapter 7 takes a different route to understanding the race-politics-religion intersection by considering members of a religion—Islam—who have been raced in the early twenty-first century in the United States. The processes of racializing members of the Muslim religion have been intense since the tragic attacks on the United States, September 11, 2001. I overheard one Muslim scholar's comment: "We are the new colored people." As I reflected on her words, I realized that the same processes are being used that crafted different African, Native, Asian, or Hispanic people into single entities. The sociopolitical treatment of Muslim communities constructs new Others that sharply belies the religious-freedom roots of the United States. Terrorist activities, including internationally, drive the process of racializing Muslims in the American imagination into a single stereotyped group; the parameters of this colorizing are defined by fear. The cultural, national, and religious diversity of those who profess Islam is lost in this construction. But white nationalists have found that mosques make clear targets for their fears.

Chapter 8 returns to the intersection of race, religion, and politics to begin discussion of what is missing from human rights and from religion to adequately address the power grid laying over people in the United States. Identifying American values provides one path toward human rights from below. Those values challenge the pain of community destruction and point toward future possibilities.

The conclusion offers another consideration of human rights from below: looking toward a future where humans are valued in the United States.

RECOGNIZING OUR SHARED HUMANITY

The chapters expose sets of relationships in the United States and point toward problems while hinting at improvements. This book is about Americans, broadly understood in a global context. Aspects of a given group's experiences are disclosed in order to arrive at a fuller discussion of human rights. Human rights in the United States are not about legislative processes, although they could involve such. Human rights are not the contortions of lawyers, although they could involve such. Human rights are about the realized humanity of each other, demanding that we work at the tasks of understanding.

I attended a symposium on diverse spiritualties at the University of Pittsburgh. One of the presenters was Rudolph T. Ware, whose research focuses on stating some of the unique dimensions of African Islam and their relations to the American black and Muslim communities.[22] He threw out a challenge at the end of the talk that has quite resonated with me: the concepts of epistemology, ontology, and cosmology are western European terms from philosophy. Ware's challenge is to rethink our use of other academic terms: how we know what we know, how we are in the world, and how we understand the universe. We are too often bound up by Western philosophical terms. Left out of epistemology, cosmology, and ontology are the historical and contemporary intellectual works of scholars of color who operate in non-European frames. Of note are compassion (heart) and intuition or instinct (gut), prevalent in the organic genius of people of color. In this, his challenge is in line with another groundbreaking thinker, Dr. Charles H. Long, who challenged the meanings of the word "religion."[23]

The advantage of writing this book at this moment in time points toward an understanding of human rights in the United States. Even as I highlight some issues of multiple cultural/ethnic/racial groupings, these alone will not answer or resolve the diverse needs. To be clear, this book will not exhaust the stories of each people nor raise all issues across the country. Instead, these broader intellectual perspectives become springboards for the conversations I hope to engender. These can become beginning points to aim toward solutions.

While there are multiple questions I will raise throughout this study, I will return repeatedly, in some form, to these: How can we recognize our shared humanity? How do we honor our rights as humans? Can we agree to be human together?

NOTES

1. Mark Potok, "The Year in Hate and Extremism," The Southern Poverty Law Center, February 15, 2017, https://www.splcenter.org/fighting-hate/intelligence-report/2017/year-hate-and-extremism.

2. As Lani Guinier and Gerald Torres point out, these legal scholars worked to develop this idea in the 1970s, following the Civil Rights Movement. "They experienced a growing sense that the structure of conventional doctrinal analysis could not come to grips with the continuing problems of deeply embedded racism." Lani Guinier and Gerald Torres, *The Miner's Canary: Enlisting Race, Resisting Power, Transforming Democracy* (Cambridge, MA: Harvard University Press 2002), 34.

3. Angela Y. Davis, *Women, Race and Class* (New York: Random House, Vintage Books edition, 1983); Gloria Hull and Barbara Smith, eds., *But Some of Us Are Brave: All the Women Are White, All the Blacks Are Men* (New York: Feminist Press, 1982); Audre Lorde, *Sister Outsider* (New York: Crossing Press, 1984)

4. I am indebted to George Lipsitz, *How Racism Takes Place* (Philadelphia: Temple University Press, 2011) and his focus on locating racism in places throughout the United States with the different faces it takes. While my focus is broader, Lipsitz's insight is important for my own considerations of embodied oppressions and material power grids that lead to a call for human rights that is also localized.

5. Bill Davis, "Crafting a Blueprint for Better Schools," *Statehouse Report*, August 7, 2015, http://www.statehousereport.com/2015/08/07/news-crafting-a-blueprint-for-better-schools/.

6. Nikole Hannah Jones, "Segregation Now," *The Atlantic*, May 2014, https://www.theatlantic.com/magazine/archive/2014/05/segregation-now/359813/.

7. Alexander G. Weheliye, *Habeas Viscus: Racializing Assemblages, Biopolitics, and Black Feminist Theories of the Human* (Durham, NC: Duke University Press, 2014), 3.

8. "Resources: Glossary," American Anthropological Association, http://www.understandingrace.org/resources/glossary.html.

9. Sander L. Gilman, "The Racial Nose," in *The Body Reader, Essential Social and Cultural Readings*, eds. Lisa Jean Moore and Mary Kosut (New York: NYU Press 2010), 220.

10. Ada Maria Isasi-Diaz, *En La Lucha / In the Struggle: A Hispanic Women's Liberation Theology* (Minneapolis: Fortress Press, 1993), 27–28.

11. Cheryl Townsend Gilkes, "A Conscious Connection to All That Is: *The Color Purple* as Subversive and Critical Ethnography," in *Personal Knowledge and Beyond, Reshaping the Ethnography of Religion*, eds. James V. Spickard, J. Shawn Landres, and Meredith B. McGuire (New York: NYU Press 2002), 176.

12. "Race: Are We So Different?," American Anthropological Association, http://www.understandingrace.org.

13. Ray Sanchez, "After ICE Arrests, Fear Spreads among Undocumented Immigrants," CNN, February 2017, http://www.cnn.com/2017/02/11/politics/immigration-roundups-community-fear/.

14. "Race: Are We So Different?"

15. Angela Y. Davis, *Freedom Is a Constant Struggle: Ferguson, Palestine, and the Foundations of a Movement* (Chicago: Haymarket Books, 2016), 34.

16. Russell T. McCutcheon, *Critics not Caretakers: Redescribing the Public Study of Religion* (Albany: SUNY Press, 2001), 131–32.

17. Douglas Jacobsen and Rhonda Hustedt Jacobsen, *No Longer Invisible: Religion in University Education* (New York: Oxford University Press, 2012), 56.

18. Jacobsen and Hustedt Jacobsen, *No Longer Invisible*, 59.

19. "History Unveiled," University of South Carolina website, November 30, 2017 and updated December 5, 2017, http://www.sc.edu/uofsc/posts/2017/12/history_unveiled.php#.WuswW8gh29Q.

20. Jana Winter and Sharon Weinberger, "The FBI's New U.S. Terrorist Threat: 'Black Identity Extremists,'" *Foreign Policy*, October 6, 2017, http://foreignpolicy.com/2017/10/06/the-fbi-has-identified-a-new-domestic-terrorist-threat-and-its-black-identity-extremists/.

21. Edward Said, *Orientalism* (New York: Vintage Books, 1978).

22. Rudolph T. Ware III, *The Walking Qur'an* (Chapel Hill: University of North Carolina Press 2014).

23. Charles H. Long, *Significations: Signs, Symbols, and Images in the Interpretation of Religion* (Milwaukee: Fortress Press, 1995).

Chapter One

Human Rights and Religions in the United States

Some years ago, in Detroit, Michigan, I was invited to a talk by the great actor, civil rights activist, and playwright Ossie Davis. One of the points that he stressed was that they, of the Civil Rights Movement, were wrong: the real fight was not for *civil* rights, but for *human* rights. Mr. Davis emphasized that Dr. Martin Luther King, near the end of his life, also had reached that conclusion and was beginning to focus his work differently with a focus on the poor. (I will explore this in greater detail in chapter 8.) Mr. Davis stressed that the critical and basic distinction between human and civil rights is that the humanity of black Americans is still unrecognized by some in our society and still questioned. That talk, that moment of listening to one of the icons of the Civil Rights Movement speak frankly about a shortfall of the movement, impacted my understandings of human rights as I consciously applied the concept to U.S. contexts.

In the United States, we tend to collapse civil rights into the same category as human rights. *Civil* rights are legally established rights that protect citizens against legally defined inequalities: the right to vote, to fair housing and education, to nondiscrimination based on categories such as race, ability, age, and sex. These rights shift according to legal definitions. *Human* rights include civil rights but are broader, beyond law but inherent in the dignity of each person. The U.S. Declaration of Independence identifies three such rights when it defines life, liberty, and the pursuit of happiness as inalienable for all human beings. From the Declaration's issuance in 1776, these words have held a statement of human rights, potent to people around the world as well as at home. These words have tantalized all those who have been left out of American social structures and national decision-making: they were not considered human enough to have inalienable rights. Human rights imply recognition of shared humanity.

In United States "human rights" are often deemed only pertinent to people of other nations, not "us." Americans too often see ourselves as exemplars of human rights, when that is a misrepresentation of our nation's realities or when we mean civil (legally defined and granted) rights. A closer look at the history of human rights through the United Nations will shed some light on contemporary predicaments in the United States and how this is connected to the intersection of race, politics, and religion.

HUMAN RIGHTS AND THE UNITED NATIONS: U.S. PROBLEM AND OPPORTUNITY

World War II added new dimensions to the global comprehension of the need for diplomacy and communication among nations. The horrors of the Nazi death camps were flung across the pages of newspapers and seared the consciences of nations. New weaponry, especially the atomic bomb, created new horrors and fears. Biological and chemical weapons were used and the stories told on radio, expanding our consciousness to the myriad of evils inflicted among humans. Bombings of civilian areas became too common, no longer an exception. Eastern and Western Europe were remade. China and Japan would need decades to recover the ravages of the war. War had always been ugly and mean, but World War II particularly led people across the globe to desire an ending to all wars.

The idea of the United Nations was not just hatched after this war but had a history of other attempts at international diplomacy. For instance, after World War I the League of Nations tried to establish such lines of communication; World War II proved that international group inadequate to achieve peace.

Discussions about the formation of the United Nations actually began in 1942 before the Second World War ended in September 1945. The United Nations Charter was signed in October 1945.[1] One important difference between the League and the United Nations was written and presented to that body three years later: The Universal Declaration of Human Rights. (See Appendix A.)

The thirty articles of the Declaration were intended as "a common standard of achievement for all peoples and all nations." Article 1 sets a tone and direction for the document: "All human beings are born free and equal in dignity and rights. They are endowed with reason and conscience and should act towards one another in a spirit of brotherhood." Rights are defined: life; freedom of movement; of expression and thought; to receive an education; to seek asylum; health and well-being; rest and leisure; a nationality and participation in the life of a country. This Declaration is the basis of international human rights law because of subsequent treaties that defined legal components. With these treaties, political problems for the United States are exposed.

The Covenant on Civil and Political Rights was a treaty drafted at the United Nations in 1958 and adopted by the General Assembly in 1966. The Universal Declaration of Human Rights was the foundation, stated in general terms; but the Covenant specified meanings and expected actions. So, the Declarations states, "No one shall be subjected to arbitrary arrest, detention or exile" (Article 9); "Everyone is entitled in full equality to a fair and public hearing by an independent and impartial tribunal" (Article 10); and "Everyone charged with a penal offence has the right to be presumed innocent until proved guilty according to law in a public trial" (Article 11).

The Covenant on Civil and Political Rights went much further, defining rights in judicial matters, spelling out minimum guarantees in the event of criminal charges. Technically, some of these guarantees are already in some form in U.S. court systems. However, it could be argued that some items— such as the right to an interpreter, to be "tried without undue delay," and promoting rehabilitation of charged juveniles[2]—have been weakly developed in this country. The Covenant also includes a section on the death penalty, to "be imposed only for the most serious crimes." Further, "Anyone sentenced to death shall have the right to seek pardon or commutation of the sentence. . . . Sentence of death shall not be imposed for crimes committed by persons below eighteen years of age and shall not be carried out on pregnant women."[3] Clearly, some of the states in this country continue the practice of imposing the death penalty—sometimes on juveniles, sometimes on flimsy evidence, impacting people of color and the poor the most.

The Covenant was established within the structure of the United Nations in 1976. More treaties and structures developed that defined U.N. human rights law. But in the United States, the Covenant on Civil and Political Rights was not ratified until 1992 by the Senate and then with five "reservations, understandings, and declarations."[4] The five reservations addressed areas of disagreement, including that "the United States reserves the right, subject to its Constitutional constraints, to impose capital punishment on any person (other than a pregnant woman) duly convicted under existing or future laws permitting the imposition of capital punishment, including such punishment for crimes committed by persons below eighteen years of age." The five understandings include that "subparagraphs 3(b) and (d) of Article 14 do not require the provision of a criminal defendant's counsel of choice when the defendant is provided with court-appointed counsel on grounds of indigence, when the defendant is financially able to retain alternative counsel, or when imprisonment is not imposed." The four declarations include this blanket statement: "That the United States declares that the provisions of Articles

1 through 27 of the Covenant are not self-executing."[5] Simply put, the reservations, understandings, and declarations on this and other treaties severely limit the impact of U.N. human rights law within the United States.

Yet the strongest argument presented against the United Nations' human rights laws is the United States Constitution. By U.S. law, particularly the Constitution, Americans have protections and rights that people in other nations may not have. It was on the strength of the Constitution in a sovereign nation, that the Senate, in its advise and consent role, could place limits on U.S. involvement in U.N.-led human rights law. But there was no parallel discussion of human rights in the United States, and so we too easily absolve ourselves. After all, *we* are not like *the people in that country*, or, as a colleague stated—we consider comparative atrocities and sigh with relief that we are so much better off.

There is one aspect of the U.S. Senate's argument to limit involvement in treaties that should be considered as relevant and that is the term "universal" to describe the charter's view of human rights. Much of contemporary scholarship has moved away from trying to determine what the universal idea might be that applies to all human beings in all places at all times. "All human beings have bodily functions between birth and death" might be the only universal that can be confidently stated. The rest of the things that happen over the course of lives depend on regions, cultures, incomes, educations, social structures, religions—in short, who and where our communities and we, collectively and individually, are. Therefore, defining and accepting "universal" human rights may always present a problem. There is another way to think about the difficulty and the solution that has immediate significance for this book. The Senate was clear that the "universals" did not fit our specific situations. Other countries resist the application of "universal human rights" to their situations as well. The United States is powerful enough to simply state, "We aren't doing that." Then perhaps this country is also strong enough to be the ones to think of ways to establish "human rights from below" to realistically fit multiple situations.

HUMAN RIGHTS FROM BELOW

"From below" is a term borrowed from the discipline of history. For many decades, history was developed with the "Great Man" perspective and the stories of a given era were told based on one significant person who was usually the male leader of the time. The American Revolutionary War became the story of George Washington or Benjamin Franklin. The story of the Civil War was often that of Abraham Lincoln or Robert E. Lee. By the middle of the twentieth century, historical scholarship shifted to the perspective of history from below, the story of a given time told in the voices of those who were not the great leaders. This shift in perspective has been very significant for women and people of color, who were often those who were invisible within those historical narratives. Contemporary historical scholarship has been enriched by the incorporation of these excluded people. The use of letters, journals, folktales, gravesites, art, clothing, music, and even recipe books gives more complete pictures of American history.

The development of concepts "from below" enters an argument that scholars have had about the challenge of different cultures and the maintenance of macro-level, or attempted, definitions of universal, human rights. Those scholars or nations who challenge universal human rights are often termed cultural relativists, defined "in general as [those who are] inclined to endorse the idea that all values and principles are culture-bound and that there are no universal standards that apply across cultural divides."[6] Cultural differences become significant departure points for universal human rights. The initial idea of "a common standard of achievement for all people and all nations" was developed by a very limited group with broad ideas based on their own era and cultures. The nations who were foundational in writing the document add another dimension to understanding.

The Universal Declaration of Human Rights was signed in 1948. Since that time, the continents of Africa and Asia have witnessed the development of innumerable new nations, particularly as colonizing nations withdrew and new sovereignty was granted. The Soviet Union was broken from a single Communist bloc and changed the face of Eastern Europe into multinations. Both China and India have gained strength, while the Middle East has been riven with continuous wars. The nations of South America and Central America have suffered wars and redefinition several times over. The ongoing global realities have only gotten more complicated since World War II. At the time of the writing of the Declaration, there were clear leaders with the clearly defined elite members of society. Today, people around the globe are seeking to define themselves and redefine their nations even as they are plugged into multiple media, both receiving and disseminating information.

The United States is not immune and has seen massive social changes since 1948. Family structures have changed; educational levels have risen; and more citizens live in cities with fewer involved in agriculture. The racial changes—in diversity, demographics, and abilities to impact the country—are profound as well. As reported in a study by the Economic Policy Institute, "People of color will become a majority of the American working class in 2032. This estimate, based on long-term labor force projections from the Bureau of Labor Statistics and trends in college completion by race and ethnicity, is 11 years sooner than the Census Bureau projection for the overall U.S. population, which becomes 'majority-minority' in 2043."[7]

The global and, for this book, national shifts mean that the people who wrote the Universal Declaration of Human Rights may speak less for current populations, even as we in the twenty-first century realize significant ideal-izations beyond that Declaration that lift our consciousness in new ways. But achieving such ideals is difficult. One recent example in the United States has brought new questions. For instance: Is health care a human right? If so, should the state be responsible for health care? The only relevant statement of the Declaration is Article 25: "Everyone has the right to a standard of living adequate for the health and well-being of himself and his family, including food, clothing, housing and medical care and necessary social ser-vices." The arguments about health care in the United States are beyond this article of the Declaration. But the issue remains, reflecting current political and religious values: What is justice on the issue of health care for the United States? Should we desire national health coverage, is it fair? Can we afford it? Should able-bodied, but nonworking people be covered? What procedures or medications should be covered? Which excluded? Whose life is valued?

These national questions defining one sociopolitical problem also demon-strate that universals need not be pitted against local human rights, for the general idea housed in the United Nations' Human Rights Declaration can still hold some relevance when local considerations are made. However, a more foundational problem to understand human rights within the United States is the very route by which human rights flow into the United States' legal systems.

PROBLEMS WITH CIVIL RIGHTS

I began this chapter with a story about civil rights activist Ossie Davis, who asserted that civil rights had not addressed the issue of human rights in the United States. But it has been through civil rights legislation that the enforce-ment of "human rights" has been claimed in this country. The civil rights bill of 1957 was the first since that of the Reconstruction era[8] and was focused on establishment of voting rights for black Americans.

Public Law 88-352 (78 Stat. 241) is commonly known as the 1964 Civil Rights Act that prohibited discrimination in employment based on race or sex. The Equal Employment Opportunity Office (EEOC) became the place where complaints of discrimination were filed. Each state established civil rights offices as well, some of which are called human rights offices.[9] On the federal and state level, in 2016,

> EEOC secured more than $482 million for victims of discrimination in private, state and local government, and federal workplaces. This included:
>
> - $347.9 million for victims of employment discrimination in private sector and state and local government workplaces through mediation, conciliation, and settlements;

- $52.2 million for workers harmed by discriminatory practices obtained through litigation; and
- $82 million for federal employees and applicants.

This included 273 resolutions of systemic investigations and 21 resolutions of systemic lawsuits totaling more than $58.3 million in remedies for workers harmed by discriminatory practices and policies. [10]

But discrimination happens beyond voting and employment. The Civil Rights Act of 1968 focused on elimination of housing discrimination. The Fair Housing Office is also under the U.S. Civil Rights Office and states its basic policy simply: "It is the policy of the United States to provide, within constitutional limitations, for fair housing throughout the United States." [11]

Arguments for the legal protections of different persons in the United States have expanded discussions of rights for persons of color, different religions, sexual orientation, and so on. But, as Ossie Davis asserted, we still are missing a sharp focus on human rights. Perhaps it is time to think of "human rights from below," instead of "universals" developed from the minds of national leaders. It will be messier, while not always reaching clearly stated conclusions that could be applied in all places and at all times. Locally developed human rights are still human rights and invest communities in their outcomes. To state this more explicitly, human rights should not be simple theories, but should be embodied and applied.

Firmly embedded in our American consciousness is Otherness, that is, creation of categories of people who are considered outsiders: black, brown, immigrant, not Christian, the list goes on. In the United States, race and religion are primary drivers of Otherness. Many of the ideas about the Other are embedded into American consciousness through popular representations; derived from different academic areas and acted out, consciously or unconsciously, in daily interactions. In the United States, a distinction could be made between the anthropological "Other" and the sociological "Other." "Anthropological 'Others' have traditionally lived in far off places and been seen either as restless natives or as exotic relics that need preserving. So we control them or protect them, keeping them at arm's length, because they are not 'Us.'" [12] What happens when that exotic native immigrates to the United States? The people from Korea or Mexico may still experience being the anthropologically created Other, especially when being told to "go home."

But there are also those who live next door or down the street in designated "ghettoes." The aim of such designation is to claim that they are not "like us." These are sociological Others. "We get to know them in order to change them—to make them copies of ourselves . . . a little wealth and education; a better accent; a few more middle-class values, perhaps a little soap behind the ears . . . [giving us] a choice between social uplift and intellectual zoology—not conscious, mind you, but lying just beneath the surface. Both are colonial relics."[13]

Othering, ultimately, defames and denies the very humanity of the persons being judged as "not us." Othering happens through religious ideas as well as political ideologies; both are central to construction of the race-religion-politics intersection. Getting past and resolving ideas of us/them become important ways to begin to act for human rights from below.

One important ideology must be added to the discussion of human rights in America today: neoliberalism. During the time discussions of human rights began during World War II, there were alternate discussions that birthed the germ of the idea of neoliberalism. Bluntly stated by one author, "Neoliberalism sees competition as the defining characteristic of human relations. It redefines citizens as consumers, whose democratic choices are best exercised by buying and selling, a process that rewards merit and punishes inefficiency. It maintains that 'the market' delivers benefits that could never be achieved by planning."[14] While the seeds of neoliberalism began in the 1930s, it was not until the 1970s that they began to flower in the United States within political circles.

This concept has a decided impact on any discussion of human rights in the United States. Scholar and educator Henry Giroux analyzes the impact of neoliberalism on American democracy. "Neoliberalism . . . considers any claims made for equality, justice, and democracy quaint, if not dangerous. It seeks to trivialize all things public, to eviscerate public life, and to destroy any notions of the common good. . . . [C]ontemporary neoliberalism represents a confluence, a historical conjuncture, in which the most vicious elements of capitalism have come together to create something new and more punishing."[15]

Pushback against liberatory activities is to be expected. A platitude states, "Privilege sees liberation as oppression" and this idea will be given greater attention in the next chapter. For this discussion, perhaps it is not a coincidence that neoliberalism became a path in the United States about a decade after the passage of the 1964 Civil Rights Act. Neoliberalism serves to cement the intersectionality of race, politics, and religion together. Racial difference is deemed inconsequential in neoliberal eyes, unless it can be turned to profit. For example, on the one hand, products are aimed at black consumers, from shoes to cars to foods. On the other hand, because racial rights are deemed inconsequential, large corporations or governmental agencies easily trample them. Product safety, environmental justice, and contractual integrity are considered externalities or collateral damages in the drive for profits, as one of my conversation partners, artist and counselor Barbra Fitzgerald, explains: if people of color cannot be used as consumers, then people of color become externalities.[16]

In these ways, neoliberalism, with an ideology of the primacy of the free market and radical individualism, serves several political purposes. First it knocks back any protests of oppressed groups as un-American, damaging to commerce, eviscerating, as Giroux states, any notion of the common good. Second, neoliberalism serves to further American tribalism and divisiveness that demands, "Whose side are you on?" Third, neoliberalism stresses individualism combined with personal choice, above all. Each of these combines to craft a social ethics of allegiance to self and the tribe-of-choice. Of a certainty, all Americans have not adopted a neoliberal ideology. Yet there is one place where even those who seek an ethical life turn: the study and practice of religion, which could be central to action for human rights. Thus, might religions end social divisiveness? But this idea is merely theory as, too often, religions end up complicit in the race and politics intersection.

RELIGIONS IN THE UNITED STATES: FEEDING (OR STARVING) THE INTERSECTION

Religions are often considered private matters: "my" belief, church, pastor, or congregation. This is normal because the process of converting to a specific religion is sometimes defined as "dying" to an old way of life and being born anew. Believers commit to a religion that encompasses a way of life, perhaps changing one's dress, foods, ritual, worship, or language. There are varieties of religions in America and a myriad of ways that a person can make wholehearted or lukewarm commitment. Yet, when we think critically of religion, finding objectivity becomes difficult because of "my" belief commitments.

Most religions enshrine a statement of the goodness of human beings at the core of their beliefs. However, if religions only define the rights of humans as those within their religions' boundaries, greater divides are established, firmly grounding religious intolerance into the intersection. But it is more complicated than that because religious life and religions have significantly shifted along with other institutions of the United States in the past decades. To explore the complicated changes in religions in the United States, a closer look at current trends is needed, beginning with patterns of religious belonging and belief.

The Pew Research Center provides statistical snapshots of the United States including American religious life. Their analysis of religion in America indicates that there has been a small drop (6 percent) in the number of religiously affiliated people: mainline Protestant and Catholic membership went down. At the same time, the number of the religiously unaffiliated or the "nones" has grown by about 9 percent. Overall, younger Americans are less religious, less likely to attend services or pray daily than older

Americans.[17] "While nationwide surveys in the 1970s and '80s found that fewer than one-in-ten U.S. adults said they had no religious affiliation, fully 23% now describe themselves as atheists, agnostics or 'nothing in particular.'"[18]

The above data indicate several practical realities, underlining the missing qualitative aspects of the information. Other data begin to fill in missing pieces. If membership has lessened and attendance is sporadic, the ability of congregations to support buildings and staff members is lessened. In the United States and Canada, 270 seminaries and theological schools prepare ministers for service to many Catholic and Protestant mainstream congregations. If younger people are more likely to embrace the unaffiliated category, then ministry to those congregations must change. The 2015 Annual Report of the Association of Theological Schools (ATS) presents a clear picture of the changes:

> Mainline Protestants are now in the minority among North American Christians. The US Roman Catholic Church will become majority Hispanic and Asian before 2030, and while the number of Catholics continues to increase, the number of weekly mass attenders lags. Thirty years ago, a significant majority of all students in ATS member schools comprised white males who were pursuing one of a limited number of degrees on main seminary campuses in weekday classes. For the most part, graduates pursued predictable forms of congregational ministry. The majority of students were enrolled in mainline Protestant schools. Schools were not financially flush, but most had revenue in excess of expenses, and students had negligible amounts of educational debt. Changes were in the air and around the edges of this settled time, but they seemed distant. Today we face a different reality. The edges have overtaken the center, and from a relatively settled cul-de-sac in higher education, theological schools find themselves in a new educational world.[19]

Two other facts from this annual report stand out. First, the majority of seminarians leave school with student debt; second, half of the member ATS schools have expenses that exceed their income. A given school with its own debt burden may offer fewer scholarships and fewer classes with teachers distracted by their low pay. Therefore, it is possible that students without wealthy families often take on the burden of their own debt unless they attend one of the wealthier schools where more scholarship money is available. Ministry becomes a much less attractive career choice for a young person with a bachelor's degree and, perhaps, debt from that first degree. (Prosperity churches are exceptions, but I will turn to these later in the chapter.)

To say that there have been significant changes in American religious life in the last thirty years is an understatement. Religions, including but not limited to Christianity, like all social institutions, have changed in the United

States. Some of those changes among diverse religions will be seen in chapters that follow. Yet, the greater social landscape must be noted here as more mobile populations move across the country more often and family ties to each other and to the land are more difficult to retain. Americans are more urban-based and often working in jobs that pay less. While the internet and social media provide access to unimaginable amounts of information, the use of cell phones keep us endlessly plugged in, even during a church service. Any religion may be identified as important, but it competes for our time and attention.

Overall, this abbreviated portrait of established religions points to the impact of the social shifts. For centuries, ministers had respect with power and authority wherever they went. In the United States, as people become less religious, that respect can no longer be expected. Some years ago, a minister went into a local police station to raise a concern for his congregation's safety. He went into the police station in professional clerical garb. Afterward, the minister was practically in tears: "The police didn't care! They didn't *respect* me!" Individual ministers may occasionally experience disrespect despite or because of their office. Seeming lack of respect by other authority figures, lack of money, shifting ministerial roles and populations—none of these can fully terminate the importance of religions in the United States.

The First Amendment of the Constitution states that no religion is to be established as the state religion. This is the basis of the concept of freedom of religion, referred to as the establishment clause. At the same time, this clause does not prohibit religions from working to further their group's goals through legislation. Many mainstream religions have lobbying groups working on their behalf to insert "my" religious beliefs into legislative form. Arguments about laws or court cases may take on hidden texts of religious views; the caveat is that religious views around any subject can only be turned into laws if they do not privilege or discriminate against one religion.

The Pew Research Center also tracked the belief patterns of U.S. legislators and in 2017 found, "The share of U.S. adults who describe themselves as Christians has been declining for decades, but the U.S. Congress is about as Christian today as it was in the early 1960s, according to a new analysis by Pew Research Center. Indeed, among members of the new, 115th Congress, 91% describe themselves as Christians."[20] The preponderance of those who share beliefs in political positions may give one or another religion friendly ears to listen to suggestions.

These data—about American belief patterns, seminary survival, ministry as a career, congregational makeup—underline a core fact: Religion is a social institution. Individual religions are not and have not been separate from the rhythms of daily life. Even if a particular religion takes a theological nonparticipation stance on some issue, there are still webs of laws and commercial interests tying their members in. These are ways to understand religion as a social institution, woven into the web of American life. As a social institution, religion can be studied in different ways.

The explorations of religion at colleges and universities also may take a different tack than that which is found in a seminary where studies are dedicated to a given faith tradition. Even seminaries offering multi-faith studies still center on their own faith, especially in their role to prepare ministers for a given tradition. But at a public university, the questions will and have ranged far outside the seminary classroom, crossing multiple disciplines. As a prominent scholar of religion stated,

> Precisely because some of our colleagues presume religion, or more properly, religious experience, to be a universal human impulse of fundamental, deep, real, and therefore self-evident value, they lack the ability to see that their comments on, for example, Chinese religions or the religion of Islam are already highly abstract redescriptions of indigenous social systems and categories. . . . [W]e must confront the fact that the category "religion" has no explanatory value whatsoever.[21]

This language may cause people who are dedicated members of any given faith to cry out against such thought as "godless." Yet the line of thinking is not to end religion but to recognize the diversity of human experience and how we might study it. If the approach to people of other religions is only from "my" faith perspective, terms like "primitive" or "pagan" or "infidel" may terminate communication before it has even begun.

Additionally, preparation to achieve positive results in the world is not the exclusive realm of churches. People, religiously affiliated or not, may be motivated to create positive change but may not want to work through an organized religion. With the growth of religiously unaffiliated people, there is growth in the concept of effective altruism, or "a philosophy and social movement which applies evidence and reason to working out the most effective ways to improve the world."[22] In other words, action can be ethically centered, but religion is itself a personal and optional inclusion. Further, no community is needed; the altruism is self-directed and based on reason.

Again, public and private colleges and universities, in addition to seminaries, may provide routes for students to develop careers in service, particularly through religious studies or ethics programs. The ideas and practices taught in colleges and universities' religion and ethics programs include the study of historic religions; promotion of religious literacy and interfaith etiquette; study of public religion which assists in framing knowledge and in understanding civic engagement; and a study of personal religion which analyzes convictions with embodied aspects, character development, and vocational choice.[23]

In the age of "spiritual but not religious" or the "nones," organized religion may yield to personal exploration of spirituality. Self-directed spirituality is often informed by various books written to aid the seeker in locating personal power, a positive state of mind, mental health, or physical healing, while aiming for spiritual enrichment. Angels, mysticism, shamanism, or dream interpretation all become processes by which people explore spirituality outside the settings of established religions. Eckhart Tolle is an example of an author who promotes personal self-fulfillment as its own spiritual lineage. Tolle draws from Buddhism and psychology to craft texts of personal transformation. It also helped sales that one of his books was promoted as an Oprah Winfrey Book Club selection.[24] Broadcasts of movies and television programs have spiritual themes without connection to specific religions— people who survive near death and then have healing power or the ability to bring others joy; dogs from heaven; or unexplained miracles. "My" spirituality becomes another choice available to Americans.

There are two smaller but no less important groupings of Americans who pursue routes other than organized religion. Atheism is lack of belief in a divine being. The Pew Research Center indicates that the number of atheists has grown from 1.6 percent in 2007 to 3.1 percent in 2014 among Americans.[25] But atheists face rejection among other Americans who believe in a particular religion. Where there is "a push by religious Americans to reinsert their faith into the nation's laws . . . there is a growing risk that this stigma will result in discrimination and oppression of atheists being enacted as law."[26]

Humanists are also part of the religiously unaffiliated group. The Humanist Association defines humanism as "a progressive philosophy of life that, without theism and other supernatural beliefs, affirms our ability and responsibility to lead ethical lives of personal fulfillment that aspire to the greater good of humanity." Their slogan is: "Good without a God."[27]

Both atheism and humanism can be held up as ethical options to religions that do not fulfill their support of human rights. But one author points out the flaw in that argument regarding humanists as always upholding human rights, and the same can be said of atheists. "People may know full well that those whom they treat in inhumane ways are fellow human beings, underneath a more or less thin veneer of convenient false consciousness. And yet, under certain social conditions—the surface of which I have just barely scratched in this paper—they may massacre, torture, and rape them *en masse* anyway."[28] In other words, no religious or nonreligious group has perfectly applied human rights; solutions are not the property of any group.

To be clear, all Americans are not kicking religion aside. Some find other ways to bring religious conceptualizations into political life, sometimes operating as individuals and not necessarily connected with an established religion. Prophetic activism is a term used to describe how people, singly or in groups, seek to put the principles of their faith into action. "In the midst of the chaos and pain of the present, prophetic politics envisions an altered future in which human relationships to one another and the natural world are repaired. Within Judaism, this is known in Hebrew as *tikkun olam*, which means repairing the world."[29] The author specifies that this idea of progressive activism is intentionally committed to nonviolent social change. Prophetic activism comes as a response to "the steady reversal of both formal and substantive rights triggered by the shift from national to global capitalism and the accompanying rise to power of conservative free-market politics."[30]

Americans do not have to depend on connections through the social institution of religions as they did one hundred years ago. There are more options for community services beyond church groups. Social media produces an incessant flow of information about any subject on all platforms, twenty-four hours a day. Americans can develop social connections with people across the country as well as around the globe. These are new identity builders that add to the radical and rapid changes of the United States' socioreligious landscape.

In a sense, the rise of religiously unaffiliated people is a product of the shifts in the American social landscape. The contours of neighborhoods have changed. Family groupings have expanded but many neighborhoods have eroded. "The expansion of personal equality and acceptance [of] minorities, women, gays, lesbians, and now even transgendered individuals are far more visible to popular culture and public life. . . . However, since the 1970s this expansion of personal equality and acceptance has been matched by an equally striking growth of socioeconomic inequality."[31] The growth of inequality erodes neighborhoods, cultural memory, community ties, and, yes, churches' memberships. People may move for work or because of higher costs of living or a lowered income. Lack of access to health care or good schools might inhibit the growth of communities. Regentrification of poorer neighborhoods may result in longtime residents' being forced out of older homes for newer high-rise buildings. The broken community ties are especially painful for people of color and those with low incomes who have fewer available institutions to provide information and service.

Prosperity churches represent another dimension of the radical changes to American religions. Churches that promote the idea of "be rich, you deserve it!" are not new, going back to the Great Depression in the 1920s. They multiplied across the American social and political landscape in the 1970s, but they were expansions, not innovations. As one example, Norman Vincent Peale was a Methodist minister who penned *The Power of Positive Thinking* in 1952.[32] The book gave a new twist on Christianity: you can do and achieve anything through prayer to Jesus Christ. The human mind, without worry or hatred, became Peale's key to success and positive thinking. Salvation in this view was tied to right thinking and success. This kind of positive thinking stands in sharp contrast to traditional Christian values such as humility, temperance, and compassion. Moreover, in Peale's vision, traditional vices, such as greed, pride, and gluttony, are turned into virtues when coupled with a mask of humility. Peale was not the first of these help-yourself thinkers, but his books, lectures, and radio programs ensured the widest possible distribution of his ideas.

Today, prosperity preachers, such as Joel Osteen, can be found in their own churches with books available to take the message beyond the church doors.[33] Osteen is also on the web, with radio and television programs.[34] He is considered one of the wealthiest pastors in the United States. He is selling what Americans want, as David Gutterman and Andrew Murphy stated,

> The Prosperity Gospel, then, represents an extreme variation on some fairly conventional American themes. Americans still feel that God plays a major role in their life . . . . Most Americans also profess the belief that God intercedes and controls outcomes in everyday life . . . . Prosperity preachers, then, are not necessarily teaching a new faith, but speaking a message that Americans want to hear, catering to the thoughts and feelings of the general Christian population and their deep desire to believe that there is order and meaning even in the midst of the recent economic downturns.[35]

Prosperity preaching is just one more choice for American religious life. Although prosperity preaching has been exported to other countries, it remains an American phenomenon, one based on the values of life, liberty, and the pursuit of happiness. These values come into play in terms of perceived national rights. Depending on the group, "life, liberty, and pursuit of happiness" may signal several things including those things that have been denied or have been a source of struggle or inspiration—or, more dangerously, viewed as exclusive rights.

The endless choice between religious beliefs and practices—or none—is one of the most radical changes in the landscape of American religions. Gutterman and Murphy present prosperity churches in terms of "neoliberalization theology to emphasize its individualistic ethos and equation of market success with divine favor."[36] Expanding this idea, I assert that not only prosperity churches are driven by individualism and the glamor of market success; neoliberalism has impacted all religious life in America with the specter of tantalizing "choice" of everything. Some Catholics have termed those members who pick and choose what they want to believe in their religion as "cafeteria Catholics." But this cafeteria is not limited to Catholics; America has become the religious and spiritual life fast-food center. Commitment to a religion once meant conversion as the dying of an old way of life and fully embracing a new one. Now pragmatic Americans give up only what we choose to give up and, yes, we can take it back. I attended a gospel sing at a college where members over the years came together in the songs of their generational classes. Earlier hymns had lyrics such as "Jesus, I will do what you want." More current prayers might be composed of a different chant: "Jesus, give me what I want."

In this new American religious world, to be holy is to be self-fulfilled. To be self-fulfilled is to be free. To be free is to choose. Self-fulfillment, freedom, and choice are not inherently evil. However, if there is no character balance, if these things are sought exclusively, then self-fulfillment becomes narcissism, freedom becomes license, and choice becomes conscienceless. Neoliberalism becomes a sacred ideology, affirming the race-religion-politics intersection. But there are other layers that construct this intersection.

HUMAN RIGHTS AT THE
U.S. RACE-POLITICS-RELIGION INTERSECTION

I once belonged to a church community where the board wished to state the church's support for a bill for a pro–death penalty proposal that was floating through the state legislature. This board-led effort was disturbing on several levels, the first being that the religion itself was opposed to the death penalty. It was equally disturbing that the pastor had nothing to say that informed the community of the wider opposition to the bill, including that of the religion's bishops. Further, as indicated above, the United Nations charged that the death penalty be "imposed only for the most serious crimes." Today, as I reflect on that mostly white church community in an urban area, I ask: was an agreement with the death penalty a mask for racist beliefs about who commits crimes in cities?

My question of that church decision is not far-fetched. A candidate for office stated in September 2016, "Our African-American communities are absolutely in the worst shape that they've ever been in before, ever, ever, ever. You take a look at the inner cities, you get no education, you get no jobs, you get shot walking down the street."[37] The same arguments get stated about Mexicans, Muslims, immigrants, and other people of color who dwell in the cities. It would seem that religions are natural places for human rights discussions to happen—but they may not happen. Instead, religions and their leaders may support political and racial divides in the name of their faith, seeking safety for themselves and their members in the face of fears.

Some religious leaders view the current state of the world and express outrage and condemnation of interracial marriage, affirmative action, immigration, urban violence, or welfare. An argument against any of these items often holds implicit racial bias without delineating that race is a factor. These ministers shepherd their congregations into their points of view.

Two authors discuss how these ministers move their communities into political/racial stances. "The capacity for conservative religious leaders to mobilize their constituents in defense of traditionalist values (be they racial, sexual, or religious) transformed local and state-level politics across the country. It also paved the way for the Moral Majority."[38] They indicate specific tools for crafting these communities. "Just as political parties provide tools and resources for the organization and mobilization of politically like-minded citizens, so did churches and religious institutions provide human, material, and communication resources necessary to mobilize political action."[39]

As religions intersect with politics and race, contours of power are born: personal belief becomes political prescription for the entire country. In May 2017, in response to his vote to cut back health care, Congressman Raul Labrador stated, "No one dies because they don't have access to health care."[40] During that same month, the Secretary for Health and Urban Development, Ben Carson, said, "Poverty is a state of mind."[41] The American myth of self-directed self-fulfillment combines with an ethical judgment of self-responsibility that leads to blaming victims and simultaneously deeming compassion as "soft" on lazy people. Oppression, with multiple ethical quandaries that religions should address, is alive and well in the United States.

What keeps racial oppression in place? If religions can fall into complicity, and politics can write the rules, what else happens? Stated bluntly by Howard Winant, "Today racism must be identified by its consequences. Racism has been largely although not entirely, to be sure—detached from its perpetrators."[42] This is the operation of hegemony that Winant defined elsewhere: "Hegemony is a system in which politics operates largely through the incorporation of oppositional currents in the prevailing system of rule, and culture operates largely through the reinterpretation of oppositional discourse in the prevailing framework of social expression, representation, and debate."[43]

As domination moved to racial hegemony, "it is racism's reinforced structural role, its 'cleaned-up,' 'streamlined,' and 'mainstream' manifestations, that allow it to survive and indeed go largely politically unchallenged at the dawn of the twenty-first century."[44] However, avoidance of political challenges needs tools. One tool is semantic infiltration, which used to silence dissent from either side of an argument, such as "affirmative action for whites."[45] Angela Davis presents an excellent functioning example of racial hegemony in combination with semantic infiltration. When African Americans decry state-sponsored violence in their communities, some people, both white and black, point to black people and charge that it is "black-on-black crime" that is the crisis in African American communities. The argument deflects from "state-sponsored violence," charging that crime within black communities has nothing to do with racism. Davis defines black-on-black crime differently, as more evidence of racism's impact:

> One of the major examples of the violence of racism consists of the rearing of generations of Black people who have not learned how to imagine the future—who are not now in possession of the education and imagination that allows them to envision the future. This is violence that leads to other forms of violence—violence against children, violence against partners, violence against friends . . . in our families and communities, we often unconsciously continue the work of larger forces of racism, assuming that this violence is individual and sui generis. [46]

The idea of oppression in the United States does not sit well with some people who want to see the nation through rose-colored glasses. Too often, the scope of oppression is reduced when it is defined as only violent encounters. As a place to begin the discussion about religion and human rights, the political philosopher Iris Marion Young's definitions of the five faces of oppression provide a helpful frame. She identified exploitation, marginalization, powerlessness, cultural imperialism, and finally, violence. [47]

Young used the term exploitation to mean that the values assigned to any work or those who perform it are inherently unequal in a capitalist society. For instance, the 200 to 300 percent gap between workers and CEOs is an established fact. [48] Young specified how exploitation combines with racism to exploit the labor of people of color. "Whenever there is racism, there is the assumption, more or less enforced, that members of the oppressed racial groups are or ought to be servants of those, or some of those, in the privileged groups." [49] Since Young penned these words, an African American man has been elected president, twice. It might seem that his election is evidence that Young's claim of exploited labor for the privileged group is no longer true. But some white people depicted President Obama as not a "real" American or as a stereotypically African witch doctor or even a lynched figure. Those who made these assertions might represent a small portion of white Americans. But during Obama's tenure as president, the Republican and mostly white Congress actively worked to subvert anything he proposed, even when the idea for the project or legislation came from Republican legislative think tanks.

Young identifies marginalization as the second form of oppression and this, she states, is the most dangerous kind. "A whole category of people is expelled from useful participation in social life and thus potentially subjected to severe material deprivation and even extermination. The material deprivation marginalization often causes is certainly unjust especially in a society where others have plenty." [50]

Powerlessness is the next form of oppression, which Young describes as follows: "The powerless are those who lack authority or power . . . situated so that they must take orders and rarely have the right to give them . . . [and] lack the authority, status, and sense of self that professionals tend to have."[51] Yet this description, while it paints powerlessness in many socially structured situations, does not encompass all life, all social settings, or, most importantly, all knowledge. If this definition were strictly true, Dolores Huerta and Cesar Chavez would never have founded and led the National Farm Workers Association in 1962.[52] To be designated as powerless by those in power does not automatically become acquiescence.

Cultural imperialism is the fourth face of oppression that Young identified. The attempted reduction of those deemed outside the mainstream culture might involve the imaginary understanding of that group that then becomes stereotypes. "The oppressed group's own experience and interpretation of social life finds little expression that touches the dominant culture, while that same culture imposes on the oppressed group its experience and interpretation of social life."[53] Yet, the oppressed group's music, food, language patterns, dress, and religion can be appropriated, without recognition of its source, for the dominant culture's pleasure. The boundaries between cultures in the United States are more porous than may be recognized at first glance. Some of these cultural appropriations will be seen in the next chapters.

Violence is one form of oppression, the most graphic and most easily understood.

> Members of some groups live with the knowledge that they must fear random, unprovoked attacks on their persons or property, which have not motive but to damage, humiliate, or destroy the persons. In American society women, Blacks, Asians, Arabs, gay men and lesbians live under such threats of violence and in at least some regions, Jews, Puerto Ricans, Chicanos, and other Spanish speaking Americans must fear such violence as well.[54]

However, violence has a major difference from exploitation, marginalization, powerlessness, and cultural imperialism. These four are systemic, denied or able to be denied. Each of these four has the blessing or curse of any given religion; for instance, a religion may limit the roles of women or people of color as divinely prescribed. Violence is different because it can be seen and documented. Seeing violence, however, does not mean it will be corrected or that justice will be given. So, without surprise, the number of recorded violent acts against people of color by white police officers often do not result in legal punishment because the question is asked if "they" deserved it.

We Americans need greater sophistication in our discussions of oppression. Oppression is not a single thing, done by evil people, in countries that are not the United States. Knowing different aspects of oppression, as carefully identified by Young, helps us name our realities with greater specificity.

Discussion of Young's categories brings this initial discussion of human rights at the intersection of religion, race, and politics to a conclusion. I contend that the lack of human rights discussions in the United States actually supports the race-politics-religion intersection. If we always define human rights as the problem of people in other countries, how do we ever look to and at ourselves? We hold to a set of American values that are in themselves forms of human rights: life, liberty, and the pursuit of happiness. However, how do these values give way to a cynical neoliberalism? How do we recognize the concept of universal human rights but make way for human rights from below? Can shifts in religions stand up to the brutality and subtlety of oppressions today?

Human rights are concepts that cut through the negatives, craft ethical approaches, and embody justice. The need for such an approach in the United States will be explored in the final chapter as possibilities to unbind the race-politics-religion intersections. The next chapters consider the people involved in the present, sticky webs of unresolved issues.

NOTES

1. The history and charter are given in more detail on the United Nations' webpage, "Charter of the United Nations," http://www.un.org/en/charter-united-nations/index.html.

2. "International Covenant on Civil and Political Rights," United Nations, Treaty Series, No. 14668, Article 14, no. 3 (a) and (c) and no. 4, 177, https://treaties.un.org/doc/publication/unts/volume%2099/volume-999-i-14668-english.pdf.

3. "International Covenant on Civil and Political Rights," Part III, Article 6, nos. 2, 4, 5, 174–75.

4. "U.S. Reservations, Declarations, and Understandings, International Covenant on Civil and Political Rights, 138 Cong. Rec. S4781-01 (daily ed., April 2, 1992)," University of Minnesota Human Rights Library,http://hrlibrary.umn.edu/usdocs/civilres.html.

5. "U.S. Reservations, Declarations, and Understandings, International Covenant on Civil and Political Rights, 138 Cong. Rec. S4781-01 (daily ed., April 2, 1992)," section III, no. (1).

6. Ann Elizabeth Mayer, *Islam and Human Rights: Tradition and Politics* (Boulder, CO: Westview Press 2013), 8.

7. Valerie Wilson, "People of Color Will Be a Majority of the American Working Class in 2032," Economic Policy Institute, June 9, 2016, http://www.epi.org/publication/the-changing-demographics-of-americas-working-class/.

8. Two civil rights bills temporarily became laws, dealing with the aftermath of enslavement of black people following emancipation. Questions of the citizenship and status of black persons and the development of these laws are discussed in detail in W. E. B. Du Bois, *Black Reconstruction in America 1860–1880* (New York: Atheneum, 1975), 270–71 and 281–83. Du Bois also indicated a successful, early use of the race, politics, and religion intersection as black people fought "the battle of all the oppressed and despised humanity of every race and color, against the massed hirelings of Religion, Science, Education, Law, and brute force," 708.

9. "State Civil Rights Offices," FindLaw, http://civilrights.findlaw.com/enforcing-your-civil-rights/state-civil-rights-offices.html.

10. "What You Should Know: EEOC's Fiscal Year 2016 Highlights," U.S. Equal Employment Opportunity Commission, https://www.eeoc.gov/eeoc/newsroom/wysk/2016_highlights.cfm.

11. "Fair Housing Act," The United States Department of Justice, August 6, 2015, https://www.justice.gov/crt/fair-housing-act-2.

12. James V. Spickard, "On the Epistemology of Post-Colonial Ethnography," in *Personal Knowledge and Beyond: Reshaping the Ethnography of Religion*, eds. James V. Spickard, J. Shawn Landres, and Meredith B. McGuire (New York: NYU Press, 2002), 238.

13. Spickard, "On the Epistemology of Post-Colonial Ethnography," 238–39.

14. George Monbiot, "Neoliberalism—the Ideology at the Root of All Our Problems," *The Guardian*, April 15, 2016, https://www.theguardian.com/books/2016/apr/15/neoliberalism-ideology-problem-george-monbiot.

15. Henry Giroux, *America's Addiction to Terrorism* (New York: Monthly Review Press, 2016), 18.

16. Barbra Fitzgerald, conversation with author, June 2017.

17. Pew Research Center, "U.S. Public Becoming Less Religious," November 3, 2015, 6–7, http://www.pewforum.org/2015/11/03/u-s-public-becoming-less-religious/. This information is taken from the larger study by Pew Research Center, "America's Changing Religious Land-scape," May 12, 2015, http://assets.pewresearch.org/wp-content/uploads/sites/11/2015/05/RLS-08-26-full-report.pdf.

18. Gregory A. Smith and Alan Cooperman, "The Factors Driving the Growth of the Relig-ious 'Nones' in the U.S.," Pew Research Center, *Fact Tank*, September 14, 2016,http://www.pewresearch.org/fact-tank/2016/09/14/the-factors-driving-the-growth-of-religious-nones-in-the-u-s/.

19. "2015 Annual Report," Association of Theological Schools, 2015,http://www.ats.edu/uploads/resources/publications-presentations/documents/2015-annual-report%20FINAL.pdf.

20. Aleksandra Sandstrom, "Faith on the Hill, the Religious Composition of the 115th Congress," Pew Research Center, January 3, 2017, http://www.pewforum.org/2017/01/03/faith-on-the-hill-115/.

21. Russell T. McCutcheon, *Critics Not Caretakers: Redescribing the Public Study of Relig-ion* (Albany: SUNY Press, 2001), 23.

22. Peter Singer, *The Most Good You Can Do: How Effective Altruism Is Changing Ideas about Living Ethically* (New Haven, CT: Yale University Press, 2015), 4–5.

23. Douglas Jacobsen and Rhonda Hustedt Jacobsen, *No Longer Invisible: Religion in Uni-versity Education* (New York: Oxford University Press, 2012), 56.

24. Eckhart Tolle, *A New Earth: Awakening to Your Life's Purpose* (New York: Plume 2005).

25. Pew Research Center, "America's Changing Religious Landscape," 4.

26. Alan Payne, "Redefining 'Atheism' in America: What the United States Could Learn from Europe's Protection of Atheists," *Emory International Law Review* 27 (2013): 701.

27. "Humanists and Humanism," The Humanist Society, http://thehumanistsociety.org/about/humanism/; "About the Humanist Society," The Humanist Society, http://thehumanistsociety.org/about/.

28. Kate Manne, "Humanism: A Critique," *Social Theory and Practice* 42, no. 2 (April 2016): 415.

29. Helene Slessarev-Jamir, *Prophetic Activism: Progressive Religious Justice Movements in Contemporary America* (New York: NYU Press, 2011), 4.

30. Slessarev-Jamir, *Prophetic Activism*, 4.

31. Stephanie Coontz, *The Way We Never Were: American Families and the Nostalgia Trap*, rev. and updated ed. (New York: Basic Books, 2016), 375–76.

32. Norman Vincent Peale, *The Power of Positive Thinking: A Practical Guide to Mastering the Problems of Everyday Life* (1952; repr., New York: Touchstone, 2003).

33. Such as Joel Osteen, *The Power of I Am: Two Words That Will Change Your Life* (New York: FaithWords, 2015).

34. Joel Osteen Ministries webpage, https://www.joelosteen.com/Pages/Home.aspx.

35. David S. Gutterman and Andrew R. Murphy, *Political Religion and Religious Politics: Navigating Identities in the United States* (New York: Routledge, 2016), 89.

36. Gutterman and Murphy, *Political Religion and Religious Politics*, 82.

37. Bryce Covert, "Donald Trump's Imaginary Inner Cities," *The Nation*, November 7, 2016, https://www.thenation.com/article/donald-trumps-imaginary-inner-cities/.

38. Gutterman and Murphy, *Political Religion and Religious Politics*, 108.

39. Gutterman and Murphy, *Political Religion and Religious Politics*, 109.

40. Kristine Phillips, "'Nobody Dies Because They Don't have Access to Health Care,' GOP Lawmaker Says. He Got Booed," *Washington Post*, May 7, 2017https://www.washingtonpost.com/news/powerpost/wp/2017/05/06/nobody-dies-because-they-dont-have-access-to-health-care-gop-lawmaker-says-he-got-booed/?utm_term=.b64a387d5b56

41. Yamiche Alcindor, "Ben Carson Calls Poverty a 'State of Mind,' Igniting a Backlash," *New York Times*, May 25, 2017, https://www.nytimes.com/2017/05/25/us/politics/ben-carson-poverty-hud-state-of-mind.html?_r=0.

42. Howard Winant, *The World Is a Ghetto: Race and Democracy since World War II* (New York: Perseus Books, 2001), 308.

43. Howard Winant, *Racial Conditions* (Minneapolis: University of Minnesota Press, 1994), 29.

44. Winant, *The World Is a Ghetto*, 308.

45. Phrase developed by Fred Ikle. See his article "Semantic Infiltration," *American Spectator*, July 10, 2010, https://spectator.org/23113_defense-jim-manzi-and-tnr/.

46. Angela Y. Davis, *Freedom Is a Constant Struggle: Ferguson, Palestine, and the Foundations of a Movement* (Chicago: Haymarket Books, 2016), 89.

47. Iris Marion Young, *Justice and the Politics of Difference* (Princeton, NJ: Princeton University Press, 1990).

48. See, for example, Sarah Anderson, "This Is Why Your CEO Makes More than 300 Times Your Pay," *Fortune*, August 7, 2015, http://fortune.com/2015/08/07/ceo-pay-ratio-sec-income-inequality/; or Lydia Dishman, "Does a Huge Pay Gap between CEO and Staff Affect Employee Satisfaction?," *Fast Company*, August 25, 2015, https://www.fastcompany.com/3050281/does-a-huge-pay-gap-between-ceo-and-staff-affect-employee-satisfaction.

49. Young, *Justice and the Politics of Difference*, 52.

50. Young, *Justice and the Politics of Difference*, 53.

51. Young, *Justice and the Politics of Difference*, 56–57.

52. The National Farm Workers eventually broadened its base and became the United Farm Workers. The organization has sometimes been successful in fighting unjust, dangerous practices on industrial farms. The organization's history is available online at "History," United Farm Workers, http://ufw.org/research/history/.

53. Young, *Justice and the Politics of Difference*, 60.

54. Young, *Justice and the Politics of Difference*, 61.

Chapter Two

Driven by the Original Identity Politics

People who imagine history flatters them (as it does, indeed, since they wrote it) are impaled on their history like a butterfly on a pin and become incapable of seeing or changing themselves or the world. This is the place in which it seems to me, most white Americans find themselves. Impaled. They are dimly, or vividly, aware that the history they have fed themselves is mainly a lie, but they do not know how to release themselves from it. [1]

James Baldwin, August 1965

In one of my first college ethics classes, I remember a student asked the professor a question during a discussion about moral development: What is the worst sin one human can commit against another? The question seemed to catch the professor off guard; he stood and thought for a few moments. "To lie. To tell another person a lie. Because it affects the mind and life of that other person." I don't remember if discussion continued, but I have often thought of that question and answer during the 2016 political season as race has come to the foreground of discussions, the outlines colored in with religious overtones. As I write this book, I remember that question and answer from a long-ago class and realize that our current racialized controversies are based on a series of lies, told through history and still believed by some. The beautiful, good, right, important, valuable, holy aspects of humanity too often wear white guises in our American imaginations. Conversely, any who are not white are subject to the correction or censure of those who are. One of my conversation partners and a mentor, Ifáṣèyí Bamgbàlà, Yorùbá Ifá-Òrìṣà Priestess stated it well: "The lie will build a community of lies around itself."

As the opening quote from James Baldwin eloquently stated, the history that white people have written about themselves seduces them into immobility, but I go further in my understanding: The lie brings white people to defensiveness and anger. Beyond a history, the core lie about being white in

America is that white people are superior. From this superiority, it follows that white people are smarter, should rule, deserve money and power, and have God on their sides—after all, God made them superior.

Now, I can hear some of my white students arguing this premise: *they* don't feel superior, are unpopular with their peers, not accepted by their families, or are poor. Yet I am not talking about personal experiences. In order to understand better the American situation early in the twenty-first century, I am analyzing systems that have created the ideology of white superiority. Some studies focus sharply on racism or white supremacy. Both of these analytical frames have limits because individuals (like students) can deny the existence of either in their lives or experiences. The long-term effects of racism can be traced, but personal or social responsibility can be denied. White supremacy can be ignored because too many white Americans are poor or oppressed themselves. Studies of racism and white supremacy are important and have their own trajectories. However, I am focused on two related points. The first is that the lie of white superiority has created systems of oppression in the United States, one aspect of which is the powerful intersection of race, politics, and religion, and this needs critical analysis. The second point is to argue for clearer understandings and discussions of human rights in the United States as was begun in the first chapter. Drawing from the decades of work in whiteness studies will assist these efforts.

Whiteness studies became a focus of scholarship since publications in 1991.[2] At issue is analysis of what it means to be white and how being white has crafted advantage for one race in American society. However, the deconstruction of white privilege has not happened yet. There is still a powerful, well-funded group of Americans insisting on the merited opportunities for white people, one of whom is Representative Steve King of Iowa. In a televised interview King stated,

> "This whole white-people business, though, does get a little tired, Charlie," King said. "I'd ask you to go back through history and figure out where are these contributions that have been made by these other categories of people that you are talking about. Where did any other subgroup of people contribute more to civilization?"
>
> "Than white people?" Hayes (the host) asked, taken aback. "Than Western Civilization itself," King said.[3]

After the public began to demand his apology, King went further in a tweet: "Culture and demographics are our destiny. We can't restore our civilization with somebody else's babies."[4]

White identity, then, as seen in King's comments, carries a weight that is not benign or, as James Perkinson stated, "White identity assumed the form of a hegemonic force within the social and cultural organization of political space in the country that admitted no easy alteration. It reproduced itself afresh in each new historical situation and gave vent to the violence of its fantasies on whoever got in its way."[5]

Whiteness is defined by Clarke and Garner as "a location from which the Others of whiteness—'blackness,' 'Asianness,' 'Jewishness,' etc.—have been constructed, both psychologically . . . and socially in a project going back centuries."[6] In this light, diverse voices are denied and denigrated. The creation of whiteness inhibits science, commerce, and the arts through exclusion of anything that does not match a closed set of facts and ideology.

Baldwin stated that history impales white Americans into inaction. I am expanding that concept to name the lie of white superiority, the creation of a tribal sense of belonging to the winning team. Perkinson, Clarke, Garner, and King referenced, like Baldwin, the importance of history. A closer look at some aspects of the history that created the lie will highlight the foundations of the current race, politics, and religion intersection.

THE HISTORY IN/FORMING THE WHITE LIE

What are the roots of the lie of white superiority? Americans did not invent it. Rather, it was imported with the European colonists' sociocultural and religious views. Like looking through sepia-toned photographs, strands of European beliefs, experiences, and thoughts came together in ways such that race, politics, and religion intersected, meshed, and continue to impact our lives today.

England, Spain, and France were the primary nations colonizing the American new world, sometimes competing with each other. England had superior naval power and became the most dominant of the three. While many contemporary political and religious contexts originated there, England subsumed the ideological bents of other nations in a colonizing competition. For instance, in the 1490s, Spain initiated the Inquisition to drive all Jews and some Muslims from the country in a struggle to wrest southern areas from Muslim rule and to send those conquerors back to Morocco. Brutal exclusion or control of conquered peoples became standard operating procedure in the Europeans' push to expand their nations.

European colonizers sailed to conquer and, in the process, encountered others who were different from them. Spanish friars traveled with their country's colonizers, some of whom left profound written records of these encounters, records full of the contradictions of their own superiority, their religious beliefs, and the indigenous people's inferiority.

An example is found in the 1588 writing of Friar Diego de Landa. His writing on the encounters of Spanish colonizers with the Mayans would become a source of written records of a people reduced and enslaved by that contact. The writings of de Landa also make clear how religion was used to make judgments against the Mayan people:

> After the people had been thus instructed in religion, and the youths benefit-
> ed . . . , they were perverted by their priests and chiefs to return to their
> idolatry; this they did, making sacrifices not only by incense by also of human
> blood. Upon this, the friars held an Inquisition . . . ; they held trials and
> celebrated an Auto, putting on many scaffolds, capped, shorn, beaten, and
> some in the penitential robes for a time. Some of the Indians out of grief, and
> deluded by the devil, hung themselves; but generally they all showed much
> repentance and readiness to be good Christians.[7]

Religion's doctrines became primary methods to cast judgment on any people encountered; simultaneously, the colonizers' Christianity became justification for their Inquisitions of other cultures.

In the 1500s, in tandem with social and political changes, European understandings of religion radically changed and wed politics in new ways. The Protestant Reformation began with the publication of Martin Luther's *95 Theses* against the abuses of the Catholic Church in 1517. Luther, a former Catholic monk, was the first domino to fall, which set off a chain of events. Roman Catholicism had been the primary religion throughout Western Europe before Luther's writings. After Luther's writing, religious groups that were not Catholic formed and pivotal religious thinkers arose, including John Calvin and Zwingli. Henry VIII was more of a religious opportunist. His motivation for establishing the Anglican Church and naming himself its head was driven by a need to separate from the Roman Catholic Church in order to obtain another divorce and another wife who would produce heirs for the throne. Similar to King Henry, other nobles throughout Western Europe saw breaking with Catholicism as a good way to establish nations and to acquire lands that Catholics had held as monasteries or convents.

With the end of the dominance of Catholicism, new dimensions of intellectual life, especially throughout Europe came into being. No longer limited by the Catholic hierarchy, the expansion of knowledge created a new placement for philosophy. The sixteenth-century philosophers began to speak new languages about personhood, responsibility, nation, and reason. René Descartes in France, Thomas Hobbes and John Locke in England, and Baruch Spinoza in the Netherlands were but a few who inspired the next generations of more specifically political philosophers and ethicists: Jean-Jacques Rousseau, Immanuel Kant, and Adam Smith. These thinkers were often dismissive of religion as significant to the development of social life; at best, religion was to remain in a private sphere.

Science, like all else in this period of social and intellectual ferment, was envisioned as grounded in reason, unlike the past eras' centering in religion. The problem with completely redoing a world is that items from the old world don't disappear. One such conceptual frame informed the development of science—namely, the interpretations of human races.

The Great Chain of Being was formed in earlier theological or philosophical ideas, such as Thomas Aquinas identifying God as Prime Mover or Aristotle/Plato/Plotinus identifying a natural order of things. Both the Prime Mover and natural order concepts depended on typologies that defined sets of things or beings in hierarchical order. The Chain of Being defined a hierarchy of all matter and all life-forms, from the least to the greatest, and strengthened itself with a claim that God had so decreed this structure. The Chain of Being was developed at a time when theology was considered the queen of the sciences in the medieval Western university system. These ideas changed shape a bit as theology was dethroned and replaced with a search for scientific information. But the old Chain of Being was transported into the new, rational science and infested the intellectual efforts of seventeenth- and eighteenth-century European theorists to define differences among human beings. The concept of race served as a scientific frame to discuss human difference. Transferring the Great Chain into the discussion created hierarchical understandings of all humans, even defining some humans as "sub-species."

One lecturer in 1795 Manchester, England, defined racial ordering. He offered scientific "proof" by pointing out diseases from which Europeans survived in some fashion when encountering other races. He claimed that black West Indian children died in large numbers from tetanus, "either due to intemperance of the mother during pregnancy, or to the irritation of the navel after birth, or to the smoke of the lying in room . . . . Some people even attribute it to the wickedness of the mother."[8] That 234 out of 358 native people of Nantucket died in 1765 from smallpox, whereas the Europeans may have sickened but did not die, was another of his proofs. He pointed to cases of leprosy and some fevers that caused the deaths of black people but not Europeans. The author then incorrectly concludes,

> Taking the European man as a standard of comparison, on the one hand, and the tribe of simian on the other; and comparing the classes of mankind . . . they may be so arranged as to firm a pretty regular gradation, in respect to the differences in the bodily structure and economy, the European landing at the head, as being farthest removed from the brute creation. That the African . . . approaches to the ape.[9]

Such bad science was not singular. Historian Nell Irvin Painter points out that the perceived beauty standards of white women and men were constructed into scientific proof of white superiority.[10] The hatred of dark skin, wide noses, and thick lips has been a unique form of violence against people of color. The "redskin" and the "colored" were stereotyped and derided by white Americans. Both Native and black communities became particular targets of white racial violence; these were the original "race riots."

The high-minded, glossy wrappings of philosophies of reason and personhood infused the educated European colonizers. These philosophies were not alone as some groups fled religious persecution in their home countries. The concept of religious freedom was a significant motivation for many groups that agreed to the colonization experiment. Catholics, Quakers, Anabaptists, Lutherans, and Puritans received tracts of land, came in groups, and sought that something, which eluded them in their home countries, called religious freedom.

But their ideas of religious freedom were for themselves; they did not necessarily offer such freedom to others. "The convention was that Christians would not enslave their fellow Christians, but [eventually] an exception would be made in the case of 'Negroes.' What would come to be called 'race' already trumped religion."[11] The Native peoples were, as de Landa's excerpt indicates above, often subjects of forced conversions to Christianity. Control of colonized people, intolerance and misreading of difference, and unscientific reasoning for European superiority: each concept transferred throughout the new world colonies, creating an incredible lack of genuine curiosity about those deemed Other.

Also confounding the high-minded ideals of European colonizers were the practicalities of how they could eke out a living in a new land. Colonizers were granted rights to land use by various crowns; their task was to obtain resources for the home nation of England, Spain, or France. The colonists retained their citizenship in their home country and fealty was expected. However, many of these settlers, ideals or not, had to live differently from those who remained in their homelands. The plants, the soil, the animals, the climate, the topography were all different from what they knew. The Native peoples gave basic, practical information on how to live. But the Native populations were decimated "by conquest, warfare, forced labor, and diseases spread from Europe and Africa for which they had not immunity."[12] The European slave traders specifically sought those who had specific skills, such as the farming of red soil, rice cultivation, or indigo dye making.

> Enslaved Africans were blacksmiths, metallurgists, toolmakers, sculptors and engravers, silversmiths and goldsmiths, tanners, shoemakers and saddle makers. They were designers and builders of warehouses and docks, barracks and homes, public buildings, churches, canals, and dams. They were coopers, draymen, and coach drivers; breeders, groomers and trainers of horses; and cowboys skilled in cattle rearing and herding.[13]

That Native and black people were used for their knowledge also pierces the lie of white superiority and affirms the humanity of people of color.

Native Americans and enslaved or freed Africans became part of the construction of whiteness and the furtherance of the superiority lie. White people constantly took stances as *not* those Others, defining themselves over against the Others. Distinctions were made through legislation, tradition, and practice. Separations were enforced by designated housing locations. Access to land, goods, and travel predetermined that white people would benefit from all dimensions of citizenship, even as citizenship was limited or denied to Native and African Americans. For the legislation against each group was based on a raw understanding of the superiority of white people and the questionable humanity of those Others.

Yet, among the many evidences of the lie was one indisputable fact: sexual relations occurred between people of color and white people. These sexual relations were not termed bestiality; a blind eye was often turned toward white men's activities (not so if white women expected the same sexual freedom). Children resulted. Those children were called mulatto or mestizo, and sometimes given a form of freedom. The only legislative action against these activities was prohibition of intermarriage or, as it was called, miscegenation.

It became a practice to identify people of color by the so-called "one drop rule"—that is, if any antecedent of a person was known to be Native or black American, that person was also considered Native or black. Appearances did not matter; genealogy did. This practice from the nineteenth century became law in the twentieth when the Virginia legislature formalized the practice in 1924 with the Racial Integrity Act. Its purpose, "W. A. Plecker, State Registrar at the Bureau of Vital Statistics in Richmond, Virginia, explained, was to 'postpone the evil day when this is no longer a white man's country.' He was obsessed with race mixing, as he believed that it would eliminate 'the higher type.'"[14]

White people consistently imposed their views, values, and definitions as the only correct ways to be human and civilized. When people of color had their own conceptualizations, there was no effort to discuss difference; the ideas of those deemed Other were wrong or unimportant.

For example, during the eighteenth century, the early European colonists attempted to buy land from native peoples, but actually facilitated deep cultural misunderstandings. "Negotiations which Europeans took to involve acquisition of land from Native people often involved a high degree of intercultural misunderstanding. When the English colonists of New England thought they were *buying* land, Native Americans often took the same agreements to mean that they were agreeing to *share* it."[15]

By the early nineteenth century, the colonies had become a nation and the constructions of white superiority fueled concepts of westward expansion and manifest destiny. "Racial anxiety and violence were abundant in these lands. From the fights over slavery in Bloody Kansas to the subjugation of

Mexicans in Texas to the contained forced migration and battles with indigenous American peoples, the expansion westward radicalized the rhetoric and actions of white supremacy between 1830 and 1860."[16] During the westward expansion, as part of the rhetoric, the idea of the "frontier" was formed.

In the spaces of contact between white settlers and Native peoples, the frontier was a moveable imaginary, "able to be moved from one place to the next as was necessary to do so for the settler colonials understanding of it."[17] The imagined frontier was to be conquered as were the savages within it. There were two stereotypical versions of the savages. "The Noble Savage, to a degree is allowed to exist on the civilized side of the border whereas the Ignoble Savage lives beyond the border, residing in uncivilized territory, or the far side of the boundary. By this reasoning, the approved context of Indian-ness as represented by the Noble Savage is an acceptable form of the Indian. . . . The Ignoble Savage is the vilified version of the ideal."[18]

Perhaps the United States' Civil War helped to solidify the race-politics-religion intersection, giving it tremendous, if embedded, unseen power over the citizenry. The legislative arguments over citizenship and enslavement extended to Native Americans and African Americans. How should the Native peoples already on the land be removed? Reservations became kinds of internment camps for Native people. Indian boarding, or assimilation, schools sought to assimilate the Savage children.[19] Many of those boarding schools were owned and operated by religious communities. Should the expansion into Western territories allow new states to identify as slave-owning states? State by state, legislation to define and justify enslavement was argued, often with religious themes, often with a view to the humanness of black people. As the vice president of the Confederacy, Alexander H. Stephens, stated,

> Many governments have been founded upon the principle of subordination and serfdom of certain classes of the same race; such were and are in violation of the laws of nature. With us, all of the white race, however high or low, rich or poor, are equal in the eye of the law. Not so with the negro. Subordination is his place. He, by nature, or by the curse against Canaan, is fitted for the condition which he occupies in our system. . . . The substratum of our society is made of the material fitted by nature for it, and by experience we know that it is best, not only for the superior, but for the inferior race, that it should be so. It is indeed in conformity with the ordinance of the Creator.[20]

In this statement, called Stephens's "cornerstone speech," race, politics, and religion are neatly woven together. The question is: why did this view, informed by bad science, policy, and politics, shaped by cultural ignorance and misreading history, persist?

A saying referenced in chapter 1 is: "Privilege sees liberation as oppression." With the support and blessing of science, legislation, and a misinformed history, white Americans felt justified in maintaining their social positions and the lie of their superiority. The illusion that mistreatment of any people of color all happened in the past, so long ago, is a comfortable support for a view of history that says equality happened. Instead, the processes of holding on to privilege were reenacted in violent ways. Grace Elizabeth Hale gave this example of "lynch carnivals." During the 1930s, these were

> communal spectacles of torture that helped ease white fears of a raceless consumer society even as they helped structure segregation. . . . Spectacle lynchings brutally conjured a collective, all-powerful whiteness even as they made the color line seem modern, civilized, and sane. Spectacle lynchings were about making racial difference in the new South, about ensuring the separation of all southern life into whiteness and blackness. . . . Racial violence was modern.[21]

The use of violence to maintain the imaginary separation of color lines is not just used against black Americans but also against any who may be deemed different or Other. The "lynch carnival" resonates with video after video of black people brutalized by police, indicating that black people deserve violence. The "carnivals" extend to other people today, as immigrants are accused of murder or terrorism and deported. As with lynch carnivals, white racial violence is permitted.

Eugenics may have had positive ideals when Francis Galton developed the idea in the 1880s, drawing from Darwin's ideas about selective breeding of animals and applying them to humans. Into the twentieth century, however, eugenics came to be applied as a biological mandate in the United States for breeding selection of physically and mentally healthy white people and tied to Protestant social reform.[22] Despite the horrors of Nazi Germany's attempted destruction of peoples who were not fitting their Aryan ideal, the movement in the United States helped to shape modern racism.

> The eugenics movement united various localized racist practices into a broad network of institutions that crucially affected the lives of literally millions of people world-wide. It was scientific racism operationalized at a national and global level. The other is that reaction against some aspects of the eugenics movement gave us the term racism and initiated a continuing public discourse about racial prejudice and bigotry that . . . actually worked to mask institutionalized mechanisms of sexualized, race-driven social control.[23]

The process by which eugenics' racial purity was to be assured included the practice of sterilization, which had begun in the 1920s and 1930s in the United States as public health systems were established in each state. The argument in support of sterilization is that it humanely solved social problems of poverty, insanity, and physical or mental "defects," when those who had such conditions could not reproduce children. Of course, this solution was based on the bad science that poverty, insanity, and disability were all hereditary. The sterilization processes, however, easily slid into ensuring that women of color were unable to bear children. Puerto Rican women became particular targets, especially if they had two or more children and were thus "denied access to hospitals to give birth unless they first agreed to be steril- ized. By 1965, over thirty-four percent of Puerto Rican women of child- bearing age had been permanently sterilized." Native American women were targeted for sterilization. "Between 1973 and 1976, the Indian Health Service sterilized 3,406 Native American women, some without their knowledge."[24] In California, welfare benefits were used as leverage to force Mexican American and African American women to consent to sterilization.[25]

The processes of finding ways to sterilize the unwanted Others continues: "A judge in Tennessee is giving inmates a unique way to reduce their sen- tences: Have a vasectomy." Glenn Cohen is a lawyer for the American Civil Liberties Union, which is bringing a suit to end the practice. Cohen stated, "While the judge appears to couch this in 'helping the inmate by not burden- ing them with extra children' one worries that it actually reflects primitive conception of heritability of criminal behavior."[26]

THE LIE CONTINUES

All forms of maintaining the color lines are not physically violent; oppres- sion also has faces of exploitation, marginalization, cultural imperialism, and powerlessness.[27] The extreme violence of lynching or sterilization did not account for the daily, persistent *threats* of violence. The psychological term "microaggression" seems too polite, minimizing the costs of living under a steady stream of abuse. Today, we still see these threats of violence, from the desecration of Jewish cemeteries[28] to graffiti vandalism of mosques.[29]

The pressures on people of color have ratcheted up in recent years. Lee Bebout analyzes the juxtaposition of whiteness and Mexicanness as played out at the U.S. border, connecting race and nationalism. He states that "whiteness and Americanness are coterminous. . . . As such, the innocence, benevolence, fears, anxieties, fantasies, and desires of whiteness may be expressions of not simply a racial imagination but also a nationalist one.[30]

James Perkinson reminds us that whiteness is not just a theory: it is about power that affects human life in America. "Race is not a problem of skin. It is a problem of the body, of its place of dwelling, of its source of nurture, of its social scripting, its educational training, its resources of protection, its erotics of desire, its politics of control, its ecology of energy."[31]

It is important to remember, as American studies scholar George Lipsitz reminds us, that whiteness actually created the singular tribe, and therefore, the original identity politics.

Whiteness recruits white people to be defenders of white group position and privilege rather than opponents of exploitation and injustice. It directs their fears toward the gains that might be made at their expense by subordinated racialized groups, while deflecting their attention away from the grossly unequal and unjust distribution of resources and power in society in general. It is nearly impossible to create a subject position that is both white and anti-racist, for whiteness is not so much an embodied identity as a structured advantage tied to the racial subjugation of others.[32]

Each cultural or religious group encountering white superiority through law or custom has had its own encounter with the American processes of creating "exotics." Exclusions become encoded in law and fiction gets enshrined through tradition. "As a Chinese-American woman remarks, 'In America, Everyman—the universal human being—is white.'. . . The will to annihilate the Other through a false incorporation can be detected in every language sign that tends, by its ever-widening scope of encompassment, to be taken for granted."[33]

Even a seemingly innocent discussion of "American" can have the hidden meaning of white/normal American. If that seems farfetched, reflect on the ways news, academic studies, and even everyday conversations specify a race for the Mexican/Korean/Haitian/African American over against how often such reference is made to indicate the race of a white American. The message is subtle but clear: "normal" Americans are white.

Part of whiteness is, as indicated above, that it renders itself invisible, normative, embedded in daily life as the "right" way to do things. In this, there is a decided impact on white Americans. Philosopher Shannon Sullivan wrote, "White people generally don't know how to live their racial identities in ways that promote racial justice. Even worse, their ignorance often poses as knowledge, making it all the more insidious. This is particularly true in the early twenty-first century and is true of the majority of white people, not just a small subset of them."[34]

At the center of the lie of white superiority is the deeper question of who is human. The answer under the lie imputes all humanity to white people and something lesser to all others. "Humans are exploited as part of the Homo sapiens species for the benefit of other humans, which at the same time yields a surplus version of the human: Man. Man (sic) represents the western configuration of the human as synonymous with the heteromasculine, white, propertied, and liberal subject that renders all those who do not conform to these categories as exploitable, nonhumans, literal legal no-bodies."[35]

The difficulties in living white identity have particular impact on American religious life. The religious complications are tied to the intersection of race and politics and ultimately to questions of human rights.

WHITENESS AND RELIGION

When Christopher Columbus encountered the Native people on Hispaniola, he claimed that they could easily be converted to Christianity because "they had no religion of their own."[36] The excerpt from Friar de Landa (shown above) indicated a brutal form of forced conversion to Christianity used on the Native populations.

Thornton Stringfellow was a Baptist pastor in Virginia. His writings shortly before the Civil War shed light on how theological approval was given to the inhumanity of enslavement. Using arguments from Christian Scripture, Stringfellow stated,

> We have shown from the text of the sacred volume, that when God entered into covenant with Abraham, it was with him as a slaveholder. . . . We have also shown from authentic history that the institution of slavery existed in every family . . . at the time the gospel was published to them. We have also shown from the New Testament that all churches are recognized as composed of masters and servants; and that they are instructed by Christ how to discharge their relative duties.[37]

Too regularly, organized Western religions aided the construction of whiteness. Established mainstream religions generally supported the lie of the superiority of their core membership, white Americans. Particularly, the leadership of pastors provided a foundation for mistreatment of all those deemed Other—whether black, Native, Chinese, Jewish, Italian, or Irish.

The last three groups—Jewish, Italian, and Irish—were eventually accepted as white under expanding conceptions of whiteness. Even so, remnants of their Otherness lingered as could be seen when Irish Americans, especially Roman Catholics, celebrated the 1961 election of John F. Kennedy as president of the United States. Kennedy became a symbol of their own social acceptance.

Religion became part of the political negotiation around whiteness. Were Roman Catholics, as were the majority of Irish and Italian immigrants, acceptable as Americans? Could they share the values of Anglo-Saxons? However, disdain for Italian and Irish Americans was eliminated or turned to admiration during the 1960s as black Americans and Native Americans began to tout racial pride and to advocate for their rights. White Americans began to celebrate their own ethnic pride, as St. Patrick and even Christopher Columbus became celebrated as "American" icons, although neither was.

Jewish people are considered white but still suffer religious discrimination known as anti-Semitism. The reasons given for anti-Semitism are vague: "They have more power than whites" or "They are not Christian" or, worse, "Jews killed Christ" (a theologically and historically incorrect statement). Anti-Semitism lives in pockets of racist white people, as the white nationalist marchers, August 2017, Charlottesville, Virginia chanted, "Jews will not replace us."[38]

I admit that I have never understood anti-Semitism in the United States. Jews, after all, are white and most are from European situations in which they themselves experienced great oppression, including systematic genocide from the Spanish Inquisition (ca. 1230–1820) to the Holocaust (1933–1945). In the process of writing this book, I begin to wonder if the reason is that too many Jewish people have been willing to step outside the American white box of segregation. After all, Jewish people had experienced great violence and hatred in Europe and they do not forget when they move to the United States. As home- and landowners, Jewish people were often the ones who would sell property to black people. I know this from my own experience in the Detroit area, where, on the west side, Jewish populations lived for some time. When they moved, usually toward suburban areas, their homes were sometimes sold to black people.

I am not suggesting that all Jewish people have been kind or non-racist. But the possibilities of business transactions with a Jewish business or home-owner were more likely than with other white people. Perhaps this is the reason for the slogan, "Jews will not replace us"? Perhaps, in this book on the intersection of race, politics, and religion, anti-Semitism is sometimes a re-sponse to white people (Jews) who do not toe the line.

Jim Wallis is a white, Christian evangelical theologian today who has written extensively on issues of injustice, especially around issues of race, in the United States. He wrote of the questions he raised as a teenager in Detroit, Michigan, during the 1960s:

> I felt the tension and hostility that pervaded the conversations among whites whenever the subject of blacks, race, the city, or crime would come up. People that I knew to be otherwise kind and loving would be transformed, uttering vicious words of intolerance and fearful hatred. I wanted to know why. Why did whites and blacks live completely divided from one another? Why did most whites seem prosperous and most blacks poor? Why didn't I know any families who sometimes went without a meal or had loved ones in jail, when I heard that black families had those experiences? And why didn't we go to church together? . . . What about our Christian faith? Doesn't God love all people? . . . I was told that we were all better off separated. Some even used the Bible to undergird their argument.[39]

The term "race traitor" is sometimes applied to people like Wallis who ques-tion the racial status quo. This occurs when white people speak up on behalf of injustices against other races. Shannon Sullivan pointed out that the term "appears to have originated during the civil rights movement in the United States, when white Southerners who opposed voting rights and equal educa-tion for black people verbally attacked white supporters of black civil rights by calling them traitors to their race. The origins of the term are clearly maliciously destructive in their intent."[40]

Even use of the word "traitor" implies a broken trust, especially in relation to a country, thereby tying whiteness to the very identity of the United States. The lie of the imagined superiority of white people becomes tied to the imagined superiority of the United States. The disenfranchisements of those who are deemed Other become necessary political games in order to retain power. Wallis's questions puncture holes in the lie and all its manifestations. Admittedly, people of color have asked such questions before Wallis was born. One of the most famous was from Frederick Douglass, who had escaped enslavement and become a noted abolitionist. On July 5, 1852, at a speech for the celebration of the nation's independence, Douglass asked a question and then exposed the lies:

> What, to the American slave, is your 4th of July? I answer: a day that reveals to him, more than all other days in the year, the gross injustice and cruelty to which he is the constant victim. To him, your celebration is a sham; your boasted liberty, an unholy license; your national greatness, swelling vanity; your sounds of rejoicing are empty and heartless; your denunciations of tyrants, brass fronted impudence; your shouts of liberty and equality, hollow mockery; your prayers and hymns, your sermons and thanksgivings, with all your religious parade, and solemnity, are, to him, mere bombast, fraud, deception, impiety, and hypocrisy—a thin veil to cover up crimes which would disgrace a nation of savages.[41]

There have been opportunities and places in American history where the lie could be called out and ended, where the intersection could have been dismantled—such as at the end of the Civil War or after Japanese internment camps closed. Instead, Wallis's questions still draw out those who want to brand any white person who exposes the lie as traitorous.

Jim Wallis's questions—"Why didn't we go to church together? . . . What about our Christian faith? Doesn't God love all people?"[42] —exposed a particular dimension of white American Christianity's role in maintaining the lie. One author, Robert P. Jones, drew from the statistics showing the lessening of congregational membership to declare an end to white Christian America. He argued that such loss is actually creating a sense of insecurity and a "crisis of confidence. . . . More than anything else, the death of White Christian America has robbed its descendants of the security of their place and beliefs."[43] Yet it is exactly that place of changing demographics that is assisting a deeper embedding of a white Christian view of the world into politics. As will be seen in the chapter on Muslims, the "Christian" is shown as the "good" American and therefore to be in a pitched battle with those Muslims waging wars of terror on us.

Ultimately, the lie of superiority tears Christianity from its ethical roots, beginning with shaping white people into false gods. Hatred is justified. Violence is condoned. Jim Wallis has begun to answer his youthful questions as he later wrote, "Whiteness is not just an ideology; it is also an idol. For people of faith, this is not just a political issue but a religious one as well. Idols separate us from God, and the idolatry of "whiteness" has separated white people from God. . . . This idol blinds us to our true identity as the children of God, because, of course, God's children are of every color that God has made them to be."[44]

Shannon Sullivan points out another truth—that in the processes of living this lie, white people have injured, not just people of color, but themselves as well. "Out of all the damage that white racism has done to African Americans and other people of color, the most damaging of all would be for it to turn them into the debilitated, deplorable people that white folk generally are."[45] Instead Sullivan calls for something new.

> The social fabric does not so much need ripping up as it needs reweaving. This creative act will involve a great deal of unraveling of what currently exists, but unraveling should not be the final goal of racial justice and related liberatory projects. Something new needs to be created and . . . that something new includes a positive racial identity for white people.[46]

WHITENESS AND POLITICS

Politics is the very pragmatic way that whiteness protects its power. It seems an obvious statement, but it is easy to think "that's just the way it is." But it is not. Our American politics are engineered to keep Others out of power.

One way is through the law and legal structures. For instance, on a national level, the 115th Congress seated in January 2017 had the following racial composition:

Out of 100 Senators, three are African American (3 percent); three are Asian American (3 percent); four are Latino/Latina American (4 percent); and there are no Native Americans.

Out of 435 Representatives: forty-six are African American (10.5 percent); thirty-four are Latino/Latina (7.8 percent); twelve are Asian American (2.6 percent). And there are no Native Americans.[47]

These numbers mean that voices are not heard, perspectives are lost, and the layers of American meanings get reduced to single notes of white. Laws are made that do not encompass the reality of the United States, but support very limited and selective points of view.

The processes of gerrymandering or structuring voting districts into strange shapes in each state in order for one political party to retain control, especially when one political party is more connected to white and upper-

class interests, is being challenged, but is still in place. Some state legislatures find ways to restrict access to the polls, or purge voting rolls of voters
of color. In other words, between gerrymandering and voter restrictions,
voting rights remains an issue that must be addressed. The reduction of this
very basic human right, voting, leads some people of color to become fatalis-
tic about the processes, "My vote doesn't matter anyway." Such fatalism
plays right into the hands of those who want to keep black, Latino/a, Native,
and Asian American voters from the polls.

When there are laws made from white perspectives, rather than incorpo-
rating multiple voices, one current theme arises that is meant to hammer that
law's perspective into place: the rule of law. "Rule of law" simply means that
the United States is governed by law, rather than arbitrary decisions made
from single perspectives. Rule of law is a very good thing; it rejects chaos
and maintains order in society. Yet, when such numbers as are reflected in
the 115th Congress indicate *who* is making laws and *who* is left out, a kind of
neo-apartheid society is set up. Voting rights has become a central issue for
many of the groups that will be discussed in the next chapter.

STILL HERE? AND A HUMAN WAY FORWARD

Whiteness was not just a choice of something to study at colleges. Whiteness
was a concern that infected some white American communities, particularly
after the election of a black man, Barack Obama, as president in 2008. A
cover of *The Atlantic* showed a picture of the new president with the glaring
headline, "The End of White America?" The article was not really about the
new president but explored the conditions of being white in America, especially through popular culture references. "We're going through a period
where whites are really trying to figure out: 'Who are we?' The 'flight from
whiteness' of urban, college-educated, liberal whites isn't the only answer to
this question. You can flee *into* whiteness as well. This can mean pursuing
the authenticity of an imagined past."[48] The author drew a sharp distinction
between the greater cultural diversity of the 1990s and the efforts of some to
uphold an imagined past where whiteness was entitled. This kind of fleeing
into whiteness meant that "another form of identity politics crystallized. Hip-
hop may have provided the decade's soundtrack, but the highest selling artist
of the 1990s was Garth Brooks. Michael Jordan and Tiger Woods may have
been the faces of athletic superstardom, but it was NASCAR that emerged as
professional sports' fastest growing institution."[49]

As the article indicated, the white lie of superiority found new ways to
justify its own existence, thereby reestablishing the intersection of race/white
superiority using politics and religion. The lie uses ahistorical readings of
contemporary contexts, claiming that we are all postracial now and have

assured the removal of all hindrances for the socioeconomic success of people of color. There are forms of broken community trust when concepts like race traitor or race card get played to silence dissent from white people.

These dimensions could be seen in Alabama with a 2017 Senate candidate's using the radical logic of justifying white superiority. He was asked to name a time in the past when America was great. The candidate pointed to a time when slavery was the law.[50] Can human rights be held up in the face of such commitment to whiteness?

Whiteness has been called an "eye. . . . And like any eye, the one thing it cannot do is see itself."[51] A more recent term for the responses of white people to racial conflict is white fragility.

> White Fragility is a state in which even a minimum amount of racial stress becomes intolerable, triggering a range of defensive moves. These moves include the outward display of emotions such as anger, fear, and guilt, and behaviors such as argumentation, silence, and leaving the stress-inducing situation. These behaviors, in turn, function to reinstate white racial equilibrium.[52]

Here is an echo of the beginning of this chapter with James Baldwin's framing of the idea of white immobility: "The history of white people has led them to a fearful, baffling place where they have begun to lose touch with reality—to lose touch, that is, with themselves—and where they certainly are not truly happy, for they know they are not truly safe."[53]

But whiteness studies themselves assist the eye to see and assist in naming the fearful and painful parts of American history. The lie of white superiority is being punctured by white people, with collaborators of color, using many truths. Is truth a human right for white Americans?

One of the ways that the lie is maintained is for "tradition" to be invoked as rationale for maintaining the privilege of white Americans. These calls are especially loud in the South, as enslavement is excused with such drivel as "we took good care of our slaves!" as a white male student shouted at me during one class. Or the argument that the Civil War was not about enslavement but about heritage. The variety of these statements has continued to support the lie of white superiority even as the possibilities of conversations across races is hampered, if not terminated.

Yet in May 2017, in New Orleans, Louisiana, Confederate monuments were removed from the city by the order of the Mayor Mitch Landrieu. The Mayor gave an address during which he named African Americans as well as various ethnic and Native tribes that comprise New Orleans.

> The historic record is clear: the Robert E. Lee, Jefferson Davis, and P. G. T. Beauregard statues were not erected just to honor these men, but as part of the movement which became known as The Cult of the Lost Cause. This "cult" had one goal—through monuments and through other means—to rewrite his-

tory to hide the truth, which is that the Confederacy was on the wrong side of humanity. . . . Consider these four monuments from the perspective of an African American mother or father trying to explain to their fifth grade daughter who Robert E. Lee is and why he stands atop of our beautiful city. Can you do it? Can you look into that young girl's eyes and convince her that Robert E. Lee is there to encourage her? Do you think she will feel inspired and hopeful by that story? Do these monuments help her see a future with limitless potential? Have you ever thought that if her potential is limited, yours and mine are too?[54]

Mayor Landrieu's words, then, puncture several holes in the lie of superiority and, as Sullivan named it, begins to reweave white identity. The human potential of all of us is at stake. The idealism of the United States encompasses life, equality, liberty, and justice. Those words were intended for a limited audience, but time has brought this country to the point where everyone wants to participate. Landrieu is inviting a fully enfranchised participation from all citizens. This Sullivan calls "dissenting with whiteness out of love . . . out of a loving relationship *with oneself*" (emphasis added).[55]

Forms of reconciliation for the past may create other human rights paths. Georgetown University provides one other example that demonstrates a sharper religious connection to addressing the blindness of the past. In 1838, Georgetown's president arranged a major sale of enslaved Africans in order to raise needed money for the university.[56] But by 2016, the university sought to make amends to the descendants of those who were sold, beginning with recognition of its role in the sale. Some names of Jesuits involved in the sale were removed from buildings. Scholarships were offered to descendants. The university held a variety of events to discuss the truth of the past with students, faculty, administration and alumni. A working group presented a report to the university president in the summer of 2016. They arrived at some conclusions that choked off the lie of superiority but, more, they made a deliberate connection with their religious beliefs. They stressed the importance of reconciliation.

> Reconciliation implies forgiveness sought and offered, but the parties directly involved in the offenses—perpetrators and victims—are long deceased. It also requires an understanding of how persons two centuries after the events could adopt for themselves a personal responsibility for the perpetrators and the victims that makes the seeking or the offering of forgiveness authentic and appropriate to the outrage and disillusionment caused by the misdeeds.
>
> . . . . In the final analysis, the Working Group found its most meaningful encouragement to pursue reconciliation in resources that are intrinsic to the university's Catholic identity: the centrality of reconciliation to the mission of Jesus Christ, the moral imperatives of contrition and forgiveness, the virtue of hope as an inspiration to and precondition for reconciliation, and the specific commitment of Jesuit schools to a faith that does justice. These tenets have

analogs in the diverse religious faiths and philosophical commitments embraced in our community.[57]

Mayor Landrieu's and Georgetown University's responses to the no-longer-denied history of injustice offer reweaving of white identity that is based on clear-eyed recognition of truth, not lies. These actions do not end the lie; the candidate calling for a return to slavery shows that there is not a definition of the very humanity of all people. Yet, Landrieu and Georgetown's actions point toward hope for a new human rights movement in the United States.

Jim Wallis, who has spent years as an activist for justice, identified the center of how change begins, and it is not at the level of politics. "Things change when hearts and minds across the country change. Things change when social movements begin, when people's understandings change, when families rethink their values, when congregations examine their faith, when communities get mobilized, and when nations are moved by moral contradictions and imperatives."[58]

Yet those who have been oppressed find their own ways to make change, fighting against limits even when they do not have control of systems and have little power. The Native American communities were the first to experience the lie of white superiority, and it is to those communities the next chapter turns.

NOTES

1. James Baldwin, "The White Man's Guilt," in *Collected Essays* (New York: Library of America, 1998), 723.

2. David R. Roediger, *The Wages of Whiteness: Race and the Making of the American Working Class* (London: Verso, 1991).

3. David A. Graham, "Steve King's Improbable Ascendance," *The Atlantic*, March 13, 2017, https://www.theatlantic.com/politics/archive/2017/03/steve-king-nearer-the-throne/519336/.

4. Graham, "Steve King's Improbable Ascendance."

5. James W. Perkinson, *White Theology: Outing Supremacy in Modernity* (New York: Palgrave Macmillan, 2004), 160–61.

6. Simon Clarke and Steve Garner, *White Identities: A Critical Sociological Approach* (London: Pluto Press, 2009), 18.

7. Friar Diego de Landa, *Yucatan: Before and after the Conquest*, trans. William Gates (1566 manuscript; New York: Dover Publications, 1978), 30.

8. Charles White, "An Account of the Regular Gradation in Man, and in Different Animals and Vegetables, and from the Former to the Latter," read to the Literary and Philosophical Society of Manchester at different meetings, in the year 1795, accessed December 2016, https://archive.org/details/b24924507. 76.

9. White, "An Account of the Regular Gradation in Man," 83.

10. Nell Irvin Painter, "The White Beauty Ideal as Science," chap. 5 in *The History of White People* (New York: W. W. Norton, 2010), 59–71.

11. Robert Bernasconi, "Crossed Lines in the Racialization Process: Race as a Border Concept," *Research in Phenomenology* 42, no. 2 (2012): 218.

12. Gwendolyn Midlo Hall, *Slavery and African Ethnicities in the Americas: Restoring the Links* (Chapel Hill: University of North Carolina Press, 2005), 19.

13. Hall, *Slavery and African Ethnicities in the Americas*, 20.

14. Bernasconi, "Crossed Lines in the Racialization Process," 221.

15. Bruce Johansen, ed., *Enduring Legacies: Native American Treaties and Contemporary Controversies* (Westport, CT: Praeger, 2004), xv.

16. Carl A. Zimring, *Clean and White: A History of Environmental Racism in the United States* (New York: NYU Press, 2015), 42.

17. Michael Taylor, *Contesting Constructed Indian-ness: The Intersection of the Frontier, Masculinity, and Whiteness in Native American Mascot Representations* (New York: Lexington Books, 2015), 29.

18. Taylor, *Contesting Constructed Indian-ness*, 30.

19. Life both on reservations and in the Indian boarding schools are well-documented, such as Adam Fortunate Eagle, *Pipestone: My Life in an Indian Boarding School* (Norman: University of Oklahoma Press, 2010); Clifford E. Trafzer, Jean A. Keller, and Lorene Sisquoc, eds., *Boarding School Blues: Revisiting American Indian Educational Experiences* (Lincoln : University of Nebraska Press, 2006); Keith Burich, *The Thomas Indian School and the "Irredeemable" Children of New York* (Syracuse, NY: Syracuse University Press, 2016); Nicholas Christos Zaferatos, *Planning the American Indian Reservation: From Theory to Empowerment* (Syracuse, NY: Syracuse University Press, 2015); David LaVere, *The Tuscarora War: Indians, Settlers, and the Fight for the Carolina Colonies* (Chapel Hill: University of North Carolina Press, 2013). In addition, numerous reports on reservations are available on the United States Senate Committee on Indian Affairs, https://www.indian.senate.gov/.

20. Alexander H. Stephens, "'Corner Stone' Speech, Savannah, Georgia, March 21, 1861," Teaching American History, http://teachingamericanhistory.org/library/document/cornerstone-speech/.

21. Grace Elizabeth Hale, *Making Whiteness: The Culture of Segregation in the South, 1890–1940* (New York: Vintage Books, 1998), 203.

22. Dennis L. Durst, *Eugenics and Protestant Social Reform: Hereditary Science and Religion in America, 1860–1940* (Eugene, OR: Pickwick Publications, 2017).

23. Ladelle McWhorter, *Racism and Sexual Oppression in Anglo-America: A Genealogy* (Bloomington: Indiana University Press, 2009).

24. Deborah Ummel, "Dream or Nightmare? The Impact of American Eugenics, Past and Present," *Cross Currents* 66, no. 3 (September 2016): 394.

25. Ummel, "Dream or Nightmare?," 394–95.

26. Kalhan Rosenblatt, "Judge Offers Inmates Reduced Sentences in Exchange for Vasectomy," NBC News, July 21, 2017, http://www.nbcnews.com/news/us-news/judge-offers-inmates-reduced-sentences-exchange-vasectomy-n785256.

27. Iris Marion Young, *Justice and the Politics of Difference* (Princeton, NJ: Princeton University Press, 1990), 52–57.

28. Kayla Epstein, "The Disturbing History of Vandalizing Jewish Cemeteries," *Washington Post*, February 21, 2017, https://www.washingtonpost.com/news/acts-of-faith/wp/2017/02/21/the-disturbing-history-of-vandalizing-jewish-cemeteries/?utm_term=.2ee3d3c02716.

29. Jordan Tidwell, "FBI Investigates Graffiti Vandalism at Two Mosques, Suspects Wanted," 5News KFSM, October 20, 2016, http://5newsonline.com/2016/10/20/fbi-investigates-graffiti-vandalism-at-two-fort-smith-mosques-suspects-wanted/.

30. Lee Bebout, *Whiteness on the Border: The U. S. Racial Imagination in Brown and White* (New York: NYU Press, 2016), 4.

31. Perkinson, *White Theology*, 154.

32. George Lipsitz, "Walleye Warriors and White Identities: Native Americans' Treaty Rights, Composite Identities and Social Movements," *Ethnic and Racial Studies* 31, no. 1 (January 2008): 101–2.

33. Trinh T. Min-ha, *Woman, Native, Other: Writing, Postcoloniality, and Feminism* (Bloomington: Indiana University Press, 1989), 66–67.

34. Shannon Sullivan, *Good White People: The Problem with Middle-Class White Anti-Racism* (Albany: SUNY Press, 2014), 3.

35. Alexander G. Weheliye, *Habeas Viscus: Racializaing Assemblages, Biopolitics, and Black Feminist Theories of the Human* (Durham, NC: Duke University Press, 2014), 135.

36. Clara Sue Kidwell, "Ethnoastronomy as the Key to Human Intellectual Development and Social Organization," in *Native Voices: American Indian Identity and Resistance*, eds. Richard A. Grounds, George E. Tinker, and David E. Wilkins (Lawrence: University Press of Kansas, 2003), 16.

37. Thornton Stringfellow, "A Scriptural View of Slavery," in *Slavery Defended: Views of the Old South*, ed. Eric L. McKittrick (Englewood Cliffs, NJ: Prentice-Hall, 1963), 97–98.

38. Yair Rosenberg, "'Jews Will Not Replace Us': Why White Supremacists Go After Jews," *Washington Post*, August 14, 2017, https://www.washingtonpost.com/news/acts-of-faith/wp/2017/08/14/jews-will-not-replace-us-why-white-supremacists-go-after-jews/?utm_term=.210a60416589.

39. Jim Wallis, *The Soul of Politics: Beyond "Religious Right" and "Secular Left"* (San Diego: Harvest Book, 1995), 88–89.

40. Sullivan, *Good White People*, 139.

41. Frederick Douglass, "What to the Slave Is the Fourth of July?," July 5, 1852, reprinted in *The Nation* July 4, 2012, https://www.thenation.com/article/what-slave-fourth-july-frederick-douglass/

42. Wallis, *The Soul of Politics*, 89.

43. Robert P. Jones, *The End of White Christian America* (New York: Simon and Schuster, 2016), 228.

44. Jim Wallis, *America's Original Sin: Racism, White Privilege, and the Bridge to a New America* (Grand Rapids, MI: Brazos Press, 2016), 80–81.

45. Sullivan, *Good White People*, 122.

46. Sullivan, *Good White People*, 140.

47. Sheryl Estrada, "The 115th Congress Is Not a Model for Diversity," Diversity Inc, January 4, 2017, http://www.diversityinc.com/news/115th-congress-not-model-diversity/.

48. Hua Hsu, "The End of White America?," *The Atlantic*, January/February 2009, 49.

49. Hua Hsu, 50.

50. Philip Bump, "Roy Moore: America Was Great in the Era of Slavery, Is Now 'Focus of Evil in the World,'" *Washington Post*, December 8, 2017, https://www.washingtonpost.com/news/politics/wp/2017/12/08/roy-moore-america-was-great-in-era-of-slavery-is-now-focus-of-evil-in-the-world/?utm_term=.96437d66c569.

51. Perkinson, *White Theology*, 153.

52. Robin DiAngelo, "White Fragility," *International Journal of Critical Pedagogy* 3, no. 3 (2011): 57.

53. James Baldwin, "The White Man's Guilt," 724.

54. Derek Colson, "Transcript of New Orleans Mayor Landreiu's Address on Confederate Monuments," *The Pulse*, May 19, 2017, http://pulsegulfcoast.com/2017/05/transcript-of-new-orleans-mayor-landrieus-address-on-confederate-monuments.

55. Sullivan, *Good White People*, 161.

56. Rachel L. Swarns, "272 Slaves Were Sold to Save Georgetown. What Does It Owe Their Descendants?," *New York Times*, April 16, 2016, http://www.nytimes.com/2016/04/17/us/georgetown-university-search-for-slave-descendants.html?_r=0.

57. Working Group on Slavery, Memory, and Reconciliation, *Slavery, Memory, and Reconciliation* (Washington, DC: Georgetown University, Summer 2016), 26–27, https://www.documentcloud.org/documents/3038068-Georgetown-University-Working-Group-on-Slavery.html.

58. Wallis, *America's Original Sin*, 170.

Chapter Three

Broken Treaties, Resistance, and Decolonization

Life circumstances have been arrayed against Native peoples since European settlers arrived on the shores of the land that would become the United States. They are sometimes called the First People; their experiences are both unique and diverse. This was and is their land. The Native Americans have had a distinctive experience of colonization. "Colonialism is not simply a system of economic and military control, but a systematic cultural penetration and domination" that encompasses the historical, political, psychological, intellectual, and cultural lives of the people.[1]

The first act of colonization was naming these new people "Indians." In 1492, Columbus did set sail from Spain. But, "the original purpose of the voyage was not to discover new lands but to open up a trade route to the 'Indies' or Asia, that would allow Spanish merchantmen to bypass the hostile Muslim fleets sailing out of the Middle East."[2] Columbus set sail in 1492, arriving in mid-October at a small island that the Natives called Guanahani. Because Columbus did not know where he was, he assumed he had arrived at his destination, Asia. As he wrote in his journal, "On the thirty-third day after leaving Cadiz I came into the Indian Sea, where I discovered many islands inhabited by numerous people."[3] Hence, Columbus misnamed the indigenous peoples of the New World "Indians," an appellation they disliked or hated.

America's indigenous people under the strictures of colonialism served as the start-up for more people to be politically oppressed by race and religion in the construction of the nation; they were the first, not the last. To consider ways that the intersectional constructions of race, politics, and religion have worked against Native peoples' interests, I begin with two stories.

Years ago, in New Orleans, Louisiana, I attended a prayer service to memorialize enslaved Africans, many of whom would have come through that port. Those who planned the service decided to make it "multi-faith" and included various Christian denominations, traditional African religions, a rabbi, an imam, and a Native American shaman. The shaman began by enumerating the number of indigenous peoples dead through colonial encounters. He ended with something like, "At least you all still have a people."

At another time, I attended an art fair, and among the artists showing their creations was a Native American woman who crafted jewelry. I was looking at her wares as a white American woman purchased several items, gushing, "These are perfect! I'm descended from an Indian princess, you know." The white woman left the booth and the Native woman looked at me. "They *all* claim to be from Indian princesses."

Each of these stories can bring dismissive responses—Why not forget about them? They don't mean anything! However, I am using the stories to point to common ways that crucial areas impact the race-politics-religion intersection in Native peoples' lives. The first story highlights treaties/sovereignty, and the second, cultural/religious appropriation.

TREATIES AND SOVEREIGNTY

The first treaty was signed September 17, 1778, at Fort Pitt (that would later become Pittsburgh, Pennsylvania) between the Delaware people and the American colonies. The American Revolutionary War did not end until 1783; the British and Americans each sought alliance in order to win. In this case, the colonial forces wanted to assure that the Delaware did not fight with the British. "The treaty with the Delaware gives insight into Indian and U.S. relations at the very beginning of the treaty making process. The Delaware treaty was a treaty of peace and mutual protection. . . . As peaceful allies, the Delaware and United States of America agreed to supply military aid to each other in any just war."[4]

Treaties between white men in American leadership and the different tribal groups were not based on a boilerplate format but varied by region and century. However, the ability of the United States' governmental agencies to break the treaties has remained consistent. While the Native people were considered independent and sovereign according to the treaties, both of those terms—independent and sovereign—have had definitions that were changed over time, most often to the Native people's detriment.

From the beginning of the process of forming treaties, language and culture were barriers to honest communication. "Treaties, at least until early in the nineteenth century, were state-to-state negotiations regarding rights and property. . . . Many treaty negotiations were conducted not only in a language

(English) that many native participants did not completely understand, but according to assumptions of European property rights that were foreign to them."[5]

"Independent and sovereign" may seem to be terms of honoring the people, yet the language more precisely came to mean "domestic dependent nation status" to the U.S. government. But the language papered over the consistent portrayal of Native peoples as infantile and barbaric. By the 1820s, the Chief Justice of the Supreme Court, John Marshall, wrote, "The tribes of Indians inhabiting this country were fierce savages, whose occupation was war. . . . To leave them in possession of their country, was to leave the country a wilderness. . . . Indians are inferior [to Christian Europeans] as a matter of law."[6]

The combination of legal gravity and everyday vilification became a pattern that flowed through white America's approach to people of color. The disparaging ideas about Indians, as Native Americans have come to be commonly called, were accompanied by "a powerful technology. For much of the first four hundred years of contact, technology dealt Indians the hardest blows. Mechanical devices from the musket to the iron kettle to the railroad made it a certainty that Indians would lose the military battle to maintain their independence."[7] These words were from the preeminent Native American scholar Vine Deloria, who challenged the impact of Western science on Native life. He challenged how Western science had treated the Native people as possibilities for science experiments rather than human beings. "Scientists may not have intended to portray Indians as animals rather than humans, but their insistence that Indians are outside the mainstream of human experience produces precisely these reactions in the public mind."[8] The relationship he saw between Western science and Indian spirituality will be considered in greater detail in the next section.

The 562 federally recognized tribes do not include all the tribes in the United States. Those that are recognized span the nation including Alaska and are considered separate nations; therefore, entering treaties with each was necessary to clarify the sets of relationships among the federal government, tribe, and state in which the tribe is located. The issue of sovereignty is related: the tribes should be able to regulate their own lands, based on their tribal system. These regulations do not include maintaining armies or printing their own money.

As Joseph Kalt and William Singer explain, sovereignty is simply self-governing. They ask a set of questions that cut through pretense:

> Who is going to decide what constitution we will operate under? Who will decide what environmental rules will govern? Who will decide whether that natural resource gets developed? Who [will] decide if a gaming casino is opened? Who will decide what is taught in the reservation high school? Who

will decide what taxes are collected and from whom? Who can regulate and
enforce contracts, provide remedies for negligent conduct, and adjudicate dis-
putes over property? Who will decide the speed limit on the road into the tribal
headquarters? Who will decide how to decide questions such as these?[9]

If the answer to these questions is any agency or group other than the tribal
government, then "sovereignty" is not realized but is damaged. To be clear,
however, some tribes had found the idea of sovereignty distasteful, for why
would outsiders give the owners the rights to their own land? As an example,
there is a known tribal group in the state of South Carolina that wants nothing
to do with the world outside their tribe. Such ideas have kept some groups
from participating in any aspect of the United States government. But as the
world shrinks, the ability to stay disconnected becomes more contentious—
particularly between younger and older generations.

The push by some Native people for realized sovereignty against federal
and state governments often takes place in courts. For example, a decision
was made in the case of the *Dollar General store v. Mississippi Band of
Choctaw* about the issue: "Whether Indian tribal courts have jurisdiction to
adjudicate civil tort claims against nonmembers, including as a means of
regulating the conduct of nonmembers who enter into consensual relationships with a tribe or its members."[10] Which entity has the right to hear a case
of alleged sexual assault when one of the parties is non-Indian? The tribal
courts argued that they had that authority. The Supreme Court rendered a
decision in June 2016, allowing authority to remain with the tribal court.[11]

The back-and-forth from tribal groups to federal government or to states
is politically fraught and socially burdensome at best. Treaties aren't just
agreements on paper but work through sets of relationships in life. "More
than 500 treaties have been made between the government and Indian tribes
and all were broken, nullified or amended."[12] Even when Native Americans
attempted to have treaties upheld through the courts, precedents were set that
gave all power to the United States.

The landmark case of *Lone Wolf v. Hitchcock* is such an example. An
1867 treaty defined millions of acres as Indian land but, by 1892, Congress
had decided to open two million of those acres to settlement by non-Indians.
Lone Wolf, a Kiowa chief, brought suit that went all the way to the Supreme
Court. The Court stated that the Congress could take such action under the
Due Process Clause of the Fifth Amendment. "Justice Edward D. White
described the Indians as 'the wards of the nation,' and matters involving
Indian lands were the sole jurisdiction of Congress" that could "abrogate the
provisions of an Indian treaty."[13] Obviously, breaking treaties generally will
not engender trust; rather, distrust is engendered. When the severance exclusively benefits one side of the agreements, damage to trust may be irrepara-
ble.

The National Council of American Indians presents a version of a Native American history timeline from their own perspectives. I will highlight four of their designated time periods: the Indian Reorganization Period; the Termination Period; the Self-Determination Period; and the Nation-to-Nation Period. These four are not comprehensive but do present snapshots of relationships between the United States government and various tribal groups.

The Indian Reorganization Period (1934–1945): The federal government "began to restore Indian lands to tribes." Yet this restoration was not so straightforward. The so-called reorganization period had been preceded by a legally mandated "mainstreaming" of Native peoples in 1887 under the Dawes Act. The aim of the Dawes Act was to take the lands of Indians, and more than ninety million acres of reservation land were taken and given to settlers. In 1934, tribal lands were "restored" by defining the lands' boundaries. At the same time, federal programs were set up intended to aid economic development.[14] The end result was still a loss of Indian lands and control.

A perfect illustration of this "reorganization" that bridges into the next time period was the 1944 passage of the Pick-Sloan act. The Act established the Missouri Valley Authority (MVA) and approved at least "a total of 107 dams. . . . In addition to giant flood-control dams numerous earthen levees and concrete floodwalls were constructed on both sides of the river from Sioux City to the Mississippi. . . . The plan also aimed at irrigating 1.5 million acres of precious bottomland in the lower basin [and] 5 million in the upper basin."[15] The impact of the Pick-Sloan Act on the "sovereign" Native tribes was not considered. The projects along the river were not completed until 1966 and crossed the Standing Rock, Cheyenne River, Crow Creek, Lower Brule, and Yankton Reservations. "Army dams in the Missouri inundated more than 202,000 acres of Sioux land. Approximately 580 families were uprooted. . . . Their best homelands, their finest pastures, croplands, and hay meadows."[16] This Act bridged the time between the Indian Reorganization period to the next.

The Termination Period (1945–1968): Any advances to Native life in the previous period were reversed as "Congress decided that federal recognition and assistance to more than 100 tribes should be terminated. . . . [which] created economic disaster for many tribes, resulting in millions of acres of valuable natural resources and land being lost through tax forfeiture sales." The voluntary physical relocation of Indians off reservations into urban areas created another layer of economic and mental stress.[17]

The Termination Period furthered a stripping away of Indian land and rights. By 1962, Native Americans began various social movements to insist on their rights to self-determination. As stated earlier, sovereignty is self-rule. Questioning the state of affairs was not a luxury when treaties and agreements were broken. Such questioning is a response to legal violations. When legal action was not enough, activism has occurred. One action was the Trail of Broken Treaties (TBT) caravan, a bit out of the time frame but demonstrating a direct response to Termination. The title is a twist on the older Trail of Tears[18] nomenclature.

The Trail of Broken Treaties caravan began in October 1972 with families traveling from the West Coast. Eight hundred people arrived in Washington, DC, November 1. By November 2, it was clear that the protesters had inadequate shelter, so they turned to the Bureau of Indian Affairs (BIA) for assistance. It is sometimes said that the Indians "took over" the BIA building. But as one eyewitness stated, "The leaders met with BIA Commissioner Louis R. Bruce (Mohawk and Sioux), while other TBT people watched films and compared notes about problems in their territories. It is more the case that the BIA building was abandoned than taken over."[19] After a tense stand-off, the leaders did meet with representatives of the federal government.

Self-Determination Period (1968–2000): This period was noteworthy because Congress passed the "Indian Self-Determination And Education Assistance Act. The government could now contract with tribal governments for federal services."[20] This includes schools on reservations, teaching Native languages and culture. The Bureau of Indian Affairs has a Division of Self-Determination Services "to promote and advocate maximum Indian participation in the programs and services conducted by the Federal Government for Indians."[21]

Despite the time line and pro-Native legislation, seizure of treaty-designated Indian lands continued throughout the twentieth century. "The United States has used its power of eminent domain to obtain large parcels of Indian land for public works projects."[22] This process of claiming land through eminent domain has consistently happened to property where people of color reside. Where to put the freeway or the railway line? Lands where Indian or black Americans have resided have been particularly subject to the state's consideration.

There were smaller local battles during this Self-Determination Period. In 1983, a federal court decision allowed the Anishinaabe (also known as Ojibwe and Chippewa) to resume spearfishing in northern Wisconsin. Although earlier treaties (1837 and 1842) had guaranteed Indians use of natural resources on reservation land, these had been stripped away during the Termination Period. Regaining spearfishing rights was important to the tribe's identity. However, white supremacists saw these Indian rights as losses for themselves, claiming the Natives were being given special privileges.

[White supremacists in Wisconsin] demanded an end to Indian spearfishing, using in part legitimate political means to pressure elected officials, but also resorting to vigilante actions, mob violence, terror and intimidation. . . . They argued that Indians depleted the supply of game, driving tourists away from the region and leaving whites with status as second class citizens. Although the amount of fish and game secured through treaty-sanctioned practices remained infinitesimally small, Indians became convenient scapegoats for the serious economic problems that did face the region. . . . A sign displayed by members of a mob attacking Ojibwe spearfishers counseled "Save a Walleye: Spear an Indian."[23]

The Trail of Broken Treaties protest and reinstatement of spearfishing rights achieved some small success in the larger fight for Indian rights. However, like the anger at Wisconsin's spearfishers, the lie of white superiority would keep pushing against any movement aiming for a clear establishment of Indian sovereignty. I visited a nearby area in Wisconsin in the early 1980s and met with a bishop of a Christian church who sneered at the idea of including Indians in planning worship services. They, he informed me, are too warrior-like.

The Nation-to-Nation Period (2000 to present), seemed to have arrived as President Bill Clinton's Executive Order for Consultation and Coordination with Indian Tribal Governments engendered greater self-governance and self-determination, creating government-to-government communication lines. But the path was not that straightforward or rosy. The realities of American Indian lives and the related political conditions remain difficult; a few years of being in greater control will not erase centuries of oppression.

As one author stated, "Many Americans have misperceptions that poverty should not exist on reservations because Native people's basic needs are taken care of under treaties."[24] Yet poverty hits Indians hard. It should be noted that there are many Native people no longer on reservations. Pushed off reservations in the Termination Period, today, like many other groups, Indians move to cities in search of better opportunities. But jobs are not easily found and federal money does not follow them into their new living arrangements.[25]

Data on Indian poverty today presents brutal realities that are not apparent through much of the United States, as research found, "Seventeen percent of Native Hawaiians and Pacific Islanders and 27 percent of all self-identified Native Americans and Alaska Natives live in poverty. . . . [T]he Standing Rock Sioux on the border of North and South Dakota, where the poverty rate is 43.2 percent—almost three times the national average . . . the unemployment rate on the Standing Rock Reservation was over 60 percent as of 2014."[26]

So, I return to the story that began this chapter as the shaman stated, "At least you still have a people." The rip-off of Native lands over centuries, including broken treaties and flouted sovereignty, is one level of pain experienced by that shaman. But when accompanied by cultural and religious oppression, the race-politics-religion intersection snaps into place.

APPROPRIATION OF CULTURES AND SPIRITUALITY

The United States was founded July 4, 1776, but there are theories that the people we know as Native Americans have populated the land for 14,000 years.[27] Their cultures, languages, spiritualties, and sciences were well developed before Europeans ever arrived. As one author stated, "American Indians are generally the object of scientific study rather than being considered scientists in their own right." She gave the example of the medicine wheel, as "evidence of the practice of science. . . . To identify the first appearance of the sun and stars on the horizon required systematic observation for considerable lengths of time."[28]

The Indian princess story at the beginning of this chapter indicates something else: not that Native people were viewed as culturally and intellectually significant, but that there was something romantic about "noble savages" or "Indian princesses." For Native Americans, the misperceptions of their cultures and intelligence were accompanied by unique stereotypes. The negative views of "the warrior" or "the squaw" were widespread and tied to the spatial construction of the wild, needing-to-be-tamed frontier. But white Americans had captured romantic images, like princesses, into their own cultures.

The myths that developed around Indians were born from white Americans' needs to develop their own identifiable culture. From the birth of the country, a need to distinguish "American" from English or other European countries was a driving question. What is American art, music, or literature? The Indian face, male and female, was distinctive and helped to serve as foils for some distinctive American myths. The myth of the warrior had an American white male counterpart: the indomitable frontiersman. Davy Crockett, Daniel Boone, James Bowie, and even George Custer were heroes to white Northern Americans from the late eighteenth and into the mid-nineteenth century and beyond. A manly American, different from European men, was embraced as representative of the spirit of the United States.

White women found a path to participate in the mythology by claiming distant kinship with Pocahontas. But the kinship was based on a fairytale of who Pocahontas was supposed to be.

Pocahontas, Version 1: A brave Indian princess defied her father to save and then wed her true love, the English colonist John Smith. Indian lore presents a different story and that tale deserves retelling here to highlight how race and politics overlapped in the processes of misappropriation of Native peoples' cultures.

Pocahontas, Version 2: When John Smith arrived at Roanoke in the early 1600s, Pocahontas was only nine or ten years old. She was daughter of the chief but as a child, she would have had little to do with decisions made by her father. Some years later, she did marry a young warrior around the age of fourteen and had a child. The English were behaving badly, however. Because Native women might go topless during hot summer months, English-men took this as invitation to rape the women. Hostilities were breaking out and Pocahontas was demanded as a hostage to ensure peace. She was taken by a sea captain to Jamestown. There, she was raped and had a son out of wedlock. She eventually married John Rolfe in 1614. Rolfe was desperate to maintain his failing tobacco business in the colonies. He needed an alliance with the tribe to get his business off the ground. Pocahontas and her son, Thomas Rolfe, were sent to England. She died in 1617, and rumors of her murder still resound in Indian communities.[29]

By the 1920s, many white women claimed kinship with one or another Indian princess. They were not claiming relationship to Pocahontas, version 2, but to the fantasy of version 1 that fit into white women's expectations for marriage and family. The fictional Indian princess stood by her man, defied her daddy for love, and lived happily as a homemaker. The claim of kinship with the fantasy became so common that the "Pocahontas exception" was made to the one-drop rule. That rule forbade white American marriage with those who had any black or Indian antecedent. (This rule did not signify that sex was forbidden.) Those who claimed to be (distant) descendants of Poca-hontas or another princess were exempt by law from marital exclusion.[30] Part of the "scientific" reason for the exception was that Native Americans were higher on the evolutionary scale than black people and, therefore, accept-able.[31]

Yet claims were based on a twisted tale that romanticized the Pocahontas story and cleaned up the roles that the white colonizers played. Such tale-telling by the dominant race occurs again and again in their relationships with oppressed peoples. A hidden part of such narratives is an idea that the Native people (or any other group) were tamed by the will of the better people. In the process, like the Pocahontas fairytale, there is a drive to co-opt the tamed personas into the "American" cultural story. In a similar manner, co-optation of Indian spiritualty has been part of the story of relationships between Native and white Americans and has expanded since many Americans began an intense search for alternative spiritualities in the late twentieth century.

Native spirituality is earth based, very different from a Western perspec-tive of religion and what comprises a religion. One Native writer, Henrietta Mann, discusses the connection of the people to the Earth in this way:

> The Great Mysterious Life-Giver planted the first people in the ground-womb of the Great Mother Earth and gave them spiritual-rooted lifeways that are anchored in the dirt and soil of this land comprising the Western Hemi-sphere. . . . The natural people of this land, the culturally and spiritually diverse first nations, have long-standing and continuous caretaking respon-sibilities for maintaining the sanctity of the earth. This is affirmed by their beliefs that they come from the earth, that they must live in mutual relationship

with the earth, that they must constantly and responsibly observe ceremonies that revitalize and renew the earth, and that in the end, they return to the earth.[32]

The shapes of these beliefs are so far outside of the Western and Christian religious views: of relations to the land, of responsibilities of people to land, of the reasons for human existence, of death. The practices the above author referenced comprise aspects of cultures that are also out of the mainstream American experiences. It is possible for Americans to learn but that is not what often happens.

The number of religiously unaffiliated Americans has grown.[33] But there are also those who view themselves as seekers through New Age movements.[34] Some of these people may choose to explore Native American spirituality. In a Western schema, earth-based spiritualities are often considered "primitive." For those who are members of mainstream Christian religions, this may be pejorative; for those who are seeking through New Age paths, this may seem to offer a glimpse of a purer, simpler way to be—another version of a fairytale. There are a plethora of books, audio links, healing herbs for sale, and web-based videos, all claiming to represent Native spirituality or beliefs. There are even Native American tarot or vision-quest cards for sale. While there may be a small percentage of these that are genuine, too often these items are cultural misappropriations.

Another way that Native spiritual practices are misappropriated is to take aspects of prayer experiences and to try to use them within Christian services. If a Christian community is mostly Native people, they would know how to seamlessly insert their culturally based prayer into a given ceremony. Yet there are awful attempts to use Native practices. One of the worst prayer services I ever attended was within the context of a retreat as an undergraduate. The leader was a well-known speaker, a white man, who at one point asked all into a circle for a prayer that he claimed was Native American. Neither he nor the participants were Native; today, I suspect that he was using a gimmick to keep us undergraduates awake. The prayer began with his instruction that everyone turn to and salute the four directions. By the time we had flopped around looking for North, we were caught in the ridiculousness of the moment and our "prayer" moment was in shambles. The resulting silliness was far distant from the sacred experiences mentioned above by Henrietta Mann. Thankfully, the speaker was not skilled in his attempted appropriation of a Native practice. But some are.

George E. Tinker discussed contemporary commodification of Native American rituals and traditions. While participants may seek something wholesome, the leader is seeking profits. The results are not benign but commodify spiritual traditions and practices of Native Americans to "trade in the Great American Supermarket of Fetish Spirituality." However, Tinker stressed that when commodified by Westerners, "outwardly appearing Indian forms (ceremonial forms) are no longer Indian in any respect once they leave the community. Rather, they are being pressed to serve the Euro-American cultural needs of the individual." The very intent of the ritual changes. As my silly experience of "Native" ritual demonstrated, "No longer is the well-being of a whole community the focus of the ceremonial act. Indian spirituality has become the playground, then, of the liberally minded, self-affirming contemporary colonizer. For all intents and purposes, it becomes something to dabble in, a distraction from a life that is rote, or an exotic expression of the return to nature."[35] Or, a way to keep undergraduate students engaged.

Here, race and religion overlap. But all of the Native experience with religion is not merely the misappropriation of their own spiritual views. White Americans believed that there was need to force Indians to convert to Christianity.

> As tribes grew weaker militarily and lost their political and economic independence, the government and the churches quickly aligned. Soon, in spite of constitutional prohibitions, Christianity was made the official religion of Indian reservations, and traditional tribal religions were banned. Indeed, Indian students were allowed to read their language only if the Bible had been printed in it. In 1870, President Grant simply handed out religious monopolies to the respective denomination in different parts of the country. Thus some tribes are Lutheran, Catholics, Episcopalians and Presbyterians not because a missionary eloquently convinced them of the validity of Christianity but because Grant had already promised the larger tribes to another denomination.[36]

Today, with the reassertion of Indian rights, some groups more intensely renew their spiritual practices. Claiming spiritual practices to reaffirm identity has been important for individuals as well as creating a sense of community. Powwows have long been a part of Native spiritual life. Indians of different tribal lineages who live in urban areas may reconnect with their heritage through powwows. "These urban Indian communities began to formulate tribal-style interactions outside of specific tribal circumstances. The religious implications" of bringing existing powwow rituals and expressions into this new urban setting are significant. These are "community-forming efforts by urban and urbanized Indians revolv[ing] around culturally-specific activities such as singing, dancing, storytelling, traditional arts, etc., all which have religious connotations in their specific tribal contexts."[37]

The processes of rediscovering, reclaiming, and reinstituting Native cultures and spiritualities are not simply reversals of colonization. These are efforts to reach understandings of Native cultures for themselves and for these times. These processes are called decolonization, but the centuries of eroding indigenous peoples' lands, identities, languages, and religious lives cannot be magically undone.

At this late date in colonial history, we Indians are left to wonder, What is left? Who are we, culturally, religiously, politically? As a result, considerable American Indian energy is regularly invested in the question of who is what and what one is. The concern invades Indian politics, Indian social service activities, Indian entitlement determinations, Indian religious participation, and Indian social life in general.[38]

The term "decolonization" has some other difficulties as well. Most often it is used in relation to formerly colonized territories/nations where the colonizer has left, by choice or force. Then the processes of rediscovering, reclaiming, and reinstituting take on entirely different meanings as new nations carve out their own spaces. That is not really the case for Native peoples. The colonizers are still with them, promising them their own space, but still finding ways to encroach on land and identity. The question above, "Who are we?" is not a rhetorical exercise. Who are the people who are nation-to-nation sovereign but not freed of the colonizer? How can they claim their own identities at a time when their ways of living are commodified? Should they participate in American societies? What happens when they move to urban areas and are cut off from a sense of "us"?

These complications can be seen through certain congressional actions during the Self-Determination Period, when laws were passed to return artifacts to Native Americans. In 1990, the Native American Graves Protection and Repatriation Act was passed. Efforts have been made to return artifacts and remains from museums to Native groups. "No one anticipated the emotional cost of repatriation, not to mention the exorbitant expense to low-budget tribal governments and communities. In addition, the return of human remains has thrust some first nations into a cultural dilemma in terms of the absence of ceremonies for reburial. Return of sacred objects also requires serious consideration of possible health risks associated with handling such items, which may have been contaminated with hazardous substances, such as arsenic."[39]

Decolonizing theology becomes another focus for people who have been oppressed. Finding and claiming a religious identity and history, the values and meanings that are built into that way of thinking, is a struggle. Henrietta Mann's description of the "Great Mysterious Life-Giver" and her profound relationship with lifeways anchored in "Great Mother Earth," in fact, may *not* be considered a religion because it does not fit a definition of such in a Western epistemology.

Adding to these difficulties, some white Americans resented the efforts toward decolonization. Some anti-sovereignty movements began. The groups range across states where Indians are beginning to exert their sovereignty, perhaps by levying a tax to those living on property within the boundaries of Indian lands. Taking their battles into courts, the stateside groups have names such as Upstate Citizens for Equality (New York State), Montanans Opposing Discrimination, Flathead Residents Earning Equality (Montana), Protect Americans' Rights and Resources (Wisconsin), and Proper Economic Resource Management (Wisconsin). There are also national groups opposing Native sovereignty: Citizens Equal Rights Alliance, Citizens' Rights Organization, All Citizens Equal, and Interstate Congress for Equal Rights and Responsibilities. There are three major themes shared by all these groups. First, they call for "equal rights for whites." Next, the anti-sovereignty groups argue that they should have equal access to natural resources and that no group should be singled out for exclusive rights, as the spearfishing dispute above demonstrated. Finally, the groups charge the Natives with dependency on the government: "All Indians are said to wallow in welfare, food stamps, free housing and medical care, affirmative-action programs, and gargantuan federal cash payments, all tax free."[40]

The intersection of race, politics, and religion, historically, has effectively taken Indian lands and oppressed Native people culturally, socially, and physically. Law, Christianity, custom, and claims of white superiority combined. The intersection continues into the twenty-first century, as the anti-sovereignty movements show, to limit and contain them. But it is not just external to Native people; another form of the intersection has been understood as a key for Indians to decolonize themselves. While discovering a sense of their Indian identities, they also reclaim their own spirituality and they act politically. "Essentially then, a Native American theology must be a liberation theology and a theology of resistance, and as such, it must speak out of its uniquely indigenous context. Thus, it must begin and end its spiritual journey with political analysis."[41]

HUMAN RIGHTS WORKING

As mistreatment of Native people happened in the United States, mistreatment also occurred to indigenous peoples in other countries. The United Nations' Declaration on the Rights of Indigenous Peoples (2008) begins with several affirmations including the following:

> Affirming that indigenous peoples are equal to all other peoples, while recognizing the right of all peoples to be different, to consider themselves different, and to be respected as such;
> Affirming also that all peoples contribute to the diversity and richness of civilizations and cultures, which constitute the common heritage of humankind;
> Affirming further that all doctrines, policies and practices based on or advocating superiority of peoples or individuals on the basis of national origin or racial, religious, ethnic or cultural differences are racist, scientifically false, legally invalid, morally condemnable and socially unjust.[42]

Each of these affirmations emphasizes the humanity of indigenous people, and this in the twenty-first century. These affirmations lead to 46 Articles. But the Declaration is for the *world's* indigenous peoples. It does not necessarily speak to local levels, although one American Native group did apply to the United Nations as will be seen below. But, in general, there is a distance between this Declaration and the grassroots. This distance returns to the importance of human rights from below to address injustices, especially related to race, religion, and politics.

There are three examples of where human rights from below occur at the local level in the United States. The first example is the ongoing contestation between Energy Transfer Partners and the Standing Rock Sioux. In this contestation, the question of sovereignty and its relationship to human rights surfaces again. Should Native sacred places be secured and honored or are business interests more important? The second example considers how Indian cultures and ideas are preserved and communicated, looking at one museum and one Native American Studies program. Questions raised by George Tinker and Vine Deloria make these sites of ambiguity and danger: the humanity of Indians could be upheld or reduced. Finally, the third example is voting rights for and by Native Americans along with participation in all aspects of the United States government.

Standing Rock

One ongoing situation compresses and exemplifies the ideas about race, politics, and religion's intersection in Native Americans lives today. In July, 2016, the Energy Transfer Partners notified the Standing Rock Sioux that the Dakota Access Pipeline would be constructed next to their reservation.

> Many at Standing Rock saw the threat of environmental catastrophe as inextricable from racial injustice. An early proposal to route the Dakota Access Pipeline through Bismarck, 45 miles north of the reservation, was rejected by the US Army Corps of Engineers because of concerns that it could harm the municipal water supply. (Bismarck's population is 92 percent white.) "But it's okay if it poisons Natives' water, right?" said Chanse Adams-Zavalla, a 22-year-old who grew up on the Maidu reservation just north of Santa Barbara, California. [43]

Energy Transfer Partners argues that they are not laying the pipes on the reservation land. They are in fact near the river; they have no pipeline-spill emergency plans in place. Despite that reality, they have stated,

> We have great respect for the concerns of the Standing Rock Sioux Tribe and plan to continue to work with their leaders. . . . Recently, their interests have been overtaken by politically motivated, anti-fossil fuel protesters who are using the issue as a cover. . . . Their actions deny private property rights and

freedoms to the landowners who are near and adjacent to the Standing Rock Reservation and deny American citizens and businesses the energy they need to produce jobs.[44]

Their arguments suspiciously parallel the anti-sovereignty movement, not understanding Indian rights, accusing them, or in this case outside environmental agitators, of barring "citizens" from energy and jobs.

After July 2016, "members of more than 200 Native American tribes and their allies gathered to block what would be America's longest crude oil pipeline. Their encampments of teepees, tents, and RVs were mostly ignored by the media until private security guards set dogs on protesters and a few journalists were arrested, sparking a national conversation about tribal sovereignty, environmental racism, and police brutality."[45]

In August 2016, some protesters were arrested. In September, U.S. District Court Judge James Boasberg rejected the Sioux's suit to end the construction, but the Army engineers stated that further review was needed. The Standing Rock Sioux and their allies seemed to have lost the battle, after violence against protesters and against police, with wrangling back and forth in court, and physical removal of the protesters. By the end of January 2017, executive action by a new president superseded all court cases, and the construction of the pipeline began.

But the Sioux had not been standing still while these seeming losses occurred. In September 2016, the chair of the tribe, Dave Archambault, went to Geneva, Switzerland, "asking members of the United Nations Human Rights Commission to condemn 'the deliberate destruction of our sacred places.'" Because it was not simply acreage and but also sacred sites, such as burial grounds, that were in danger from the pipeline. "Archambault called on the commission and its members 'to condemn the destruction of our sacred places and to support our nation's efforts to ensure that our sovereign rights are respected. We ask that you call upon all parties to stop the construction of Dakota Access Pipeline and to protect the environment, our nation's future, our culture and our way of life,' he said."[46]

June 2017 brought two victories to the tribe. On June 14, Judge James Boasberg ruled in the tribe's favor, stating that "the U.S. Army Corps of Engineers failed to perform an adequate study of the pipeline's environmental consequences when it first approved its construction."[47]

Earlier in the month, the tribe received the Henry A. Wallace Award from the Wallace Global Fund. The $250,000 award was for the tribe's courage standing up against the "oppressive combination of corporate and governmental power." In addition, the Wallace Global Fund pledged an additional $1 million toward "the tribes' transition away from fossil fuels. That shift toward clean energy, which Archambault says began about a decade ago, involves change on the individual, community, and commercial levels. in addition to helping all seven Sioux reservations sell clean wind and solar power to out-of-state buyers, the tribe's goals include increasing their energy independence."[48]

As complex as this situation at Standing Rock has been, some aspects of reaching for human rights at a local level can be seen. The Sioux tribe persisted through the courts; the same judge that denied their request the first time later adjudged that not enough study of environmental consequences had been made. This persistence becomes part of the processes of identifying and gaining human rights, for power is never conceded easily. The tribe received recognition and a monetary award through a global fund. Ultimately, painfully, they stayed true to their own identities as connected to the earth and to their communities.

A Museum and a Native American Studies Program

Places where human rights could potentially be enacted are Native American museums and Native American studies programs. I mention only one of each here, as possible exemplars of holding up the humanity of Native American peoples.

Perhaps the most significant museum is the National Museum of the American Indian in Washington, DC. The Museum has a board of directors composed of Native people from the entire country. The focus of exhibits is to highlight Indian people across the country. The Museum is a site of pride, of holding on to history and cultures within a country that has not honored sovereignty and has too often appropriated Indian culture.

The recognition of American Indian cultures includes the architecture: "It needed to be a living museum, neither formal nor quiet, located in close proximity to nature. . . . [T]he building's design should make specific celestial references, such as an east-facing main entrance and a dome that opens to the sky." Such recognition of cultural difference includes the landscaping. "Native people believe that the earth remembers the experiences of past generations."[49] This centering of the perspectives of Indian people resounds with the United Nations Declaration on the Rights of Indigenous Peoples, mentioned above, one article of which is repeated here: "Affirming that indigenous peoples are equal to all other peoples, while recognizing the right of all peoples to be different, to consider themselves different, and to be respected as such."[50]

The issues of human rights are more focused when there is a Native American studies program housed at a university or college. Now, instead of the one-day tourist, such a program conducts research and delivers educational classes. Such programs particularly bear the weight of past relationships and the criticisms about the resulting scholarship. Some of the sharpest criticisms came from Vine Deloria Jr. He stated that the sacred and secular were placed into binary categories, and preference was given to reason over all else. Therefore, the "only referent point was the human mind and in particular the middle-class, educated European mind. . . . Scientists would come to act like priests and defer to doctrine and dogma when determining what truths would be admitted, how they would be phrased, and how scientists themselves would be protected from the questions of the mass of people whose lives were becoming increasingly dependent on them."[51] Native American Studies programs struggle with whose voice should be heard and how the information is to be delivered.

And the content always stands against the Western canon. Michelene Pesantubbe is a religion scholar who recognized the pioneering place of first-generation scholar Vine Deloria as well as others. She writes of the challenges: "As many of us engage in the intellectual pursuit of culturally centered theories, our efforts are often met with a less than enthusiastic reception by those who would maintain the status quo. . . . Before real dialogue can begin, however, some degree of equanimity between the Western and Non-Western approach must be achieved."[52] These issues of decolonizing the mind left me with more questions.

So I turned to some conversation partners at the University of South Carolina Lancaster's Native American Studies Center. The center formally began in 2012 and focuses on the Catawba tribe. Because of a donation, the center holds the largest documentation of the Catawba—including pottery. I went to the center, knowing that my questions would be better asked in person.

I met with faculty and staff: Christopher Judge, an archaeologist who holds weekly public archeology labs; Stephen Criswell, the director; Brent Burgin, an archivist; and Adam Biggs, who works with African American Studies.

My first question was based on the fact that, with the exception of Adam Biggs, these are all white men who work directly within the Center. I wondered if the arts focus of the center was reductive of the broader issues of the Catawba. I mentioned the story of the Indian princess and this brought great laughter, with the agreed-upon sentiment: If we've heard it once, we've heard it a thousand times. The discussion ranged over cultural diffusion, cultural appropriation, that we are all mixed, cultural transmission, and local tribes that are not federally recognized.

But here is the portion of the conversation that related to concepts of human rights: I wondered about the relationships between the Native American Studies Center and the tribes. Twelve years ago, the staff brought in the all the chiefs to shape the destiny of the proposed center. They asked, "How are we going to build this? How are we going to work together?" The chiefs responded, "You need to get past your Amero-centricity. Tell our true story. We need education and jobs." The center staff and faculty meet with

tribal leaders annually to check in. An annual artist-in-residence is celebrated; Catawba artifacts are preserved; the center staff work with and within the
tribal communities; there are continued efforts to improve educational options. In 2015, the first Catawba received a PhD with the encouragement,
support, and mentorship of the staff at the center. Part of what can be seen is
a beginning shift in anthropology and ethnography, or how people are studied by scholars.

Voting Rights

The Native American Voting Rights Coalition website begins with a quote of
Ben Black Elk: "Martin Luther King said, 'I have a dream.' But we Indians
didn't have a dream. We had a reality."[53] Or, as the shaman stated at the
beginning of this chapter, "At least you still have a people." How then might
Natives assert their rights as a people? Some are becoming more engaged in
American political life, and this is fully their human right.

Recognizing that some Native tribal groups reject participation in
American political processes, others have begun actions in which Native
Americans are working to assert their voting rights. In an area of Nevada, a
lawsuit charged that the "tribal citizens had to travel as many as 100 miles to
vote." Local officials opened more polling stations and, now, several other
tribal groups have begun their own lawsuits. "In Alaska, where native people
make up a fifth of the population, officials recently rolled out election materials in the Yup'ik, Inupiaq, and Gwich'in languages, following federal rulings
that found the state had failed to provide materials equivalent to those used
by English speakers."[54]

The size of the Bears Ears National Monument in Utah was recently
slashed, losing its protected status. The argument to reducing the size is for
exploration of minerals. However, the monument has ancestral connections
to five tribal groups. Though not directly related to voting rights, the processes of pursuing a lawsuit to protect the land still represent an establishment of
rights. This along with other issues, may become strong motivation for Native Americans to actively participate in voting in the future.

CONCLUDING THOUGHTS

Like history's approach "from below," research about people can take into
account the porous nature of cultures and the reality that truth is not a fixed
quantity. In the words of one anthropologist, "If 'culture' is not an object to
be described, neither is it a unified corpus of symbols and meanings that can
be definitively interpreted. Culture is contested, temporal, and emergent."[55]

These sentiments reflect the training and attitude of the staff and faculty
at the Native American Center I visited. Such attitudes are a far cry from the

challenges that Vine Deloria has thrown out to scholars. But the remnants of anti-sovereignty movements prove that the negative uses of science and scholarship have had an impact on the American public imagination of the "Indian."

Voting rights in particular have the potential to assert Native rights in some locales. But the need to combat poverty and abrogation of treaties and land grabs require more than simple voting. Legal action, as the Standing Rock Sioux have begun to use, may expand.

Yet, these tactics, recognizing that culture is neither unified nor definitively interpreted, leave room for honest conversations, ways to get over our Amero-centricity. Finding ways to honestly tell the stories of the Native Americans and other Others, especially in their own voices, are integral to building a genuine, honest, and holistic American view of human rights.

The next chapter turns to African Americans with other sets of challenges to enrich the conversations.

NOTES

1. R. S. Sugirtharajah, *Voices from the Margins: Interpreting the Bible in the Third World*, cited in Stephen Burns, introduction to *Postcolonial Practice of Ministry: Leadership, Liturgy, and Interfaith Engagement*, eds. Kwok Pui-Lan and Stephen Burns (Lanham, MD: Lexington Books, 2016), 2.

2. Tony Long, "August 3, 1492: Columbus Sets Out to Discover . . . a Trade Route," *Wired*, August 3, 2011, https://www.wired.com/2011/08/0803columbus-sets-sail-trade-route/.

3. "Columbus Reports on His First Voyage, 1493," Gilder Lehrman Institute of American History: On History Now, https://www.gilderlehrman.org/content/columbus-reports-his-first-voyage-1493.

4. Duane Champagne, "First Treaty Signed at Fort Pitt with Delaware for Trade and Alliance," *Indian Country Media Network*, February 15, 2014, https://indiancountrymedianetwork.com/history/events/first-treaty-signed-at-fort-pitt-with-delaware-for-trade-and-alliance/.

5. Bruce Johansen, ed., *Enduring Legacy: Native American Treaties and Contemporary Controversies* (Westport, CT: Praeger Publishers, 2004), xiv.

6. Johnson v. M'Intosh, 21 U.S. (8 Wheat.) 543 (1823), cited in Glenn T. Morris, "Vine Deoria, Jr., and the Development of a Decolonizing Critique of Indigenous People and International Relations," in *Native Voices: American Indian Identity and Resistance*, eds. Richard A. Grounds, George E. Tinker, and David E. Wilkins (Lawrence: University Press of Kansas 2003), 108.

7. Vine Deloria, Jr., *Red Earth, White Lies: Native Americans and the Myth of Scientific Fact* (New York: Scribner, 1995), 16.

8. Deloria, *Red Earth, White Lies*, 20.

9. Joseph P. Kalt and Joseph William Singer, "Myths and Realities of Tribal Sovereignty: The Law and Economics of Indian Self-Rule," Faculty Research Working Papers Series, Harvard University, John F. Kennedy School of Government, March 2004, 5.

10. "Dollar General Corporation v. Mississippi Band of Choctaw Indians," SCOTUSblog, June 23, 2016, http://www.scotusblog.com/case-files/cases/dollar-general-corporation-v-mississippi-band-of-choctaw-indians/.

11. "Jun 23 2016, Adjudged to be AFFIRMED by an equally divided Court," "Dollar General Corporation v. Mississippi Band of Choctaw Indians."

12. Samuel Vargo, "With More Than 500 Treaties Already Broken, the Government Can Do Whatever It Wants, It Seems . . . ," *Daily Kos*, November 21, 2014, https://www.dailykos.com/story/2014/11/21/1345986/-With-more-than-500-treaties-already-broken-the-government-can-do-whatever-it-wants-it-seems.

13. "Lone Wolf v Hitchcock," *Oyez*, https://www.oyez.org/cases/1900-1940/187us553.

14. National Council of American Indians, *Tribal Nations and the United States: An Introduction* (Washington, DC: Embassy of Tribal Nations, 2015), 15, http://www.ncai.org/tribalnations/introduction/Tribal_Nations_and_the_United_States_An_Introduction-web-.pdf.

15. Michael L. Lawson, *Dammed Indians: The Pick-Sloan Plan and the Missouri River Sioux, 1944–1980* (Norman: University of Oklahoma Press 1982), 20.

16. Lawson, *Dammed Indians*, 29.

17. National Council of American Indians, *Tribal Nations and the United States*.

18. The 1830 Indian Removal Act, covering several Southern states, was enforced by President Andrew Jackson. Working on behalf of white settlers who wanted to grow cotton on the Indians' land, the federal government forced the Indians to leave their homelands and walk thousands of miles to a specially designated Indian territory across the Mississippi River. This difficult and sometimes deadly journey is known as the Trail of Tears. Thousands of people died along this forced march. History.com staff, "Trail of Tears," History.com, 2009, http://www.history.com/topics/native-american-history/trail-of-tears.

19. Suzan Shown Harjo, "Trail of Broken Treaties: A 30th Anniversary Memory," *Indian Country Today*, November 7, 2002, https://indiancountrymedianetwork.com/news/trail-of-broken-treaties-a-30th-anniversary-memory/.

20. "History and Culture: Indian Self Determination and Education Assistance Act 1975," Northern Plains Reservation Aid, http://www.nativepartnership.org/site/PageServer?pagename=airc_hist_selfdeterminationact.

21. Division of Self-Determination Services, Bureau of Indian Affairs, https://www.bia.gov/bia/ois/dsd.

22. Lawson, *Dammed Indians*, xx.

23. George Lipsitz, "Walleye Warriors and White Identities: Native Americans' Treaty Rights, Composite Identities and Social Movements," *Ethnic and Racial Studies* 31, no. 1 (January 2008), 103–4.

24. Helen Oliff, "Treaties Made, Treaties Broken," *Partnership with Native Americans*, March 3, 2011, http://blog.nativepartnership.org/treaties-made-treaties-broken/.

25. Timothy Williams, "Quietly, Indians Reshape Cities and Reservations," *New York Times*, April 13, 2013, http://www.nytimes.com/2013/04/14/us/as-american-indians-move-to-cities-old-and-new-challenges-follow.html.

26. Julian Brave NoiseCat, "Thirteen Issues Facing Native People beyond Mascots and Casinos," *Huffington Post*, July 30, 2015, updated August 31, 2015, http://www.huffingtonpost.com/entry/13-native-American-issues_us_55b7d801e4b0074ba5a6869c#. Other issues include the following: mass incarceration and policing, the federal government still stripping Native people of land, exploitation of natural resources, violence against women and children, substandard education, poor housing, inadequate health care, economic underdevelopment, youth suicide, loss of Native languages, communities that are still unrecognized.

27. Christopher Klein, "New Study Refutes Theory of How Humans Populated North America," *History*, August 10, 2016, http://www.history.com/news/new-study-refutes-theory-of-how-humans-populated-north-america.

28. Clara Sue Kidwell, "Ethnoastronomy as the Key to Human Intellectual Development and Social Organization," in Grounds, Tinker, and Wilkins, *Native Voices*, 5.

29. Vincent Schilling, "The Story of Pocahontas: Historical Myths versus Sad Reality," *Indian Country Today*, March 21, 2017, https://indiancountrymedianetwork.com/history/genealogy/true-story-pocahontas-historical-myths-versus-sad-reality/

30. Robert Bernasconi, "Crossed Lines in the Racialization Process: Race as a Border Concept," in *Research in Phenomenology* 42, no. 2 (2012): 218.

31. Kevin Noble Maillard, "The Pocahontas Exception of American Indian Ancestry from Racial Purity Law," *Michigan Journal of Race & Law* 12, no. 2 (Spring 2007): 4.

32. Henrietta Mann, "Earth Mother and Prayerful Children: Sacred Sites and Religious Freedom," in Grounds, Tinker, and Wilkins, *Native Voices*, 194.

33. Gregory A. Smith and Alan Cooperman, "The Factors Driving the Growth of the Religious 'Nones' in the U.S.," Pew Research Center, *Fact Tank*, September 14, 2016, http://www.pewresearch.org/fact-tank/2016/09/14/the-factors-driving-the-growth-of-religious-nones-in-the-u-s/.

34. "Members of the New Age Movement," Pew Research Center: Religious Landscape Study, 2014, http://www.pewforum.org/religious-landscape-study/religious-family/new-age/.

35. George E. Tinker, *Spirit and Resistance, Political Theology and American Indian Liberation* (Minneapolis: Fortress Press, 2004), 53.

36. Deloria, *Red Earth, White Lies*, 24.

37. Dennis F. Kelley, "Ancient Traditions, Modern Constructions: Innovation, Continuity, and Spirituality on the Powwow Trail," *Journal for the Study of Religions and Ideologies* 11, no. 33 (Winter 2012): 121.

38. Tinker, *Spirit and Resistance*, 54.

39. Mann, "Earth Mother and Prayerful Children," 203.

40. Bruce E. Johansen, "The New Terminators: A Guide to the Antitreaty Movement," in *Enduring Legacy*, 306–7.

41. Tinker, *Spirit and Resistance*, 6.

42. "United Nations Declaration on the Rights of Indigenous Peoples," March 2008, 1–2, http://www.un.org/esa/socdev/unpfii/documents/DRIPS_en.pdf.

43. Wes Ezinna, "Crude Awakenings," *Mother Jones*, January/February 2017, http://www.motherjones.com/environment/2016/12/dakota-access-pipeline-standing-rock-oil-water-protest/.

44. Dakota Access Pipeline Facts, https://daplpipelinefacts.com/.

45. Ezina, "Crude Awakenings."

46. Mike Nowatzki, "Standing Rock Chairman Asks U.N. Commission to Oppose Dakota Access Pipeline," *Bismarck Tribune*, September 20, 2016, http://bismarcktribune.com/news/state-and-regional/standing-rock-chairman-asks-u-n-commission-to-oppose-dakota/article_421a94ad-d90d-5223-a1ab-fe466860d295.html.

47. Robinson Meyer, "The Standing Rock Sioux Claim 'Victory and Vindication' in Court," *The Atlantic*, June 2017, https://www.theatlantic.com/science/archive/2017/06/dakota-access-standing-rock-sioux-victory-court/530427/.

48. Abbey White, "A Major Global Foundation Just Pledged $1 Million to the Standing Rock Sioux," *The Nation*, June 19, 2017.

49. "Architecture & Landscape: The Architectural Design Process," National Museum of the American Indian, http://nmai.si.edu/visit/washington/architecture-landscape/.

50. "United Nations Declaration on the Rights of Indigenous Peoples," 1.

51. Deloria, *Red Earth, White Lies*, 17.

52. Michelene E. Pesantubbee, "Religious Studies at the Margins: Decolonizing Our Minds," in Grounds, Tinker, and Wilkins, *Native Voices*, 214.

53. "About the Native American Voting Rights Coalition," Native American Rights Fund, https://www.narf.org/native-american-voting-rights-coalition/.

54. Julie Turkewitz, "For Native Americans, a 'Historic Moment' on the Path to Power at the Polls," *New York Times*, January 4, 2018.

55. James Clifford, introduction to *Writing Culture: The Poetics and Politics of Ethnography*, eds. James Clifford and George E. Marcus (Berkeley: University of California Press, 1986), 20.

Chapter Four

Black Identities and the Weight of History

Native Americans experienced racial, religious, and political oppressions at the hands of the white colonizers in a colonizing experiment. That experiment has changed in some cosmetic ways, but has not ended, as the incidents at Standing Rock demonstrate. The processes of turning assorted African peoples into a controlled, Othered group were different: Africans were forcibly imported, becoming cheap, discredited, invisible labor pools. Today, even into the twenty-first century, African Americans experience the race-politics-religion intersection in some particular ways, born of that history. From that history, author Joy DeGruy coined the term "post traumatic slave syndrome," indicating multiple ways that contemporary African American are negatively impacted by the past.[1] This history of oppressive and controlling experiences can be seen when issues of black American identities are explored.

Unlike the Native inhabitants, the constructions of imported Africans' identities had different results. For instance, it is intriguing that when many Americans speak of race, they often are referencing *only* African Americans, for race relations are often collapsed into binary black-white American interactions. "Given the intellectual history of what was once called 'the Negro problem,' the ritualistic conflation of race matters in the United States with blackness is an unfortunate but unavoidable habit of mind."[2] In other words, as stated in chapter 2, black people have "race," and white people are "normal" Americans. Another aspect of this twisted perception of black identities is that the very humanity of black people is still questioned. In these peculiarly formed identities, the intersection of race-politics-religion is lived out. Before getting to identities, I first turn to consideration of the weight of history where the intersection continues to be built and policed.

WEIGHT OF HISTORY

The Willie Lynch letter or speech has been floating around black American communities for decades, seeming to appear during Black Power movements in the 1960s. There is no named author. The basic story is that a white planter in the 1700s counseled other planters to control the enslaved Africans by divide-and-conquer strategies, setting each black person against the other by groupings, such as men against women, field against house workers, and so on.[3] The last name—Lynch—was also a reference to lynching. The Willie Lynch letter/speech is not historical. However, it speaks to something within black communities, serving as a parable that cautions against self-hatred and community destruction. The parable gives a warning that black communities are torn apart by design. The parable serves as an instruction for black people to build community and togetherness as alternatives to defeat Willie Lynch. The parable still makes black Americans stop and think about many incidents in their communities, from crack epidemics to high rates of imprisonment: why does *this* happen to us?

To analyze contemporary black American communities, it is necessary to turn to the far-reaching, historic roots of oppression. Simplistically, misinformation is thrown around that slavery ended in 1863; therefore, there is no black oppression today. But black Americans intimately experience the dissonance between realities and ideas in their own communities as against the rest of the United States. History is a lens that keeps black Americans' thinking clear. The distinctions are seen in the 2012 presidential race between Governor Mitt Romney and President Barack Obama. President Obama wanted to make a point that we live in an interdependent social web and emphasized, "You didn't build that." He referred to business owners who use roads, bridges, gas, electricity, and so on that they did not build in order to create, construct, and run their businesses. But Governor Romney started a feud over the term, arguing, yes, we did build our businesses! In other words, if you built it, you own it exclusively and no one else can claim credit. Some historians I know sent out e-mails with historic photos of the original White House and another of some enslaved Africans, with the caption "Yes, we *did* build it." Within black communities, these counter discussions and arguments, like the Willie Lynch parable, often stand against the prevailing public perceptions.

> The truth is that enslaved Africans plotted and worked—hard—with some even fighting in the Union army for their freedom and citizenship. After the Civil War, they took what little they had and built schools, worked the land to establish their economic independence, and searched desperately to bring their families, separated by slavery, back together. That drive, initiative, and resolve, however, was met with the Black Codes, with army troops throwing them off their promised forty acres, and then with a slew of Supreme Court

decisions eviscerating the Thirteenth [ending enslavement], Fourteenth [citizenship for all born in the United States], and Fifteenth [voting for all male citizens] Amendments.[4] (Additions by author)

After Reconstruction, several states enacted Jim Crow laws, as part of the Black Codes mentioned in the previous quote. In other states, segregation became practice, if not law. Legal or not, segregation was formed with the idea of "separate but equal." The reality is that there was no equality in separation of all services into white and colored. The long term of legal or de jure segregation crafted distinctive aspects of black cultures. Within this time frame, black Americans still tried to find paths forward. One answer to the limits imposed by Jim Crow laws in the South was what came to be known as the Great Migration. Early in the twentieth century, black families left sharecropped farming with the realities of physical and economic violence for employment and greater freedom in the North. But again, history is not to be understood that simplistically. Even when black people sought to leave sharecropping for Northern industries' jobs, "white Southern elites raged with cool, calculated efficiency. . . . [M]ayors, governors, legislators, business leaders, and police chiefs . . . working hand in hand with plantation, lumber mill, and mine owners, devised an array of obstacles and laws to stop African Americans, as U.S. citizens" from leaving.[5]

The northern United States itself was not free of segregation or racism. African Americans were attracted to the North for the promise of decent-paying jobs as industries grew and needed workers. But black workers were still given skewed treatment. For instance, the primary manufacturers in Detroit were the automakers. Ford, Briggs, and Dodge auto plants began to recruit migrants from the South before World War I. The efforts to recruit and retain employees were through hometown black ministers who could vouch for the migrants' willingness to work.

> Detroit's most welcoming employer was Ford, which recruited an elite corps of black male workers through carefully cultivated contacts with leading black ministers. . . . Henry Ford's idiosyncratic paternalism toward black migrants combined with the company's interest in finding workers willing to accept the dirtiest and most grueling jobs. . . . Half of all blacks in the automobile industry nationwide were Ford employees. . . . Most blacks worked in service jobs, especially on plant janitorial and maintenance crews, or in hot, dangerous jobs in foundries or furnace rooms.[6]

As Henry Ford gathered black and white employees to his plants, he also instituted segregated housing. White employees were able to find housing in Dearborn, Michigan; black workers were to find housing in select areas of Detroit. Segregation, whether in the North or the South, was given the blessing of some Christian religions.

RELIGION IN AFRICAN AMERICAN HISTORY

For African Americans, religion, especially Christianity, is woven through-out the history. However, black American humanity was reduced in white Americans' eyes to prove God's requirement that black people are intended as servants and slaves. White theologians focused on constructing negative black identities. The so-called "Curse of Ham," for example, was used throughout the history of African enslavement to justify the institution of slavery.

In this sixteenth-to-seventeenth-century version of the biblical story of Ham, Noah invented wine, drank too much, and fell asleep—naked. Ham wandered by and laughed at his father. Two other sons, Japeth and Shem, covered their father. When Noah woke up, he cursed his son and his children. The effect of the curse began with Ham's son, Canaan. From that time, Ham's descendants exhibited the curse through, what one author terms, a Matrix:

> The Matrix consisted of three fundamental elements: (1) that black skin is the result of God's curse and is therefore a signal and sign of the African's cursed-ness to slavery; (2) that Africans embodied this cursed nature through hyper-sexuality and libidinousness; and (3) that these sinful and cursed Africans were also uncivilized brutes and heathens who were helped by slavery because they were exposed to culture and the saving Gospel of Jesus Christ. At the close of the seventeenth century, the Curse of Ham evoked a single racist image of a black skinned, hypersexualized, pagan slave. This Matrix was then used for more than two centuries to repel any attack against the practice of African slavery in the English colonies of America. [7]

The idea of black people as cursed by God easily connects with a concep-tualization of black people as subhuman beings. Maintaining subjugation of the barely humans was built into American laws and customs. Conversely, many African Americans turned the tables and used religion in self-directed, positive ways, standing against negative ideations, while affirming their own humanity. Anthropologist and author Zora Neale Hurston studied African American religious life in the 1920s. She considered folk cures and hoodoo, language usage and folk religious practices. She stated, "The Negro has not been as christianized as extensively as is generally believed. The great masses are still standing before their pagan altars and calling old gods by a new name." [8] Such practices and beliefs helped ensure black people retained a sense of their humanness. Such affirmation of humanity continued, as in the slogan of the 1968 Memphis Sanitation workers strike: "I Am a Man."

While the Curse of Ham began in the sixteenth century, the religiously negative views of black people as subhuman, as missing some foundational element of humanness, continue into the twenty-first-century United States.

For instance, in 2011, an author stated his reasons for opposition to interracial marriage. "Miscegenation is unnatural and works against God's purposes, especially when racial admixture occurs in large quantities. Therefore its default status is one of moral wrongness."[9] The author does not cite the Curse of Ham, but the "wrongness" of black people is stated quite clearly.

Negative constructions of black people through white religious thought tie into other stereotypes, are infused into the law, and are given support through research paths that start at the point of the stereotypes. Together, this pattern results in significant economic and political deprivations for many black communities.

> Black-white residential segregation remains intense. . . . Segregation remains virtually unchanged at apartheid levels. . . . Public-school segregation, after dramatically improving in the era of civil rights enforcement (1968–90), has significantly eroded. Blacks are now almost as racially isolated from whites as they were at the time of the passage of the 1964 Civil Rights Act.[10]

There is no direct correlation between black racial isolation in America and the Curse of Ham ideology. But the belief that black Americans do not need or deserve better educations or incomes is not rooted in logic or science. Logically, that schools and businesses fail or that property values fall may be the fault of the political/social/economic/educational system rather than the black people caught in it. Urban legends of black "ghettoes" remain in American society as one white presidential candidate in 2016 referred to these areas as "hell." Or the FBI's designation of "Black Identity Extremism" as a threat to the United States. The implications of designating places as "hell" or identifying the exercise of First Amendment rights to free speech as endangering society harshly hits the humanity of black Americans. Social assaults on the rights of black Americans demonstrate measures of unwarranted social control with glimpses of the Curse of Ham showing in the background.

Police officer Darren Wilson gave testimony about his perceptions before he shot unarmed Michael Brown in St. Louis in 2014 using these words: "[He] had the most intense aggressive face. The only way I can describe it, it looks like a demon, that's how angry he looked."[11] Wilson's claim of seeing a demon is not singular; repeatedly police officers see inhumanity coming at them in black faces. A police officer in Charlotte, North Carolina, claimed that he repeatedly shot Jonathon Ferrell in 2013 because he looked like a "zombie."[12] The third point in the Curse of Ham Matrix—of black people as uncivilized brutes—shows up as defense for mistreatment, perhaps with more modern wording, like "zombie," but still promoting unwarranted fear.

The persistence of anti-black racism in the United States in its many forms and structures is almost baffling. There are myriad studies countering the theological and scientific bases for racism or emphasizing the humanity of black people. Scholarship that refutes negative claims has grown since the 1950s and 1960s. The American social situation has changed as civil rights legislation has somewhat opened housing, sometimes improved education, and occasionally opened jobs. "Black folks—separated for centuries from the full resources of the American good life on the basis of race and race alone— were not supposed to occupy a level playing field of psychological good health and potential economic well-being."[13]

Progress toward full enfranchised citizenship has not been steady or consistent across the country as state-by-state legislation actively works to counter any advances, particularly with black voter suppression. Throughout American society, black people are generally viewed with suspicion. One author used the term "racecraft" to define our functionally superstitious understanding of the category of race.[14] The raced treatment of African Americans has become its own kind of faith practice for some: the devil and evil are black.

The current situation of African Americans lives under the burden of striving forward and repeatedly being pushed back. Is Oprah successful? Should Trayvon Martin have been killed? We live at a strange time in the United States when one person could answer both those questions affirmatively.

That there are some African Americans at some level of the middle class is viewed as achieving the "dream" of civil rights activists. Houston A. Baker deconstructs such thinking.

> The dream of better days ahead seemed to translate in the post–Civil Rights era in distinctly economic terms. . . . Economics was the enabler of the dream: we were free at last! Even though we had scarcely any sustainable wealth to manage, fall back upon, or pass on to succeeding generations. Many of the best middle-class denizens of the black world today are only "colored rich."[15]

Social success carries its own burden because there remains so much poverty, ill health, or environmental hazard inhibiting the majority of black American life chances.

Witness a recent report that the state of Alabama's rural communities have the worst poverty in the developed world. A United Nations expert visited several United States cities, stating that "poverty in the U.S. has been overlooked for too long."[16] Of note, hookworm was discovered to be thriving in Lowndes County, which has a 74 percent African American population.[17]

A further confusion is added because race is seldom the reason given for failing schools, underemployment, or lower property values in black neighborhoods. Blaming black people for criminality, their "broken" families, their city governments (if a black leader is in office), or their laziness is easily thrown into arguments to explain current situations. It functions as anti-racist racism: "Anti-racist racism is a pointed but logical construct able to withstand the scrutiny of scientific investigation. . . . [A]nti-racist racism manifests as the need to dominate by anti-racist rhetoric in whatever venture being considered."[18]

So the example of colleges and universities limiting their admissions to the highest SAT and ACT scorers does not necessarily mean that the most intelligent students get into college. Rather, testing measures seem scientific—but too often high schools in black communities are underperforming, and those schools do not offer test preparation services. The anti-racist SAT tests become another form of racism. Another example is found with "low-income housing projects that use federal tax credits—the nation's biggest source of funding for affordable housing—are disproportionally in majority non-white communities. What this means, fair-housing advocates say, is that the government is essentially helping to maintain entrenched racial divides, even though federal law requires government agencies to promote integration."[19] Whether SAT testing for college admissions or planting more housing projects in low-income, segregated neighborhoods of people of color, the argument might be made that these processes are anti-racist. But when the end results are racist structural maintenance, they merely provide cover as anti-racist racism.

The Civil Rights Act in 1964 won a series of rights for African Americans as citizens. Before and after that act, the activism of many African Americans helped to keep the injustices in the forefront of national and international consciousness. Since then, particularly since the 1980s, there have been intensive pushbacks utilizing anti-racist racism against black American civil rights. Black scholars and activists have begun to rename these actions as the new Jim Crow.[20]

One of the strongest uses of the term "New Jim Crow" is by Michelle Alexander, who has analyzed systems of incarceration that unfairly target black Americans. She refers to these as creating a racial caste within the United States. Law enforcement of black communities with an emphasis on drug wars or safe streets or law and order paint targets on black men and women. Recent videos of police shootings of black men or women are shared on social media and are no less than state-sponsored violence. The statements by police that they feared for their lives from "demons" or "zombies" have become standard forms of defense that, sadly, are effective in clearing the cops' names. The inability to access the constitutionally guaranteed legal defense or to pay bail further erodes the abilities of most black Americans to realize justice in the court systems. As Alexander stated,

> It may be helpful, in attempting to understand the basic nature of the new caste
> system, to think of the criminal justice system—the entire collection of institu-

tions and practices that comprise it—not as an independent system but rather as a *gateway* into a much larger system of racial stigmatization and permanent marginalization. . . . [Think of it as a] system that locks people not only behind actual bars in actual prisons, but also behind virtual bars and virtual walls . . . [that] function nearly as effectively as Jim Crow laws once did in locking people of color into a permanent second-class citizenship. [21]

The persistent legal, social, individual, and religious dimensions of racism in the United States create issues of lack of trust in the political system from the perspectives of African Americans. "These group-centric trust orientations are rooted in African Americans' racial experiences, and they are integral in their trust in government to do what is right, despite government's advances toward becoming more democratic, equitable, and inclusive of African Americans." [22] Certainly, trust levels shift by state or region. The African Americans in Flint, Michigan, for example, who have experienced years of poisonous lead in their water system, compounded by the years and layers of inaction of state officials, would conceivably have low levels of trust in their governmental institutions.

"For more than a year, Flint residents have been screaming that their water wasn't OK, that it smelled bad, tasted bad, looked bad, and was making them sick. Few listened," [Nancy] Kaffer wrote. "The state told them, again and again, that the water was safe—that contamination had been handled, and that the water was within acceptable levels." [23]

Trust of political systems certainly would be damaged in such circumstances.

Extending this decay of trust would be the processes by which oppression of black Americans is normalized. Methods of overt racism such as state-sponsored violence, anti-racist racism through laws, including erosion of citizens' rights such as voting: these are among ways that black oppression seems predetermined in America. Most importantly, the hegemonic system learns from each oppressed group how best to oppress others.

How do people find their way to wholeness when encountering persistent, systematic racism? The next section begins a discussion of black identity in the twenty-first century.

BLACK IDENTITY: WHO *ARE* YOU?

From the 1960s, questions of black American identities were revisited with renewed freedom. To be sure, such explorations of what it means to be black with debates throughout black communities were not new. Moving from the early colonizers' term of "Anglo-African" to the "colored" and "Negro" of Jim Crow to "Afro-American" was a journey over time as black people declared identities that were reconsidered in the next generations. These were not leisurely discussions; claiming and defining the humanity of black persons was at stake.

The category of colored/negro was initially cobbled together by white colonizers. Multiple tribes, from regions across the continent of Africa, were themselves colonized, deemed property, and thus, eligible to become a singly named group. Yet those diverse Africans had to work through differences by African region. Black Americans today still struggle with a larger group identity, now defining themselves by regions in the United States. But perhaps there are possibilities for shifts in perspectives.

The National Museum of African American History and Culture (NMAAHC) opened in 2016 on the National Mall in Washington, DC. Through its various exhibits, the museum tells a "we" story that does not limit identity to region but claims the United States as the base. While there are other museums of African American history throughout the country, they are mostly focused on local history. The NMAAHC marks the first time in the United States that black culture and history are given such a prominent and well-situated place to tell a fully American story.

Even with this moment, the day-to-day data on living in black bodies sketch a framework that is the result of the interactions between race and politics. In K–12 education: school readiness is not improving for black students; they are more likely to be viewed negatively by white teachers and are less likely to be exposed to advanced classes. While poor behavior in the classroom can sometimes indicate future earnings achievement for white students, black students face earnings penalties,[24] with records to prove their "thuggish" behavior shows from childhood.

The Centers for Disease Control (CDC) reported that the mortality rate gap between black and white Americans "had narrowed from 33 percent to 15 percent" among black people sixty-five and older. However, the CDC was clear "that the United States has a long way to go before it achieves health equity. Blacks in every age group under 65 continue to have significantly higher death rates than whites. Black life expectancy at birth is about 3½ years lower than that of whites."[25]

Writing of black women's pregnancies and the risks to mothers and babies, Dani McClain, herself a health worker, wrote of her own experience while pregnant: "Research suggests that it's the stress caused by racial discrimination experienced over a lifetime that leads to black American women's troubling birth outcomes, not the individual choices those women make or how much money or education they have. . . . There's something about the American experience that tears away at the black body."[26]

In the previous chapter, I discussed eminent domain as one of the governmental practices to continue taking treaty-determined lands or resources of Native Americans. Black Americans have also had their communities broken by governmental agencies, and they lack treaty agreements to resist.

For instance, Chicago, Illinois, has experienced high murder rates. One minister that I interviewed in 2015 told me her version of how such high rates developed. She said that gang problems in two housing projects—Cabrini Green and Robert Taylor—led to the city solution of redevelopment. People who lived in those projects were given vouchers to move into new housing. Gang structures, especially hierarchies, were broken. But gang behavior was not. She said that gang members, spread throughout the South Side of Chicago, declared themselves "gangs" of one or two persons and committed acts of violence without a controlling structure. Gangs did function as a kind of community for these members, and relying on the structures did provide some kind of information and direction. Poor or black communities may not fit the descriptions of "good" people or communities. *Not* finding out the existing structures translates into not utilizing community resources. When I asked the minister why the churches had not done anything, her exasperation showed: "Don't you think we would if we knew how?" In spite of these realities, two current terms attempt to define black identities today. Both are based on the visible and outstanding success of a few African Americans, such as President Barack Obama or Oprah Winfrey.

Postracial

The first term is postracial, which claims that Americans have moved to a time where race is unimportant and will not impede personal success, such as achieving the presidency. Despite the fact that most African Americans will never achieve that office, that Barack Obama did becomes myth and legend in black communities. One author put it in terms of emotion as he discussed "how I'd felt seeing Barack and Michelle during the inauguration, the car slow-dragging down Pennsylvania Avenue, the crowd cheering, and then the two of them rising up out of the limo, rising up from fear, smiling, waving, defying despair, defying history, defying gravity."[27]

But "postracial" can also refer to an ongoing project of getting beyond single, stereotypical definitions of race as categories. The term can refer to people of mixed heritage, knowing that they are the result of "blended" races. Today, the number of mixed-race births has grown: "Not only does the face of multiracial America appear to be transforming across generations, but the prevalence of mixed race Americans is changing as well,"[28] possibly fueled by the increase in mixed-race marriage.

America is becoming postracial in another way. There are multiple advertisements now for people to get DNA testing to find out national, regional, or racial heritage. The ads often show people glowing with happiness to discover they have roots in Nigeria or are 3 percent Native American. In scholarship and especially in daily life, Americans are working to figure out if the term "postracial" is helpful. But we are not there yet.

Back to the example of President Obama: for some African Americans, he was initially not considered black enough; simultaneously, for some white Americans, he was too black. Those who are of mixed racial heritage experience that tension between too much and not enough.

Postblack

Postblackness is the other term used to describe the current realities of black identity. Its best interpretation is that some people, like Oprah Winfrey, can insulate themselves from the majority of the effects of racism. The term is also used to imply, as did the author Touré, that "we are like Obama: rooted in but not restricted by Blackness. It means we love Blackness but accept the fact we do all view or perform the culture the same way given the vast variety of realities of modern Blackness."[29] This definition ignores the realities of being black at this time in the twenty-first century: the average black person can strive to be "like Obama." But another author found Touré's perspective ahistorical and out of context. "For Touré, there is no suffering, no despair, no existential angst—for that matter, no white flight, no racial conservatism, and no remnants of laws and practices that, in the case of America, divided a nation. Out of context, blackness—race—is as ridiculous as Santa Claus in springtime."[30]

"Postblackness" and "postracial" are terms that will need continued discussion. But right now, at this moment, neither applies to the majority of black Americans. The life realities of most African Americans, who are poor, disenfranchised, and excluded from mainstream society, still need to be addressed. In addition, there are several areas where black American identities in the twenty-first century overlap with equality and class.

Other Black Identities, Changed and Unchanged

The impact of neo-middle-class black people can, at times, have toxic effects on the growth of black communities or efforts to end racism. One effect is the result of the high visibility of those who have moved into professional positions, adding to questions of why those other black people cannot. However, Baker charges,

> The most published and publicized blacks on the American public scene today are well-dressed, comfortably educated, sagaciously articulate, avowedly new age, and resolutely middle class. Such black Americans are, in their own designation, men and women of color who have just said "no" to race. The evolution of their relationship to the black majority during the past three decades can be summed up in a single word: good-bye![31]

Other areas where black American identities are changing include forms of media and consumer consumption, which are often related. Black buying power is projected to reach $1.4 trillion by 2020, which is 275 percent growth since 1990.[32] Advertisements need to be "culturally relevant and nuanced. Hiring a black model for the sake of diversity isn't going to cut it."[33]

But there is the level of the so-called "digital divide"; African American millennials are closing the gap. "With $162 billion in buying power and undisputed cultural influence, Black millennials are using their power to successfully raise awareness of issues facing the Black community, and influence decisions shaping our world."[34] But this rosy picture of middle-class black Americans' spending power belies the reality that the black wealth gap endures. Even as the gap endures, social media is another consumable that expands opportunities to consume more products. But some aim to turn the Internet into a kind of empowerment.

The embrace of creative uses of social media is seen in the website of a young black woman, Natasha Marin, who began a digital art project with social consequences. The website is Reparations.me with the following invitation: "I invite People of Color to ask for what we need to feel better, be happier, be more productive by posting in this space. These may be both material and immaterial requests. I invite people who identify as White to offer services or contributions to People of Color in need of time, energy, substantive care, and support."[35] But going on the website today links to a Facebook page where entry is only possible by joining the group after completing an application. "This group is focused on bringing about healing and connection in the present tense. Reparations: Requests & Offerings is not about reparations for American Slavery (although this is a very valid pursuit) it's actually about addressing present-day income inequality, community building, community care, and about bring about much needed healing."[36]

While there are advances in relationships and changes in black American identities, there is also pushback. Because these are different ways to enter conversations about racial identity, the racist pushback has responded by falling back on threats and name-calling, rather than "bringing about healing and connection."

Transracial?

One final way to think about black identities today before moving on: Is race, especially blackness, only about blood? This is the question that had arisen when Rachel Dolezal, a woman who had been working and living as a black person, was exposed as white. She defines what she did as "self-identification" rather than passing. She continues to identify as a black woman.[37] So questions are posed from this event: "Might Blackness be something one can achieve, which is to say, something one can work toward by doing? Is it, as Dolezal seems to suggest, something that can be obtained through a series of opportunities or experiences? Something that one can 'live,' and therefore attain?"[38]

A new word is being explored and that is "transrace." Is race policed, as is gender? Should transracial become accepted, as should transgender? I turned to one of my conversation partners here. Barbra Fitzgerald believes that the category of transracial will undermine civil rights laws because it moves from work on behalf of the community to an individualism that honors only itself. So, like the destruction of black communities through eminent domain, the use of "transracial" continues semantic infiltration,[39] taking over real estate in one person's mind.

So black identity in America is developing. Amid the social and economic deprivation that most black Americans experience, neo-middle-class discussions incorporate language of postblack, postracial, and transracial among tech-savvy consumers. Identities are not exactly what they were even as Internet trolls for white racists attempt to shut down discussions. I return to an earlier question and add a new one: How do people find their way to wholeness when encountering persistent, systematic racism? Is religion the answer?

STILL AT THE INTERSECTION: BLACK AMERICAN RELIGIOUS THOUGHT

Religion, and particularly Christianity, is a place where, on the one hand, racism seems embedded, as demonstrated by the Curse of Ham and moral condemnation of interracial marriage. On the other hand, as mentioned earlier in the chapter, both rebellion and complaisance have been offered to members through black religions. Through various religious forms of Christianity, Islam, and Buddhism, as well as smaller sects, such as Black Hebrews, Spiritualism, and the Shrine of Black Madonna, African Americans have found ways to affirm their humanity. Some church communities have stepped into politics at different times in response to injustices:

> One of the great beacons within the black community in countering vote suppression has been the black church. . . . Black churches were integral to countering the Jim Crow laws in the South and the machine politics of the North and to ensuring that black votes counted. . . . Black churches and black clergy are needed now as much as they were after Reconstruction and during the mid-twentieth century.[40]

Several African American scholars point very specifically to religion as a location where racist ideology must be countered and extracted. James Cone was a theologian whose work on black power and theology in the 1960s began a field known as black theology.[41] More than that, his work delineates a clear point that began the development of black liberation theology. In a later work, Cone stated, "Black Theology is a theology of and for black people, an examination of their stories, tales, and sayings. It is an investigation of the mind into the raw materials of our pilgrimage, telling the story of 'how we got over.'"[42] Despite the historical development of this theology, Cone challenged those, scholars and pastors, who are committed to work for justice. "'A time comes when silence is betrayal,' Martin King said. That time has come for white theologians. White supremacy is one of the great contradictions of the gospel in modern times. . . . Black theologians must end their silence too. We have opposed racism much too gently."[43]

As black liberation theology developed, so too did womanist theology and ethics. In these, African American women's theological thought became a path to liberation. One of the earlier womanist ethicists, Katie G. Cannon, emphasized some aspects that call entire African American communities to wholeness: "As God-fearing women they maintain that Black life is more than defensive reactions to oppressive circumstances of anguish and desperation. Black life is the rich, colorful creativity that emerged and reemerges in the Black quest for human dignity."[44] Yet, in a later reflection on womanist ethics and theology encountering racism in academic settings, Cannon stated,

> Whenever the academy fails to take seriously valid bodies of knowledge produced at the intersection of race, sex, and class; whenever the academy desires only to systematically classify the inner workings of our embodied mining of the motherlode as questionable fool's gold . . . then we end up with education that is unbalanced, knowledge that is incomplete, and a worldview that is distorted.[45]

Another scholar analyzed the criticisms of Malcolm X against Christianity during the 1960s. However, Muoki Mbunga made a distinction between the criticisms of Malcolm X and the best path toward the future and toward improving Christianity itself. "I contend that it is only Eurocentric Christianity that is responsible for enslaving, colonizing and exploiting Africans and other Afro-descended people. I am strongly convinced of the urgent need to construct an African-centred Christianity that is built on African cultural values, that articulates the experiences and aspirations of African people, and is a tool for their liberation and unification."[46]

Despite these and other calls to end racism within Christianity and the academy, an editorial by a black Southern Baptist minister demonstrates that it has not ended. He was called names at the Baptist summer camp when he was thirteen. At a 2017 assembly, a resolution to condemn white supremacy was rejected. Academically, "Five white professors at Southwestern Baptist Theological Seminary in Fort Worth dressed in a way that mimicked gangsta rappers. They posed for a picture wearing hoodies, hats to the side and flashy necklaces. One of the professors was holding what looked like a gun." Apology by the seminary president was given. But for these and other experiences, Rev. Lawrence Ware had had enough. He has left the Southern Baptist Convention.

> I want to be a member of a body of believers that is structured around my Christian beliefs of equity, not one that sees those issues as peripheral. The equality of all people should be a fundamental principle that is a starting point of the convention's existence, not a side issue to be debated. I love the church, but I love black people more. Black lives matter to me. I am not confident that they matter to the Southern Baptist Convention. [47]

Some would find his statement that he "loves black people more" as a problem—does this mean he does not love God? But a church is not a god either.

In the development of the race-politics-religion intersection, another factor impacts religion itself: American individualism. It is easy to fall into delusion when there seems to be success with obtaining material goods and to link that attainment with proof of the rightness of belief—in a particular God, in a particular form of church, in social structures, in a nation where many others are left out. The self-righteous have a script: If *they* believed, really believed, did not question, and worked really hard, they would achieve success too. Such a delusion returns to the lie of white superiority and the lie seems to be affirmed by success. But it is not easy for African Americans to fall into this delusion. Rev. Ware tells the story of disillusionment with his church community because of experiences of persistent racism. Thousands of black Americans daily share that experience as the dissonance between the myths—of American greatness and justice—meets with unequal employment, housing, education, and application of the law. Working hard has not been the problem but getting a just wage for work is an ongoing problem for African Americans. Prosperity preaching suggests that it offers answers to these tensions.

Prosperity preaching in black communities is not new; Rev Ike and Daddy Grace were examples from the twentieth century. But today, the interpretation of Christianity as an ATM machine infects even mainstream churches. Prosperity preaching is neoliberal theology at its most effective: forget race, gender, or age. Focus on getting money and goods. After all, Jesus wants this because Jesus was rich, too. At its core, prosperity preaching promotes individualism, not community. Prayers, songs, and events are structured to support consumption—at all age levels. One church offered a preschool that taught children how to be entrepreneurs. Tithing is the central commitment so new members at some congregations must turn in W-2 forms for the previous year before they can join. Free-love offerings, over and above the weekly tenth of gross income, are offered as answers to anything, from getting a new car to avoiding miscarriage. Black prosperity churches often avoid calling themselves "black" but reference being "international." This break with a sense of "black church" helps bring memberships into a closed circle that is not in conversation with wider swaths of black communities. Money, after all, sets you free and those who are members *here* are free. Prosperity churches are not divorced from politics, but link with candidates and officials who will encourage their "freedom."[48]

Religion interacts within black communities to engage politics and race. One author stated it this way: "Where is God in the poorest neighborhoods of Grand Rapids, in the bankrupt Detroit, or on the South Side of Chicago? What is missing . . . is a more elusive, profoundly felt sense of *purpose* and calling that a care for all humanity—black, white, brown, yellow—underpins. . . . [A] response to despair."[49] Human rights expand capabilities of religion to address black oppression.

TOWARD HUMAN RIGHTS

Actions to develop human rights perspectives and actions from within African American communities are occurring, even as hard-won civil rights are being refought for and relitigated. One example is the Forward Together Moral Movement that began in North Carolina in 2012. One of the leaders of the movement is Rev. William J. Barber. He recognizes the importance of local efforts and also the significance of being in the South. "Among these United States, our history of inequality and injustice is nowhere more rigidly defined and painfully exposed than in the Southern states. But precisely for this reason, the South is also a deep well of resistance, struggle, and freedom movements."[50]

The movement began with Moral Mondays, rallies across the state of North Carolina held in response to the legislature's work to disenfranchise voters. There were integrated efforts to overturn unjust laws through legal action, some of which made it to the Supreme Court. But the broader lines for social justice were laid out as activists in other states used similar efforts. Rev. Barber does not view himself as a solitary leader, but thinks in terms of collective action and whole-group involvement. He refers to an idea of "moral fusion organizing."

> As our coalitions move from a new moral consensus toward legal and statutory changes, we know we have to put faces on the issues that our partners care about. We cannot be abstract. Directly affected people must lead the way and we must support and stand with them. . . . Even as we focus on real people's lives and issues, we must work to help people see how their issues are connected.[51]

Another U.S.-based movement that has captured much media attention is Black Lives Matter (BLM). Three black women—Patrisse Cullors, Opal Tometi, and Alicia Garza—worked to develop an online forum that would fight anti-black racism and oppression. The official web page states, "In 2013, three radical Black organizers—Alicia Garza, Patrisse Cullors, and Opal Tometi—created a Black-centered political will and movement building project called #BlackLivesMatter. It was in response to the acquittal of Trayvon Martin's murderer, George Zimmerman."[52] While beginning from a social-media platform, today there are numerous BLM chapters through the United States using similar moral-fusion organizing to engage people across the country. The movement's principles include: globalism, restorative justice, empathy, loving engagement, queer affirming. One of their principles is "Black Villages": We are committed to disrupting "the Western-prescribed nuclear family structure requirement by supporting each other as extended families and 'villages' that collectively care for one another, and especially our children, to the degree that mothers, parents, and children are comfortable."[53] Community building becomes an important focus for undoing the neoliberal emphasis on individualism, and it is a theme that I will resurface in chapter 8.

One final focus on human rights is the continued disconnection between the United States and the United Nations when it comes to ending racism. (Excerpts of some of the related documents are in Appendix B.) A 2001 document against "Racism, Racial Discrimination, Xenophobia and Related Intolerance" followed a conference held in Durban, South Africa. The declaration states that the conference "recognize[s] that racism, racial discrimination, xenophobia and related intolerance occur on the grounds of race, colour, descent or national or ethnic origin and that victims can suffer multiple or aggravated forms of discrimination based on other related grounds such as sex, language, religion, political or other opinion, social origin, property, birth or other status."[54] This is the broad view that includes people of African descent that was specifically addressed.

A report from a "Working Group of Experts on People of African Descent" in the United States in 2016 cited some positive developments but remained concerned about the "human rights situation of African Americans. In particular, the legacy of colonial history, enslavement, racial subordination and segregation, racial terrorism and racial inequality. . . . [T]here has been no real commitment to reparations and to truth and reconciliation. . . . Contemporary police killings and the trauma that they create are reminiscent of the past racial terror of lynching."[55]

While the United Nations may make these larger statements, the need to promote human rights and racial justice on local levels is still needed. The 2001 document from Durban against racism has never been ratified by the United States. We continue to pat ourselves on the back for some civil rights legislation that many are working assiduously to reverse. How can racial justice be achieved when United Nations documents are ignored? Black players from the National Football League who have "taken a knee" during the "Star-Spangled Banner" before games in 2016 and 2017 have brought more attention to racial justice and racial discord than have pronouncements from the United Nations.[56] Black players are wealthy but still black. They have been criticized for being "ungrateful" for all they have received, which is reminiscent of some white theological critiques of black morality. But what they have done is exercise their First Amendment free speech rights, thereby bringing attention to racial inequities. They have reached audiences across the country, causing discussions that might not have happened otherwise. Their activism has greater impact, emphasizing again the need for human rights from below to tackle the race-politics-religion intersection.

NOTES

1. Joy DeGruy, *Post Traumatic Slave Syndrome: American's Legacy of Enduring Injury and Healing* (Portland, OR: Uptone Press, 2005).

2. Richard Purcell, "Trayvon, Postblackness, and the Postrace Dilemma," *Boundary 2* 40, no. 3 (2013): 144.

3. The following is an excerpt: "I use fear, distrust, and envy for control purposes. . . . Take this simple little list of differences and think about them. On top of my list is "AGE," but it's there only because it starts with an "a." The second is "COLOR" or shade. There is intelligence, size, sex, sizes of plantations, status on plantations . . . whether the slaves live in the valley, on a hill, East, West, North, South, have fine hair, course [*sic*] hair, or is tall or short. Now that you have a list of differences, I shall give you an outline of action, but before that, I shall assure you that distrust is stronger than trust and envy stronger than adulation." "Willie Lynch Letter: The Making of a Slave," *The Final Call*, May 22, 2009,http://www.finalcall.com/artman/publish/Perspectives_1/Willie_Lynch_letter_The_Making_of_a_Slave.shtml.

4. Carol Anderson, *The Unspoken Truth of Our Racial Divide* (New York: Bloomsbury, 2016), 4.

5. Anderson, *The Unspoken Truth of Our Racial Divide*, 41–42.

6. Thomas J. Sugrue, *The Origins of the Urban Crisis: Race and Inequality in Postwar Detroit* (Princeton, NJ: Princeton University Press, 1996), 25.

7. David Whitford, "A Calvinist Heritage to the 'Curse of Ham': Assessing the Accuracy of a Claim about Racial Subordination," *Church History and Religious Culture* 90, no. 1 (2010): 27.

8. Zora Neale Hurston, *The Sanctified Church* (Berkeley, CA: Turtle Island, 1981), 103.

9. Nil Desperandum, "On Interracial Marriage: The Moral Status of Miscegenation," *Faith and Heritage: Occidental Christianity for Preserving Western Culture and People*, May 2011, http://faithandheritage.com/2011/05/the-moral-status-of-miscegenation/.

10. Myron Orfield and Thomas F. Luce, "America's Racially Diverse Suburbs: Opportunities and Challenges," in *Housing Policy Debate*, Institute on Metropolitan Opportunity (Minneapolis: University of Minnesota Law School, 2013), http://www.prrac.org/pdf/Myron_Orfield_-_Diverse_Suburbs_FINAL.pdf.

11. State of Missouri v. Darren Wilson, Grand Jury Volume V, September 16, 2014, p. 225, included through a link at https://www.nytimes.com/interactive/2014/11/25/us/darren-wilson-testimony-ferguson-shooting.html?_r=0.

12. Carimah Townes, "Cop Justifies Repeated Shooting of Unarmed Black Man with the 'Zombie' Defense," *Think Progress*, August 6, 2015, https://thinkprogress.org/cop-justifies-repeated-shooting-of-unarmed-black-man-with-the-zombie-defense-3fb6b17b86ba.

13. Houston A. Baker, *Betrayal: How Black Intellectuals Have Abandoned the Ideals of the Civil Rights Era* (New York: Columbia University Press, 2008), 76.

14. Karen Fields, cited in Purcell, "Trayvon, Postblackness, and the Postrace Dilemma," 143.

15. Baker, *Betrayal*, 75.

16. "Alabama Has the Worst Poverty in the Developed World, U.N. Official Says," *Newsweek*, December 10, 2017, http://www.newsweek.com/alabama-un-poverty-environmental-racism-743601.

17. Ed Pilkington, "Hookworm, a Disease of Extreme Poverty, Is Thriving in the US South. Why?," *The Guardian*, September 5, 2017, https://www.theguardian.com/us-news/2017/sep/05/hookworm-lowndes-county-alabama-water-waste-treatment-poverty.

18. Ronald E. Hall, "Anti-Racist Racism as a Judicial Decree: Racism in the Twenty-First Century," *Journal of African American Studies* 19 (2015), 321.

19. John Eligon, Yamiche Alcindor, and Agustin Armendariz, "Program to Spur Low-Income Housing Is Keeping Cities Segregated," *New York Times*, July 2, 2017, https://www.nytimes.com/2017/07/02/us/federal-housing-assistance-urban-racial-divides.html.

20. William Barber and Jonathan Wilson-Hartgrove, "The Strange Career of James Crow, Esquire," *The Atlantic*, February 4, 2016, https://www.theatlantic.com/politics/archive/2016/02/jim-crows-new-legal-career/459879/.

21. Michelle Alexander, *The New Jim Crow, Mass Incarceration in the Age of Colorblindness* (New York: The New Press, 2012), 12–13.

22. Maurice Magnum, "Explaining Political Trust among African Americans," *Journal of Public Management and Social Policy* 23, no. 2 (Fall 2016): 94–95.

23. Ashley Woods, "Nancy Kaffer Wins 2015 Scripps Howard Award," *The Detroit Free Press*, March 8, 2016, http://www.freep.com/story/opinion/columnists/nancy-kaffer/2016/03/08/columnist-nancy-kaffer-wins-2015-scripps-howard-award/81499558/.

24. Liz Sablich, "7 Findings That Illustrate Racial Disparities in Education," Brookings, Brown Center Chalkboard, https://www.brookings.edu/blog/brown-center-chalkboard/2016/06/06/7-findings-that-illustrate-racial-disparities-in-education/.

25. Joel Achenback, "Life Expectancy Improves for Blacks, and the Racial Gap Is Closing, CDC Reports," *Washington Post*, May 2, 2017, https://www.washingtonpost.com/news/to-your-health/wp/2017/05/02/cdc-life-expectancy-up-for-blacks-and-the-racial-gap-is-closing/?utm_term=.d899e809ac01.

26. Dani McClain, "Fighting for a Healthy Black Pregnancy," *The Nation*, March 6, 2017, 18.

27. Ta-Nehisi Coates, "My President Was Black," *The Atlantic*, January/February 2017, 66, https://www.theatlantic.com/magazine/archive/2017/01/my-president-was-black/508793/.

28. Gretchen Livingston, "Today's Multiracial Babies Reflect America's Changing Demographics," June 24, 2015, Pew Research Center, *Fact Tank*, http://www.pewresearch.org/fact-tank/2015/06/24/todays-multiracial-babies-reflect-americas-changing-demographics/.

29. Touré, *Who's Afraid of Postblackness? What It Means to Be Black Now* (New York: The Free Press, 2011), cited in Purcell, "Trayvon, Postblackness, and the Postrace Dilemma," 146.

30. Patrice Rankine, "'The World Is a Ghetto:' Post-Racial America(s) and the Apocalypse," in *The Trouble with Post-Blackness*, eds. Houston A. Baker and K. Merrida Simone (New York: Columbia University Press, 2015), 171.

31. Baker, *Betrayal*, 72–73.

32. Janie Boschma, "Black Consumers Have 'Unprecedented Impact' in 2015," *The Atlantic*, February 2, 2016, https://www.theatlantic.com/politics/archive/2016/02/black-consumers-have-unprecedented-impact-in-2015/433725/.

33. Boschma, "Black Consumers Have 'Unprecedented Impact' in 2015."

34. Mia Scott, "Nielsen 2016 Report: Black Millennials Close the Digital Divide," October 17, 2016, http://www.nielsen.com/us/en/press-room/2016/nielsen-2016-report-black-millennials-close-the-digital-divide.html.

35. "Meet Natasha Marin: The woman behind REPARATIONS," Reparations.me, http://www.reparations.me/about.

36. "Reparations: Requests   and   Offerings,"   https://www.facebook.com/groups/939299172870387/.

37. The Associated Press, "Rachel Dolezal: As a Child I Drew 'Self-Portraits with the Brown Crayon instead of the Peach Crayon,'" *National Post*, June 16, 2015, http://nationalpost.com/news/world/rachel-dolezal-as-i-child-i-drew-self-portraits-with-the-brown-crayon-instead-of-the-peach-crayon/wcm/8f20a4d7-4b36-4da6-967f-15568d0c9606.

38. Marquis Bey and Theodora Sakellarides, "When We Enter: The Blackness of Rachel Dolezal," *The Black Scholar* 46, no. 4 (2016): 39–40.

39. Fred Ikle–developed term; see Fred Ikle, "Semantic Infiltration," the *Spectator*, July 10, 2010, https://spectator.org/39311_semantic-infiltration/.

40. Maurice Mangum, "Black Churches and Black Voter Suppression in Florida and Ohio," in *From Every Mountainside: Black Churches and the Broad Terrain of Civil Rights*, ed. R. Drew Smith (Albany: State University of New York Press, 2013), 189.

41. James Cone, *Black Power and Black Theology* (New York: Seabury Press, 1969).

42. James Cone, *God of the Oppressed* (New York: Seabury Press, 1975), 18.

43. James Cone, *Risks of Faith: The Emergence of a Black Theology of Liberation, 1968–1998* (Boston: Beacon Press, 1999), 136.

44. Katie Geneva Cannon, *Katie's Canon: Womanism and the Soul of the Black Community* (New York: Continuum, 1995), 56.

45. Katie G. Cannon, "Structured Academic Amnesia: As If This Womanist Story Never Happened," in *Deeper Shades of Purple*, ed. Stacey Floyd-Thomas (New York: NYU Press, 2006), 27.

46. Muoki Mbunga, "Malcolm X and Christianity: Engaging the Criticisms and Moving towards an African-Centred Christianity That Can Advance Pan Africanism in the 21st Century," *Journal of Intercultural Disciplines* 13 (Fall 2013): 15–16.

47. Lawrence Ware, "Why I'm Leaving the Southern Baptist Convention," *New York Times*, July 17, 2017, https://www.nytimes.com/2017/07/17/opinion/why-im-leaving-the-southern-baptist-convention.html?src=me&_r=0.

48. Stephanie Y. Mitchem, *Name It and Claim It? Prosperity Preaching in the Black Church* (Cleveland: Pilgrim Press, 2007).

49. Rankine, "'The World Is a Ghetto,'"165.

50. Rev. Dr. William J. Barber II, *The Third Reconstruction: How a Moral Movement Is Overcoming the Politics of Division and Fear* (Boston: Beacon Press, 2016), xiv–xv.

51. Barber, *The Third Reconstruction*, 124–25.

52. Black Lives Matter, "Herstory," https://blacklivesmatter.com/about/what-we-believe/.

53. Black Lives Matter, "Guiding Principles," https://blacklivesmatter.com/about/what-we-believe/.

54. "World Conference against Racism, Racial Discrimination, Xenophobia and Related Intolerance: Declaration," Durban, South Africa, September 2001, http://www.un.org/WCAR/durban.pdf.

55. Report of the Working Group of Experts on People of African Descent on Its Mission to the United States of America, August 18, 2016, http://www.ushrnetwork.org/sites/ushrnetwork.org/files/unwgepad_us_visit_final_report_9_15_16.pdf.

56. There are myriad reports about the NFL players, including these: Steve Chapman, "Why Do Whites Oppose the NFL Protests?" *Chicago Tribune*, October 4, 2017, http://www.chicagotribune.com/news/opinion/chapman/ct-perspec-whites-nfl-anthem-protests-20170927-story.html; Benjamin Hoffman, Victor Mather, and Jacey Fortin, "After Trump Blasts N.F.L., Players Kneel and Lock Arms in Solidarity," *New York Times*, September 24, 2017, https://www.nytimes.com/2017/09/24/sports/nfl-trump-anthem-protests.html?_r=0; Juana Summers, "It's Impossible for Black Athletes to Leave Politics off the Field," September 24, 2017, http://www.cnn.com/2017/09/24/politics/trump-african-american-athletes/index.html.

Chapter Five

Hispanics? "We Know Who We Are"

Thirty years ago, I worked for a community organization dedicated to ending drug use among young people. For fieldwork, the supervisor paired me with Terry, a Mexican American (yes, really: putting black and Mexican persons together to go in "certain" neighborhoods). But we minority team members were glad; we had time to visit places in neighborhoods and to hang out. After one of the many meals at her mama's house, Terry turned to me and said, "They are trying to do to Mexican people what they did to black people." "They" were the government and/or Anglos (white people); the "doing" was erasure of identity.

At this moment in early twenty-first-century America, immigration has become the focal point for many of the discussions around Mexicans, Cubans, Ecuadorans, and Dominicans—anyone who is speaking something like Spanish; and, yes, even U.S. citizens, Puerto Ricans.

> A protest, April 2010: Several thousand gather in Houston, Texas, to protest Arizona's recent anti-immigration bill SB 1070 and the rise in anti-immigrant and anti-Latina/o discourse. They carry U.S. flags. Their signs read "We are all immigrants," "Immigrant Rights = Human Rights," and "Do I look Illegal?" A small counterdemonstration of approximately thirty anti-immigration activists lines the streets periodically. At one corner, a middle-aged couple, white and bedecked in red, white, and blue signifiers of patriotism, yell "Go back home!" A young Latina—a child of immigrants herself and armed with a voice—responds "I am home! I was born here!" For a second, the couple looks dumbstruck, then repeats "Go back home!" and other tautologies such as "Illegal is illegal!"[1]

As I have watched the anti-Mexican and anti-immigrant fever seeming to grip some sections of the United States, I recall Terry's words. I realize that "Hispanic" shrank the diversity among Latinos/Latinas into "Mexican" as a kind of American cultural illiteracy quickly shaped ethnic groups into a "brown" race. Immigration becomes the focal point for politicians to spew hatred of brown people. This is in response to the proposed DREAM (Development, Relief, and Education for Alien Minors) Act that would have granted residency to Latinos and Latinas who were brought to the United States as children and who know this country as home.

Representative Steve King of Iowa was malicious in his opposition to this idea. In one interview, he stated, "They aren't all valedictorians. They weren't all brought in by their parents. For everyone who's a valedictorian, there's another hundred out there who weigh a hundred and thirty pounds— and they've got calves the size of cantaloupes because they're hauling seventy-five pounds of marijuana across the desert. Those people would be legalized with the same act." In another interview, King pushed the stereotypes: "We have people that are mules, that are drug mules, that are hauling drugs across the border and you can tell by their physical characteristics what they've been doing for months."[2]

The race-politics-religion intersection has ideas racing from one side to another in attempts to maintain current power structures. In the case of Latinos/Latinas, human rights considerations in the United States demand a broader *American* view. I begin with questions of identities and race.

WHO'S HISPANIC?

The designation of "Hispanic" as a category to designate a group of humans in the United States began to be used in 1976 by the Census Bureau.

> In 1976, the U.S. Congress passed the only law in this country's history that mandated the collection and analysis of data for a specific ethnic group: "Americans of Spanish origin or descent." The language of that legislation described this group as "Americans who identify themselves as being of Spanish-speaking background and trace their origin or descent from Mexico, Puerto Rico, Cuba, Central and South America and other Spanish-speaking countries."[3]

Terry's sensitivity to getting named by the government, like the nomenclature "Indian" or "Negro," was real. In addition to the officially designated term "Hispanic," the term Latino/a is used, adding to a general lack of clarity in the popular American imagination. Both terms have problems:

> The term "Hispanic" is accused of overemphasizing the Euro-Spanish element of the heritage, ignoring the contributions made by non-Spanish Europeans, Africans, Asians, and Native Americans. . . . ["Latino/a"] emphasizes a Latin (European) culture while overlooking other groups. Like the expression "His-

panic," "Latino/a" is a nebulous term used as a catch-all label to homogenize diverse groups.[4]

Since my conversations with Terry, much has happened in the United States as greater diversity is celebrated while civil rights expand or contract, depending on legislative efforts by different groups. The drive to define a diverse group of people, Hispanic, is accompanied by a public lack of understanding of the richness and diversity of cultures involved.

> Non-Hispanic Americans view Hispanics and Latinos with suspicion: who are these short, brown-skin interlopers who have arrived in the country, refuse to learn English, assimilate into the mainstream of American life, and make demands on non-Hispanics to the point where it is impossible to dial any toll-free number and not be affronted by the "Oprima 2 para español" message that is as grating as nails screeching down a blackboard?[5]

Popular American culture has fostered racial and cultural illiteracy and put "Hispanic" into a single box that does not distinguish the great diversity among Latinos/Latinas. As Juan Gonzalez pointed out, movies and television crafted some very potent stereotypes during the 1970s and 1980s, particularly a "glorified . . . violent, outlaw, marginal identity. . . . Nowhere to be found in any of these films by Anglo producers was any inkling that Latinos have been a positive force in U.S. society, that we possessed a culture of any value before we were conquered, or that we contributed to or expanded the culture of this nation."[6] Unsurprisingly, Representative Steve King's language reflects this negative image. The fears of the anti-immigrant protestors at the beginning of this chapter are fueled by these images and the words of someone in leadership like King.

Such unsympathetic portrayals are adopted by Latinos/Latinas themselves, as experienced from within any oppressed group, as they promote negative views of themselves. Marco Gutierrez is Latino and was politically active during the 2016 election. In an interview, he supported *anti*-immigration: "My culture is a very dominant culture, and it's imposing and it's causing problems. If you don't do something about it, you're going to have taco trucks on every corner."[7]

Latinos/Latinas include ethnic as well as racial groups, but in the United States, the "Hispanic" designation helps to convert them into a race: brown. The racializing of Latinos/Latinas is complicated because of the route through which most were incorporated into the United States—through treaties with Spain or Mexico. "The diverse nature of Latino culture and people, however, presented both Americans and Latinos with difficulty in determining the place of Latinos within the social and racial hierarchy that defined American culture . . . [resulting] in what some have characterized as an 'ambiguous racial identity' that places them somewhere between African Americans and Anglos (whites) in the racial social hierarchy."[8]

Race and hierarchy in the United States are complicated by the black-white binary: all other races are "positioned as people of color without difference from African Americans. Such a move erases the historical specificity of oppression."[9] At its core, "the U.S. racial order relies on a fiction of purity and rigid classification that allows little room for mixed-race peoples and interracialism."[10]

Ethnicity becomes an issue: when Hispanic/Latino/as are identified as ethnic, what does it mean? In chapter 2, it was noted that some white Americans were claiming ethnic identities during the 1960s, such as Italian and Irish. Today, DNA testing helps people find some ethnically identified genetic link that they then claim. Since it can be arbitrarily assigned or claimed, ethnicity can be as socially constructed as race or gender. Philosopher J. L. A. García argued,

> Ethnicity is an inherently problematic concept, as is that of culture, and we should be much more skeptical about them than intellectuals nowadays are. We may properly want to lend some clarity to Hispanic and forms of ethnicity for ordinary and political purposes, but we should expect it to admit of much specification.[11]

Following García's warning of the use of ethnicity, I would add that we should be attentive to the use of the term as a code to limit or deny the humanity of people.

To explore these ambiguous identities further, national origins are important dimensions of a person's self-identification; these origins are not erased when living on the mainland United States. If anything, the experiences here may deepen such affiliations. Even recognizing who is or is not a citizen may add to non-Latino/a confusion. Puerto Rico, as a U.S. territory, grants American citizenship as a birthright. Mexico and Cuba are two of the most recognized countries of origin with different cultures and different social-class structures and a variety of routes to arriving in this country. But consider that all of Central America, South America, and the Caribbean have contributed to the population known as "Hispanic" in the United States. They may be citizens, sometimes for several generations; may be aiming for citizenship; may be here as students or tourists; but also could be migrants here to work or refugees fleeing oppression. Certain countries in those areas, such as French-speaking Haiti or Portuguese-speaking Brazil, fit better in the Latin category because their original languages are still derived from a Latin-derived language, but not Spanish.

From the time of the legislation to the present, "Hispanic" identity becomes more confusing because anyone who completes a census form can self-identify as desired. "One approach defines a Hispanic or Latino as a member of an ethnic group that traces its roots to 20 Spanish-speaking nations from Latin America and Spain itself (but not Portugal or Portuguese-speaking Brazil). The other approach is much simpler. Who's Hispanic? Anyone who says they are. And nobody who says they aren't."[12]

The answers to "Who is Hispanic?" provide sources for Latino/as in the United States to focus on the origin countries to provide identifications while trying to craft identities among people who misunderstand and stereotype them.

> Our definitions of ourselves are suspended in time, defined by memories of the ways of our peoples at the time that we left. We historicize our culture. In this country we began the process of treating culture like an artifact, something to be excavated and studied and copied but never lived. . . . We fear the process of assimilation, which will leave us without our roots. This would be tolerable, perhaps, for those who look like the people with power in this country. But for those who cannot pass, there is no reward for assimilation. In the end, the assimilated brown or black person will become "stateless."[13]

I spoke with Miguel De La Torre, professor of social ethics and Latinx studies at Iliff Theological School, about the complexities of "Hispanic."[14] The first question I had for this conversation partner was about his work in Latinx studies. "Latinx," he explained, is a term that is early in usage, among scholars and activists mostly, to avoid the Latino (male) and Latina (female) from the Spanish language. Latinx is gender neutral but is not yet widely used.

I wondered if the term Hispanic was succeeding in redefining or removing national origins out of people's lives. Was there pushback from within the community? Not at all, he stated. "Hispanic," as a term, is more assimilating, but "We know who we are." Dr. De La Torre told some stories of how national identities still are recognized among members of the larger Latinx communities. I asked him a question related to my own experiences as an African American about people who may be good-hearted but ask culturally insensitive question. When Americans walk up to him, a Cuban, and talk about celebrating Cinco de Mayo, how does he respond? He stated that the celebration of the Mexican victory over the French in the nineteenth century is less a celebration of culture than an opportunity to eat and drink certain foods. But we did discuss the difficulties of Latinx growing up in the United States, in school systems that do not know the differences between different national groups.

In the past few years, the Census Bureau has posted demographics that "Hispanics" are the largest minority in the United States. Does this account make any difference? De la Torre stated that the audience for that information was not Latin communities; it was African Americans. "When Anglos keep using the 'largest minority,' they are creating a zero sum rule to the detriment of African American communities," threatening economic and social advances: See, you're not important anymore.

The issue of race is more complex because there is also racism within Latinx communities. Latinx were already racialized and, depending on their national origins, often have their own way of doing racism. Light-skinned people are often given preference over darker-skinned people. And the people considered white in a given Latin American country are considered brown by U.S. racial standards. There is also a pecking order, within Latinx communities, among people from different Latin American countries.

Another aspect of racism against Latinx people needs identification. I visited a city in Texas a few years ago. Some white men in the airport van to the hotel began a discussion of all the things wrong with Mexicans who were invading their country. The black woman driving the van spoke up: "That's right! And they won't even learn English!" Class and race separated the driver and the men; after the comment, they stopped speaking, blinking in shock. She was claiming the United States as her country, too. The racism that black people sometimes extend toward other races is a reflection of white racism.

By claiming white racism, the black woman may have had hope of alliance or, at best, acceptance by white Americans. This is often true of some black Americans and as Dr. De La Torre indicated, some Latinos/Latinas. Such cross-oppressed groups' racism will surface in discussions about all Othered Americans. Yet, buying into white racism and the lie of white superiority will not end oppression; it becomes an issue to block the development of human rights from below.

I turn now to aspects of the history that shape the political edges of the intersection for Latinos/Latinas.

HISTORY AND UNSPOKEN POLITICS

Missing from the movies or the official term, Hispanics, are facts of the United States' relationships with the various Latin American countries from which American Latinos/Latinas originate. There is a quote attributed to former Secretary of State Henry Kissinger that characterizes relationships with Latin America: The United States has no permanent friends or enemies, only interests. To consider the history of the areas from which U.S. Latinos/ Latinas derive is to reflect on the foreign policies, the U.S. interests that have shaped the areas, the immigration patterns, and the people from those areas. This historical overview is not to present detailed histories of the twenty or so countries that make up Latin America but to give a glimpse into the complexities.

There are exciting and amazing stories to be told in the individual lands that make up Latin America in the individual histories. But the focus of race-politics-religion in the United States, in considering what is at stake, leads to thinking about what, as Kissinger said, those interests are. Rather, I am contending that there are certain themes that have determined current relationships.

The idea of the United States having a "Manifest Destiny" to stretch from the Atlantic Ocean to the Pacific Ocean drove the country's interests in the nineteenth century. "In a period of only five decades, the territory of the United States more than tripled, and both national rhetoric and policy invited westward migration and immigration."[15] The Louisiana Purchase in 1803 involved buying an area from France and may have whetted the desire to expand. So, through treaties or force, by 1820, Florida and the Southeast were annexed. "Texas, California, and the southwest by 1855; and finally, Central America and the Caribbean during the second half of the century, a phase that culminated with the Spanish American War of 1898."[16]

With Native Americans, acquiring lands was the primary interest. With African Americans, the use of bodies and labor was the controlling factor. But reaching into the lands around the United States was different. Not only did the expansions remake the United States but also the surrounding regions.

> Those annexations transformed an isolated yeoman's democracy into a major world empire. In the process, Mexico lost half of its territory and three-quarters of its mineral resources, the Caribbean Basin was reduced to a permanent target for Yankee exploitation and intervention, and Latin Americans were made into a steady source of cheap labor for the first U.S. multinational corporations.[17]

All these confusions are played out in race and politics. Ultimately, self-identification is critical, for, as Miguel De La Torre stated, "We know who we are." With that knowledge, awareness of a rich Latino/Latina history and culture remains within their various communities. Yet, Larry Catá Backer stated, "In the end, we are to a great extent on our own. Yet we are not on our own together. There are real differences in the local cultures of the various regions that make up what the non-Latino/a Americans perceive as Hispano-America."[18]

There is yet another layer—free trade—to the international and political dimension.

NOT REALLY FREE TRADE

The concept of "free trade" between nations has grown in particular ways since the 1940s. In some ways, the idea was born around the same time as the United Nations, in the 1940s. Two particular international organizations, the World Bank and the International Monetary Fund (IMF), have helped to shape Latin American relations with the United States. The World Bank began in 1944 at a U.N. conference, "to build a framework for international economic cooperation in order to avoid repeating the competitive currency devaluations that contributed to the Great Depression of the 1930s. The IMF's primary mission is to ensure the stability of the international monetary system."[19] The World Bank was established in 1944, originally loaning money to countries rebuilding after World War II. But "the focus shifted from reconstruction to development. . . . In 1956, the institution became able to lend to private companies and financial institutions in developing countries. And the founding of the International Development Association in 1960 put greater emphasis on the poorest countries."[20] Both of these sound like international philanthropic associations intended to assist the growth of equality. The opposite happens for Latin American countries, especially when the United States is involved in negotiations: the United States' presence and leadership dominate both the World Bank and the IMF.

The first experiments with free trade were in Panama and Puerto Rico. American corporations went to Panama and established the Colon Free Zone "where they could take advantage of Panama's 75 cents an hour wages."[21] The Zone is still operating and, in public-access areas, is considered a commercial tourist destination.[22] Puerto Rico was turned into "a virtual free trade zone," furthered by "a loophole in the Internal Revenue Service Code . . . which exempted from federal taxes the income of U.S. subsidiaries."[23] Eventually, the Puerto Rico free trade project began to fall apart, as Puerto Rico is a U.S. territory and the citizens have the same rights as other United States citizens. Therefore, "the firms started moving to other Caribbean countries."[24]

To be clear, not only citizens of the United States believed in free market theories. There were people who were from Latin American countries who bought into free trade economics. Roberto Campos, for example, was a United States–educated Brazilian who participated in the United Nations and the World Bank. He brought the International Monetary Fund to Brazil. He once stated, "Obviously the world is unequal. Some are born intelligent, some stupid. . . . Some die early, in the prime of life; others drag themselves criminally through a long useless existence. There is a basic fundamental inequality in human nature, in the conditions of things. The mechanism of credit cannot escape this."[25] This brutal view of human beings is reminiscent of the police office Darren Wilson in 2016 claiming he saw a demon instead of a man or Chief Justice Marshall in 1823 claiming that Indians were inferior.

The history of the United States interacting with Latin America, the Caribbean, and U.S. territories has been a history of inequitable relationships. But the structures of the World Bank and the International Monetary Fund use the professional jargon of economics to place all blame on individual countries.

> With the magical incantation of "monetary stabilization," the IMF—which not disinterestedly confuses the fever with the disease, inflation with the crisis of existing structures—has imposed on Latin America a policy that accentuates imbalances instead of easing them. It liberalizes trade by banning direct exchanges and barter agreements; it forces the contraction of internal credits to the point of asphyxia, freezes wages, and discourages state activity. [26]

I have teased out only a few components of historical U.S./Latin America relationships. There are many other factors that have inhibited holistic growth instead of creating healthy options for the neighbors of the United States. Some of the factors include these: the U.S. covert or overt meddling in their electoral politics; forcing devaluation of their money; or, supporting, with arms or money, rebel groups. As Eduardo Galeano stated, "The Congressional Record of the United States is replete with irrefutable evidence of interventions in Latin America." [27]

Ignoring history and past relationships, a message that supports current anti-immigration arguments is to charge our international neighbors to "get your own country/territory straightened out." Perhaps it is long past time to move beyond interests and to recognize the needs in new ways. Yet, "the system has multiplied hunger and fear; wealth has become more and more concentrated, poverty more and more widespread. That is recognized by the documents of specialized international organizations, in whose aseptic vocabulary, our oppressed territories are 'countries in process of development.'" [28]

As instability and poverty cling to these countries, both immigrants and refugees arrive across the U.S. borders. Not all of them are poor and uneducated, but too many are—especially from Mexico and Central America. Today, immigration involves sets of political debates that often focus on "Hispanics" or "Muslim terrorists." I return to the second focus, Muslims, in chapter 7. Here, when immigration is raised in terms of "Hispanics," it is very often negative and counter to the mantra on the Statue of Liberty: "Give me your tired, your poor, your huddled masses yearning to be free." Instead, in the words of the next writer, it is detrimental to the health of the United States to let all those poor, uneducated Latinos cross our borders:

Immigrants from Latin America—the largest single group—arrive with the least education: Only about 13 percent of them have a college degree or more. They too assimilate to American life, but to the increasingly disorderly life of the American non-elite. Their children make educational progress as compared to the parents, but—worryingly—educational progress then stagnates or retrogresses in the third generation. For many decades to come, Latino families educationally lag well behind their non-Latino counterparts. . . . When children of immigrants grow up poor, they assimilate to the culture of poorer America. . . . In other words, immigrants to the United States are dividing into two streams. One arrives educated and assimilates "up"; the other, larger stream, arrives poorly educated and unskilled and assimilates "down." It almost ceases to make sense to speak and think of immigration as one product of one policy.[29]

Such ideas add to confusion about the historical relationships with Latin America and induce fear in those Americans who think any "Hispanic" is coming to take away jobs or to assimilate "down" to criminality and therefore threaten their lives. The truths of relationships are reduced to personal interests. As a result, some Americans behave badly.

Two days after the election, at the Hillandale Shopping Center, I saw an elderly Latina woman being humiliated by two big white guys. They were calling her a spic and to go back to Mexico. And I was walking through the parking lot and she was standing there shaking violently, and I put my arm around her and I said, "Guys, this is unacceptable, buzz off." And they said with menace, "You don't tell us what to do!" I threatened to call the police and they scattered.[30]

IMMIGRATION, BORDERS, AND CITIZENS

Ignoring history then, leads some politicians to encourage the idea of building a southwestern U.S. border wall or to develop an immigration policy that is based on the merit of the applicant. At the same time, "In 2015 alone, 49 states and Puerto Rico enacted 216 laws and adopted 274 resolutions related to immigration. Some of these laws are enforcement-focused laws designed to control and deter the influx of unauthorized immigrants within a particular state or jurisdiction; other laws are intended to neutralize federal enforcement and integrate immigrants into local communities."[31] Some politicians strongly propose English-only legislation: "English-only campaigns of the twenty-first century exploit nativist sentiments appealing to social amnesia about historical multilingualism in the U.S. and ignorance about the benefits of bilingual English acquisition."[32]

Immigration in Latinx contexts takes on racially motivated tones. About 2,500 Nicaraguans given protected status in the United States because of a devastating earthquake in their own country will be ordered to leave in

2019.[33] Also previously given protected status, 59,000 Haitians have been ordered to leave as well.[34] And 200,000 Salvadorans who were given protected status in the United States because of destructive earthquakes in their own country have been ordered to leave.[35] The people being ordered to leave are still in need of protected status as their countries are still recovering from earthquakes or hurricanes. The brutality of ending their status can argue the rule of law—they were only here temporarily—but fails to embody human rights. The motivation for sending all these particular people back to devastated countries is clearly race motivated. That the rule of law with no mention of race is cited by those who terminate the protected status is indeed antiracist racism. Another way is being used to remove Latina/os from the United States

The so-called Dreamers are now young adults, brought to this country as children. The Deferred Action for Childhood Arrivals (DACA) program was established by an executive order of President Obama. It brought young undocumented people out of the shadows. Many of these young people are now in college, most are working, some serve in the U.S. military. They know no other country. They are undocumented and subject to deportation. And they are indeed targeted. Several states' attorneys general have fought to end DACA.[36] They are also being used as bargaining chips to terminate the diversity lottery for selecting immigrants from low-migration countries; for ending or restricting family-based migration; for building a wall across the southern border of the United States. Each of these proposals indicates a level of racism, carefully being enacted through policy.

But not all Latinx people are immigrants. In the case of Puerto Rico, after devastating hurricanes strafed the island, federal government responses have been somewhere between slow and absent. The lack of recognition of the island's status as a U.S. territory, while ignoring the American citizenship of Puerto Ricans, can only be tied to the overall negative racial perspectives that weigh against all Latina/os. But there is a difference between Dreamers and people under protected status and those from Puerto Rico. Puerto Ricans cannot vote in United States' elections while they reside on the island. They *can* vote if they move to the mainland of the United States. This has implications that I will discuss under the closing section on human rights.

RELIGION AT THE INTERSECTION

Religion, for Latinos/Latinas, is a two-edged sword that cuts both ways: benefiting their communities at the same time others are using it to undercut that work. The religious experiences in Latin American countries established negative lineages: "In the evangelization of the Americas, the Europeans, using their own culturally determined image of 'a good, mature, and civilized human being,' judged the natives to be mere children, creators of tales, liars, and totally untrustworthy. As such, they . . . could be peripheral members of the church but could never participate fully in the life of the church."[37] Some of this attitude traveled into U.S. politics, but a more effective method of Othering Latinos and Latinas is at work today.

Like the Curse of Ham tale used against African Americans, immigration is used to demonstrate that "Hispanics" have done something wrong being here—illegally. In the same vein as the Curse of Ham, Christianity is used as a tool to disempower Latinos/Latinas, making them Others who do not belong in the United States.

Today, some white Americans who try to frame Christianity against Latinos/Latinas use a heavy hand in their application of biblical ideas. "John 10:1 Verily, verily, I say unto you, He that entereth not by the door into the sheepfold, but climbeth up some other way, the same is a thief and a robber. And so it is also with illegal aliens."[38] Here, the Conservative Christians of Alabama utilize a portion of a gospel saying attributed to Jesus; the last eight words are not in the Scripture.

The following author also aims to incorporate biblical ideas to buttress anti-immigrant rhetoric:

> Biblical wisdom would protect Americans from open borders and the risks associated with amnesty; illegal entry into the country by violent Islamists, narco gangs and those who knowingly enter with dangerous diseases like Ebola. Our goal is not hostility, but hospitality. . . . While the Bible teaches us to be kind to the sojourner or "resident alien," it also teaches that kindness to the sojourner ought not to be injustice to local citizens and their unique culture.[39]

Unlike the Curse of Ham, these two examples were crafted at a time when there is greater skepticism about usage of the Christian Bible to support hatred. The general American population is also more tolerant, more educated, and more conversant with diversity. There is much still to do to improve diversity; but infusing these authors' ideas into the marrow of the American cultural milieu is not as forceful as it was during the times of African enslavement.

One commonality among the authors cited above is the exploitation of "nativist sentiments." Such sentiments are bred and nurtured with fear—of crime, of poverty, of loss of employment for American citizens, of culture— even of the English language. Such fears themselves become a form of "religion."

There are Latinos/Latinas who experience the negative forms of Christianity who then raise caution flags about the possibilities of hope through religion. The following author questions whether religion—particularly Catholicism—and language—specifically Spanish—serve Latin communities well.

> Two significant ingredients of the glue that holds [Hispanic communities] all together are language and religion. Ironically, the language and religion which serve this purpose are not the religions of our Indian and African ancestors, but rather Castellano, the Spanish of Castilla, and the Roman Catholicism of our conquering Spanish ancestors. Yet, using language and religion as affiliation fetishes creates a risk of converting us into a museum culture. [40]

Starting near the end of the twentieth century to the present, the religious demographics of Latinos/Latinas have been changing. Pew Research reported, "The Catholic share of the Hispanic population is declining, while rising numbers of Hispanics are Protestant or unaffiliated with any religion. Indeed, nearly one-in-four Hispanic adults (24%) are now *former* Catholics." [41] Such movement, from one religion to another or unaffiliated status, might reflect responses to the historical negative expressions of the European Catholicism of the colonizers; these changes also might reflect resistance to negative views here in the United States. Yet 55 percent are still Catholics, 22 percent are Protestant. [42]

However, even as religion and spirituality shift, there remains a core of religious belief, especially Christian, among Latinos/Latinas. One draw to religious communities is that identified ethnic churches may offer services in Spanish and may have connections to particular countries of origin. While second- and third-generation Latinx may lose fluency in the language, these churches provide a communal connection beyond simple language skills.

> Nearly six-in-ten Hispanic churchgoers (57%) say their church maintains close ties with countries in Latin America by sending money or missionaries to these countries or receiving clergy from countries in the region. . . . Among religious groups, churchgoing Protestants are more likely than Catholics to say that their church maintains close ties with Latin America (71% and 54%, respectively). Protestants also are significantly less likely than Catholics to say that they are unsure of their church's ties to Latin America (10% to 26%). And a plurality (44%) of religiously unaffiliated Hispanics who ever attend religious services say the place of worship they attend most often maintains close ties to countries in Latin America. [43]

Religions can offer liberatory words for Latinos/Latinas, because they do know who they are. Miguel De La Torre and Edwin Aponte explain, "Hispanic theologies are community based. Usually Eurocentric theologies reject this proposition and claim some sort of objectivity, which divorces their theological perspectives from their social location. Hispanic theologies, on the other hand, openly admit their connections to the communities from which they arose." [44] The resulting theologies incorporate many aspects of

Latino/Latina culture and history: being "exiles, aliens and outsiders";[45] cultural roots that includes popular religiosity, including Native American and African tradition;[46] and *mestizaje*, or mixture of races and cultures.[47] Central values are justice, family, and community.[48]

Latinas find specific ways to develop liberation theologies from their own life experiences. Among these thinkers and activists, Ada María Isasi-Diaz developed the idea of mujerista theology to address Latinas' needs in their own voices.

> Mujerista theology, which includes both ethics and systematic theology, is a liberative praxis: reflective action that has as its goal liberation. As a liberative praxis mujerista theology is a process of enablement for Latin women which insists on the development of a strong sense of moral agency and clarifies the importance and value of who we are, what we think, and what we do.[49]

Among Latino/as, there are also a variety of African-derived religions—diverse, diffuse, and still influential and important despite Christianity's dominance. Among these religions are Vodou, Candomblé, Rastafarianism, Obeah, and Lucumi. The national origin of each religion links back to African traditional religion, even though some may have incorporated folk Christian beliefs, as connected with and envisioned by enslaved Africans throughout the Caribbean. Taken together, these are referred to as "African Diasporan religions."[50] The religious beliefs emigrated with enslaved people or later migrants to the United States—so that Rastafarianism and Obeah travel from Jamaica; Vodou, from Haiti; Candomblé, from Brazil, and Lucumi, from Cuba. There are many variations of these religions, influencing art and culture. Using their own religions and their cultural memories, these African Latin people also retained their own humanity within hostile and dehumanizing situations.

LATINX HUMAN RIGHTS

Questions of human rights for Latinx begin to bring these areas of race, religion, and politics together. Because of the international dimensions of Latinos/Latinas in the United States, it might seem that the United Nations should be a helpful starting point. But, as seen above, on that global scale, the United States has been a foundational presence at the United Nations from its beginnings. The International Monetary Fund and the World Bank have already been "helping" to end poverty in the regions of Latin America. Free trade, development, and capital are all based on Euro/U.S. ideas of proper methods. The argument for these ideas revolves around the belief that they are objective and acultural. The arguments for free trade, development, and capital are solidly informed by neoliberalism, which "endorses profit-making as the essence of democracy and consumerism as the only operable form of citizenship—grounding both in an irrational belief in the market's ability to solve all problems and to serve as a model for structuring all social relations."[51]

As Americans, we do not like to hear such arguments about our system. Yet the results of the singular belief in the free market leads to ideations that we often hear, "Every individual is responsible for their own fate and this skewed notion of freedom is reinforced by an emphasis on possessive individualism and the notion that personal advantage is far more important than the public good. . . . [These are] driven by a survival-of-the-fittest ethic, grounded in the celebration of shark-like competition."[52] Values of justice, family, and community stand in contrast and may indicate that U.S. popular culture has something to learn from the "aliens, exiles, and outsiders" in our midst. This brings us back to human rights from below. Language, museums, and aspects of citizenship are some dimensions of human rights from below for Latino/as.

Language

Language may be the place to begin consideration of Latino/Latina human rights from below. Language has the power to create identities and to carry layers of meaning that do not necessarily translate well into other tongues. The English-only movement has not eliminated Spanish; many people are bilingual. Facility with languages is needed, especially with young citizens, as the United States moves into global dialogues. Language becomes a primary move into human rights.

> To provide social justice and cultural access for language minorities globally, it absolutely is imperative to approach language minorities not as subjects of assimilation, or as "others" distinguished by a different language, skin color, or nationality, but as people who have the human rights to equal opportunities. It absolutely is imperative to recognize and respect non-dominant languages, because they are important elements of personal and group identities, necessary for healthy socioeconomic and personal growth, and carriers of knowledge.[53]

Language introduces the larger issue of culture. While language can be argued as needed for global commerce (Spanish, with English, is a major language of commerce), understanding the diverse Latin cultures is necessary—for all Americans as well as Latinos/Latinas. Here, education is the key. This is especially true for Latin peoples in the United States. An example is found in the "Tucson [Arizona] Unified School District's (TUSD) Mexican American Studies Department (MASD). Put simply, MASD has created and has implemented a transformative education model that views diversity as resource. From our perspective, this resource can be and should be used as an academic tool. We have found that when the cultural diversity of our students is embraced, appreciated, understood, and honored, students will respond in favorable ways that many never knew they could respond."[54] The pedagogy and curriculum developed culturally and historically relevant content, social justice focuses, and community service to craft "critically compassionate intellectualism" to the benefit of the students. Such foci reflect the central values mentioned above of justice, family, and community.

Museums

As mentioned in previous chapters, both Native American and African American communities have designated museums in Washington, DC. With the opening of the National Museum of African American History and Culture in September 2016, some discussion began among lawmakers about the possibilities of a similar structure dedicated to Latino/Latina history and culture. One Latino wrote a strongly worded opinion against such a museum. Reflecting racism, he argued that African Americans could not be compared to immigrants. He argued that a museum would "cement" the idea that Latinos/Latinas are an "ethno-racial" group. He charged that racial divisions only began in the 1970s and a museum would add to the social "fragmentation" as well as "perpetuate the notion of victimhood."[55] As Roberto Campos, cited above, this author rejects the idea that there is benefit to emphasis on Latin cultures and history; instead, he pushes toward assimilation. But the Tucson Mexican American Studies Department is demonstrating that culture is a resource, not a detriment.

Perhaps the author is not aware that there is a strong, local museum, El Museo del Barrio, in New York City. "El Museo del Barrio is the preeminent forum and resource in the United States dedicated to Caribbean, Latino, and Latin American art. The museum cares for a diverse, 6,500-object Permanent Collection of Caribbean, Latino and Latin American art, unique in the United States."[56] Further, they specify that El Museo "provide[s] an educational forum that promotes an appreciation and understanding of Caribbean and Latin American art and culture and its rich contribution to North America." Establishing a national museum in Washington, DC, might significantly contribute to the education of all Americans about Latinos/Latinas.

Aspects of Citizenship

Discussing United States citizenship and Latinx surfaces some repugnant nativist sentiment. But the needs of immigrants and refugees also bring some specific work for human rights in and on behalf of Latina/Latino communities.

One organization is the Sanctuary Movement. Multiple faith communities have come together pledging support for immigrants who fear deportation. Their website states that more than one thousand communities have taken this pledge:

> As people of faith and people of conscience, we pledge to resist the newly elected administration's policy proposals to target and deport millions of undocumented immigrants and discriminate against marginalized communities. We will open up our congregations and communities as sanctuary spaces for those targeted by hate, and work alongside our friends, families, and neighbors to ensure the dignity and human rights of all people.[57]

Another organization is Clergy and Laity United for Economic Justice (CLUE). They have been "working with the National Immigration Law Center to develop rapid-response trainings. They want to train people to film encounters, interview witnesses, and build prayer walls around ICE officers. CLUE is also trying to enlist faith leaders who would be willing to go to detention centers after raids to talk to ICE officers or to serve as a source of spiritual support to detainees."[58]

Immigration is a central point that brings issues of human rights to the fore and challenges Americans' understandings of Latinos/Latinas. Even though there are some Christians against immigration and some politicians pushing various forms of removing immigrants from the United States, other Americans are organizing against the separation of families or the brutality of immigration agents. One organization is in Washtenaw County, Michigan, the Washtenaw Interfaith Coalition for Human Rights (WICHR). Their mission is "to provide a culturally sensitive and supportive urgent response to raid detainees and their families, educate the targeted and allied communities, impact local governmental policies to empower and protect immigrant community members, and to work toward humane national immigration reform that provides a pathway to citizenship for all undocumented workers and people."[59]

Their volunteers include bilingual social work students and community members who rapidly respond to "the emergency needs of families and documenting incidences of immigrant raids, detainments, and deportations." The agency and its volunteers educate immigrants of their rights while developing allies among community members. The agency also participates in local and national political action.[60]

A wall is proposed at the southwestern border to prevent Latin Americans from arriving without documentation. The result has been an increase in protests from religious people about the symbol of the wall and its meaning for our humanity. In April 2017, a three-week Caravan Against Fear began, a 2,000-mile trek that will head down California's Central Valley to Los Angeles, then south to Los Angeles, then south to San Diego, east into Arizona, . . New Mexico, and Texas. Those who stay with the caravan the whole three weeks will end up at a series of rallies in Texas at month's end. . . . The caravan is following in the moral footsteps of Cesar Chavez's great marches.[61]

Grounded in history, the work of activists like these is undoing the intersection of religion, politics, and race. In the words of one pastor in the caravan, "We're all one people, from one God. We all have God's DNA."[62] This, like the Washtenaw Interfaith Coalition for Human Rights and the Clergy and Laity United for Economic Justice and the Sanctuary Movement, is human rights from below.

But there are also larger umbrella organizations, such as the National Council of La Raza (NCLR), which began in 1968. This group has deliberately worked to make connections among various Latin American groups. In July 2017, they changed their name to Unidos US. Their website states, "We serve the Hispanic community through our research, policy analysis, and state and national advocacy efforts as well as in our program work in communities nationwide. And we partner with Affiliates across the country to serve millions of Latinos in the areas of civic engagement, civil right and immigration, education, workforce and the economy, health, and housing."[63] The organization establishes the Americanness of Latinx people.

Another website stresses Latin people as real Americans, especially within their situation. A website challenges—Define American: "It's time for a new conversation about immigrants and identity in America. Why do people come to this country? What does it mean to be undocumented? What does it mean to be a good citizen?"[64] The stories of many of the Dreamers are included. The issue of immigration is made personal; the stories can lead to human rights from below.

Finally, the issue of voting recurs for Latinx people. The immigration issue is mobilizing people to consider for whom they vote based on where the candidates stand on policies such as DACA and the diversity lottery. And people from Puerto Rico, United States citizens all, who move to the mainland can exercise their right to vote. They will not forget how they have been treated. It is not simply a matter of civil rights. It is a matter of human rights.

NOTES

1. Lee Bebout, *Whiteness on the Border: The U.S. Racial Imagination in Brown and White* (New York: NYU Press, 2016), 1.

2. Amy Davidson Sorkin, "Steve King and the Case of the Cantaloupe Calves," *The New Yorker*, July 25, 2013, http://www.newyorker.com/news/amy-davidson/steve-king-and-the-case-of-the-cantaloupe-calves.

3. Jeffrey Passel and Paul Taylor, "Who's Hispanic?" Pew Hispanic Center, May 28, 2009, http://www.pewhispanic.org/2009/05/28/whos-hispanic/.

4. Miguel A. De La Torre and Edwin David Aponte, *Introducing Latino/a Theologies* (New York: Orbis Books, 2001), 15.

5. Louis E. V. Nevaer, "The Hispanic Diaspora in the United States," Hispanic Economics, http://www.hispaniceconomics.com/overviewofushispanics/hispanicdiaspora.html.

6. Juan Gonzalez, *Harvest of Empire: A History of Latinos in America* (New York: Penguin Press, 2000), 216–17.

7. Niraj Chokshi, "'Taco Trucks on Every Corner':' Trump Supporter's Anti-Immigration Warning," *New York Times*, September 2, 2016, http://www.nytimes.com/2016/09/03/us/politics/taco-trucks-on-every-corner-trump-supporters-anti-immigration-warning.html?_r=0.

8. Henry Flores, *Latinos and the Voting Rights Act: The Search for Racial Purpose* (Lanham, MD: Lexington Books, 2015), 121.

9. Bebout, *Whiteness on the Border*, 7–8.

10. Bebout, *Whiteness on the Border*, 11.

11. J. L. A. García, "Is Being Hispanic an Identity?" in *Debating Race, Ethnicity, and Latino Identity: Jorge J. E. Gracia and His Critics*, ed. Ivan Jaksic (New York: Columbia University Press, 2015), 102.

12. Passel and Taylor, "Who's Hispanic?"

13. Larry Catá Backer, "Not a Zookeeper's Culture; LatCrit Theory and the Search for Latino/a Authenticity in the U.S.," *Texas Hispanic Journal of Law and Policy* 4, no. 7 (1998): 13–14.

14. Miguel de la Torre, conversation with author, July 2017.

15. Ines M Miyares, "Creating Contemporary Ethnic Geographies: A Review of Immigration Law," in *Contemporary Ethnic Geographies in America*, 2nd ed., ed. Christopher A. Airriess (Lanham, MD: Rowman & Littlefield, 2016), 33.

16. Gonzalez, *Harvest*, 28.

17. Gonzalez, *Harvest*, 28.

18. Barker, "Not a Zookeeper's Culture," 16.

19. "The IMF at a Glance," International Monetary Fund, http://www.imf.org/en/About/Factsheets/IMF-at-a-Glance.

20. "History," The World Bank, http://www.worldbank.org/en/about/history.

21. Gonzalez, *Harvest*, 232.

22. "The Colon Free Trade Zone, Panama Republic of Panama," Colon Free Trade Zone, http://www.colonfreetradezone.com/freezone-colon.html.

23. Gonzalez, *Harvest*, 232.

24. Gonzalez, *Harvest*, 233.

25. Eduardo Galeano, *Open Veins of Latin America: Five Centuries of the Pillage of a Continent* (1973; repr. New York: Monthly Review Press, 1997), 220.

26. Galeano, *Open Veins of Latin America*, 220.

27. Galeano, *Open Veins of Latin America*, 272.

28. Galeano, *Open Veins of Latin America*, 267,

29. David Frum, "America's immigration Challenge," *The Atlantic*, December 11, 2015, https://www.theatlantic.com/politics/archive/2015/12/refugees/419976/.

30. Dave Zirin, "A Majority-Immigrant Church Vandalized with 'Trump Nation/Whites Only,' Becomes a Site of Resistance," *The Nation*, November 21, 2016, https://www.thenation.com/article/a-majority-immigrant-church-vandalized-with-trump-nationwhites-only-becomes-a-site-of-resistance/.

31. Emily Ryo, "On Normative Effects of Immigration Law," *Stanford Journal of Civil Rights and Civil Liberties* 13, no. 1 (2017): 99

32. Teresa Pac, "The English-Only Movement in the US and the World in the Twenty-First Century," *Perspectives on Global Development and Technology* 11, no. 1 (2012): 197.

33. Ron Nixon, "About 2,500 Nicaraguans to Lose Special Permission to Live in the U.S.," *New York Times*, November 6, 2017, https://www.nytimes.com/2017/11/06/us/politics/immigrants-temporary-protected-status-central-americans-haitians.html?action=click&contentCollection=U.S.&module=RelatedCoverage&region=Marginalia&pgtype=article.

34. Miriam Jordan, "Trump Administration Ends Temporary Protection for Haitians," *New York Times*, November 20, 2017, https://www.nytimes.com/2017/11/20/us/haitians-temporary-

status.html?action=click&contentCollection=U.S.&module=RelatedCoverage&region=
Marginalia&pgtype=article.

35. Miriam Jordan, "Trump Administration Says That Nearly 200,000 Salvadorans Must
Leave," *New York Times*, January 8, 2018, https://www.nytimes.com/2018/01/08/us/
salvadorans-tps-end.html.

36. Kristen Bahler, "Here Are the 9 Attorneys General Who Led the Campaign to End
DACA," *Money*, September 5, 2017, http://time.com/money/4927838/trump-daca-attorney-
generals/.

37. Virgil Elizondo, *Guadalupe, Mother of the New Creation* (Maryknoll, NY: Orbis Books,
1997), 86.

38. "Christians and Immigration—Bible Verses," Conservative Christians of Alabama,
http://ccofal.org/TeaParty/Christians-immigration.phtml.

39. Kelly Monroe Kulberg, "How Should Christians Think about Immigration Amnesty?,"
Christianity.com, http://www.christianity.com/christian-life/political-and-social-issues/how-
should-christians-think-about-immigration-amnesty.html.

40. Backer, "Not a Zookeeper's Culture," 14–15.

41. "The Shifting Religious Identity of Latinos in the United States," Pew Research Center,
May 7, 2014, 5.

42. "The Shifting Religious Identity of Latinos in the United States," 5.

43. "The Shifting Religious Identity of Latinos in the United States," 84.

44. De La Torre and Aponte, *Introducing Latino/a Theologies*, 69.

45. De La Torre and Aponte, *Introducing Latino/a Theologies*, 46.

46. De La Torre and Aponte, *Introducing Latino/a Theologies*, 61–62.

47. De La Torre and Aponte, *Introducing Latino/a Theologies*, 13.

48. De La Torre and Aponte, *Introducing Latino/a Theologies*, 65–67.

49. Ada María Isasi-Diaz, *Mujerista Theology: A Theology for the Twenty-First Century*
(Maryknoll, NY: Orbis Books, 1996), 62.

50. Research about African Diasporan religions is growing. A few examples follow: Rachel
E. Harding, *Refuge in Thunder: Candomblé and Alternative Spaces of Blackness* (Blooming-
ton: Indiana University Press, 2000); Margarite Fernández Olmos and Lizabeth Parvisini-
Gebert, *Creole Religions of the Caribbean* (New York: NYU Press, 2005); Dianne M. Stewart,
Three Eyes for the Journey: African Dimensions of the Jamaican Religious Experience (New
York: Oxford University Press, 2005); Kamari Maxine Clarke, *Mapping Yorùbá Networks:
Power and Agency in the Making of Transnational Communities* (Durham, NC: Duke Univer-
sity Press, 2004).

51. Henry Giroux, *America's Addiction to Terrorism* (New York: Monthly Review Press,
2016), 18.

52. Giroux, *America's Addiction to Terrorism*, 19.

53. Pac, "The English-Only Movement," 205–6.

54. Augustine F. Romero and Martin Sean Arce, "Culture as a Resource: Critically Compassionate Intellectualism and Its Struggle against Racism, Fascism, and Intellectual Apartheid in
Arizona," *Journal of Public Law and Policy* 31 no. 1 (2009): 179.

55. Mike Gonzalez, "We Don't Need a National Latino Museum," *Washington Post*, September 23, 2016, https://www.washingtonpost.com/opinions/we-dont-need-a-national-latino-
museum/2016/09/23/7f5a0308-7f59-11e6-9070-5c4905bf40dc_story.html?utm_term=.
7d86b527708c.

56. "History," El Museo, http://www.elmuseo.org/history-mission/.

57. "Sanctuary   Movement,"   Sanctuary   Not   Deportation,   http://www.
sanctuarynotdeportation.org/.

58. Kanyakrit Vongkiatkajorn, "Here Are the Churches Fighting Back against Trump's
Immigration Crackdown," *Mother Jones*, February 21, 2017, http://www.motherjones.com/
politics/2017/02/sanctuary-church-movement-trump-deportation/.

59. Laura Sanders et al., "Grassroots Responsiveness to Human Rights Abuse: History of
the Washtenaw Interfaith Coalition for Immigrant Rights," *Social Work* 58, no. 3 (April 2013):
119.

60. Sanders et al., "Grassroots Responsiveness to Human Rights Abuse," 119–21.

61. Sasha Abramsky, "Caravan against Fear," *The Nation* 305, no. 3 (July 31/August 7, 2017): 16.
62. Abramsky, "Caravan against Fear," 21.
63. "We Are Unidos US," Unidos US, https://www.unidosus.org/about-us/.
64. "Join the Conversation," Define American, https://defineamerican.com/.

Chapter Six

Asian Americans at the Race-Politics-Religion Intersection

As they expanded their empires to colonize these lands, the French and British used the term "Orient" to indicate East Asia, Southeast Asia, South Asia, and the Middle East, especially during the eighteenth and nineteenth centuries. (The separation of what we think of as the Middle East is, in some ways, a more recent invention of identities.) The "Orient" began to be used. However, the Orient cannot be understood separately from the term by which the Western Europeans designated themselves: the "Occident." The peoples of the Orient—Orientals—were considered sly, hypersexualized infidels who were inferior to the logical, intelligent, Christian Western Europeans, or Occidentals. The designation of the Orient comprised Orientalism, as Edward Said wrote in the 1970s, an imaginary geography, constructed in the nineteenth century, that "is a system of representations."[1]

> It is also an influential academic tradition (when one refers to an academic specialist who is called an Orientalist), as well as an area of concern defined by travelers, commercial enterprises, governments, military expeditions, readers of novels and accounts of exotic adventure, natural historians and pilgrims to whom the Orient is a specific kind of knowledge about specific places, peoples, and civilizations.[2]

Creating this imaginary geography and defining its imaginary residents also casts the "Orientals" into the category of the Others, persons who should be excluded or feared. Edward Said began his analysis from a European stance that was focused on colonial expansion and control; but there were other dimensions added when Orientalist ideas moved to the United States.

The concept of Asia is itself a problem. Gayatri Chakravorty Spivak lists the countries of "Asia" grouped together:

> Afghanistan, Armenia, Azerbaijan, Bahrain, Bangladesh, Bhutan, Brunei, Cambodia, China, Cyprus, Georgia, Hong Kong, Indonesia, Iran, Iraq, Israel, Japan, Jordan, Kazakhstan, the Koreas, Kuwait, Kyrgyzstan, Laos, Lebanon, Macau, Malaysia, Maldives, Mongolia, Myanmar, Nepal, Oman, Pakistan, Paracel Islands, Philippines, Qatar, Russia, Saudi Arabia, Singapore, Spratly Islands, Sri Lanka, Taiwan, Tajikistan, Thailand, Turkey, Turkmenistan, United Arab Emirates, Uzbekistan, Vietnam. Asia. Diversified subject-positions produced by shifting geopolitical lineaments. So far just a list off the Internet. [3]

Although people from Arabic countries, such as Iran and the United Arab Emirates, are grouped into the category of the "Orient" occasionally, as the above list demonstrates, I will not throughout this book; Muslims are the subjects of the next chapter with distinctive realities in the United States. Despite this difference, the imaginary geographies of the "Orient" remain. In the United States, "Oriental" is most often a reference for rugs or art, although, occasionally, it is used in reference to a human. Also, we Americans are generally geographically challenged, not able to find most of the countries listed above on a map, much less admit that we have heard of them. Therefore, our abilities to connect people with places is limited.

If Orientalism was a geographical imaginary, "Asian American" is often used as a human imaginary. It is shorthand for "them" to avoid the long discussions of place in the United States. One writer stated succinctly described this imagined Asian American as lacking cultural connectedness:

> Nobody grows up speaking Asian-American, nobody sits down to Asian-American food with their Asian-American parents and nobody goes on pilgrimages back to their motherland of Asian-America. . . . We share stereotypes, mostly—tiger moms, music lessons and the unexamined march toward success, however it's defined. My Korean upbringing, I've found, has more in common with that of the children of Jewish and West African immigrants than that of the Chinese and Japanese in the United States—with whom I share only the anxiety that if one of us is put up against the wall, the other will most likely be standing next to him. [4]

Sorting out some of the dimensions of the race, politics, and religion intersection for people that we call "Asian Americans" in the United States begins with some observations about the diverse histories of the many Asian people in the United States.

"ASIAN AMERICANS":
HISTORIES OF THE OFTEN IGNORED/INVISIBLE

At various times, from 1870 on, the United States' census groupings official-ly included the following: Chinese, Japanese, Filipino, Korean, Asian Indian, Vietnamese, other Asian Pacific Islanders, with brief appearances from the categories of "part Hawaiian" and "Hindu." The blanks on the forms were filled in by the census takers and based on their observations of the persons being counted; not until 1960 did citizens self-select racial designations.

The number of immigrants from Asia to the United States grew over the years:[5]

- 1820–1869: 90,698;
- 1870–1919: 836,704;
- 1920–1949: 180,564;
- 1950–1969: 494,4007;
- 1970–1989: 3,797,882;
- 1990–1999: 2,859,899;
- 2000–2009: 3,479,835.[6]

The number of years in each grouping range from fifty (first two groups) to ten years (the last group). The numbers demonstrate that immigration from Asian countries has dramatically increased.

These numbers reflect changes in U.S. immigration laws over the years. Chinese laborers were needed to build railroads through the 1800s, reflected in the first two numbers. However, in 1882, "Congress passed the Chinese Exclusion Act. . . . [T]heir entry was perceived to be a threat to existing laborers, especially in California."[7] Congress identified the "barred Asiatic zone" in 1917, covering an area from Afghanistan to the Pacific; this zone designated the people who were ineligible for U.S. citizenship. However, Japan, which had already agreed to prevent emigration, and the Philippines, which was a U.S. territory, were the exceptions in the Asiatic zone.[8]

Shifts in immigration numbers after 1950s reflect responses to World War II and refugees.

> In 1965, the Asian-American share of the U.S. population stood at less than 1 percent—having been held down by a century's worth of exclusionary policies explicitly based on race. That was the year—at the height of the civil rights movement and in the heat of a roaring economy—that the U.S. government opened the gates to immigration from all parts of the world, Asia included.[9]

With the fall of Saigon in 1975 and Pol Pot's reign of terror in Cambodia, as one of the major powers of the United Nations, the United States received refugees for resettlement. "Over the next fifteen years, the United States became the world's largest resettlement country, receiving approximately one million refugees from Southeast Asia."[10]

The growing flow of immigrants from Asian countries is not solely based on the changing laws in the United States or international refugee asylum needs. From the mid-nineteenth century, the United States became involved in Asian countries seeking to develop resources and goods, simultaneously impacting international trade balances. "The U.S. military involvement in Asia through military bases, military intervention, or temporary occupation of Asian countries also accounts for Asian immigration to the United States. For instance, the entrance of Koreans, Vietnamese, Cambodians, Hmong, and Laotians to the United States as military brides, refugees, adoptees, or immigrants cannot be fully explained without considering U.S. involvement in the Korean War and the Vietnam War."[11]

ETHNICITY, OPPRESSION, AND RACISM

The discussion of ethnicity that concerned the previous chapter is also pressing for people from Asian countries. At the beginning of this chapter, the "Asian" countries were listed. Ethnicity is multiplied substantially when considering the diversity within each country. So India includes more than fifty ethnic groups, including Tibetan, Parsi, Bengali, and Pashtun. Vietnam, a much smaller country than India, has more than fifteen defined ethnic groups, including Hmong, Khmer, Kinh, and Thai. When these diverse groups relocate to the United States, the fact of ethnicity as a social construction is underlined when all these distinctions are removed: these multiple people become "Asian."

One author notes that the concept of Asian and Pan Asian originated between 1895 and 1945 when "Japan used the rhetoric to 'save' or 'liberate' Asia from the Western aggressors" while promoting their own colonial efforts among their Eastern neighbors.[12] But the terms "Asian" and "Pan Asian" took on different shades of meaning in the United States, born of racial oppression.

Racism

The United States' immigration laws were significant for shaping the presence or absence of people from different Asian countries. The first Chinese Exclusion Act lasted for ten years (1882–1892). Using the practice of severely limiting the number of immigrants from all Asian countries, the act was initially focused on Chinese workers brought to the United States as cheap labor to build the railroad system, especially through the West coast. The anti-Chinese sentiment among white Americans expanded to Japanese, Koreans, and Indians, so that the 1917 Immigration Act barred entrance to anyone from an "Asiatic Barred Zone."[13] This was effectively hanging a "you are not welcome here" sign outside the country.

The racist ideas among white Americans were driven by a belief that "the yellow people" were coming to take "our" jobs. This was bolstered by the belief that Chinese people were coming to destroy "our" country. (Both arguments are reminiscent of the arguments against Mexican immigrants.) At several times in American history, these fears resulted in violence against people from Asian countries. In 1885–1886, anti-Chinese riots occurred in Washington state, Alaska, Wyoming, South Dakota, and Nevada. Several anti-Asian movements, called exclusion leagues, were formed—often through railroad unions.

By the time of the Japanese Pearl Harbor bombing in 1941, all Japanese Americans were forcibly removed to internment camps by order of President Franklin Roosevelt. Yet there was at least one report at the time that argued against such incarceration:

> In January 1942, a naval intelligence officer in Los Angeles reported that Japanese-Americans were being perceived as a threat almost entirely "because of the physical characteristics of the people." Fewer than 3 percent of them might be inclined toward sabotage or spying, he wrote, and the Navy and the FBI already knew who most of those individuals were. Still, the government took the position summed up by John DeWitt, the Army general in command of the coast: "A Jap's a Jap. They are a dangerous element, whether loyal or not."[14]

In 1998, the United States government did apologize and gave each survivor a cash payment. But all Asians' experience of racism and oppression do not end with such an apologetic resolution. The general anti-Asian climate persisted from the nineteenth century and was reflected in raced systems including segregated schools or the right to own land.

The racism that Asian peoples experienced was of a different flavor than that of Native, African, or Latino/Latina Americans. As Asian people were Othered, they were defined as competent but unsociable.[15] There was no tap dancing or salsa music, no soul food and no tortillas—no easily accessible culture pieces for Americans to assimilate, except for parts of religions. (I will return to this in the section below on religion.) There was so much diversity that the creation of a group, Asian Americans, Orientalized a people. The term "Asian American" is relatively new for the U.S. context. Historian Yuji Ichioka began to use it in the 1960s to bring the various ethnic groups in America together into a Pan-Asian political bloc. Ichioka's research focused on the stories of Japanese Americans. Contrary to stereotypes, "Asian immigrants weren't docile people who only worked hard and kept to themselves, Ichioka once said, but instead they fought the injustice of exploitive employers with strikes and demonstrations."[16]

Counterweights to Racism

Like Latinos/Latinas, people of Asian descent are still more likely to self-identify by region or national origin, even as their sense of boundaries is more fluid. A Pew Research report states, "The Asian-American label itself doesn't hold much sway with Asian Americans. Only about one-in-five (19%) say they most often describe themselves as Asian American or Asian. A majority (62%) say they most often describe themselves by their country of origin (e.g., Chinese or Chinese American; Vietnamese or Vietnamese American, and so on)."[17] The report also states that the number of Asian Americans who call themselves "just American" has also grown, to 28 percent.

Unlike Latinos/Latinas, the range of languages among those called "Asian American" is much wider. Regional dialect along with social class can create significant language barriers. "Two Filipinos, for example, may have to communicate with each other in English because one's native language is Tagalog while the other's is Ilocano. In a group of Chinese, one may have come from rural China; another, from cosmopolitan Hong Kong; a third, from war-torn Vietnam; a fourth, from Jamaica; and a fifth, from Ohio—each with obviously distinct stories to share."[18]

With these layers of information, I spoke with another conversation partner. Brett Esaki is a professor at Georgia State University.[19] I wondered about Asian Americanness and if it is related to an updated kind of Orientalism. As Dr. Esaki explained, the issue is more complex as Asian Americans are highly bifurcated:

> This is often related to the colonial history of the Asian nations and how the postcolonial nations did or did not retain ties to the former colonial powers. China and India maintained their ties to Britain; the Philippines, Japan, and S. Korea maintained their ties to the USA, therefore, all these countries have access to English, capitalist economies including trade, and technology. Those who rejected Western influence, mostly Southeast Asia, ended up poorer and less educated.[20]

There is also a split between wealthier immigrants who have "money, skills, and education and their children who do far better than older-generation Asian Americans." At the same time, there are "refugees who largely have great trouble learning the language and getting educated and finding housing in areas with good schools," as Dr. Esaki explained during our conversation.

Esaki's words echo those of author Frank Wu: "The lines of division among the groups were as obvious to them as they were obscure to outsiders: Chinese from Japanese, and vice versa; among the Chinese, the Mandarin-speaking, middle-class professionals who arrived as students on scholarships from the Cantonese-speaking lower-class laborers who had opened restaurants and operated laundries in the inner city."[21]

The dynamics that shaped them into Asian Americans are part of the race, politics, and religion intersection. The intersection works as seen in this:

> Asianization refers to racism specific to Asian Americans. . . . Asian Americans are hence "perpetual foreigners" or "forever foreigners," who can never be American and whose presence in America is not desired. It is this sense of foreignness that distinguishes the particular type of racism aimed at Asian Americans. And this racialization has been a common underlying cause of much historical and contemporary anti-Asian violence, oppression, and discrimination.[22]

Added to these layers are ways that each group is defined in the popular imagination in terms of the black-white binary. As stated in the previous chapter, this framing "position[s] people of color without difference from African Americans. Such a move erases the historical specificity of oppression."[23] This relationship to black Americans, the practice of treating the "raced" in one way, extends to Asian people when they become the "model" minority of the nation:

> [Asian Americans] pull themselves up by their bootstraps without complaining. Although seemingly flattering, this racialization is dangerous for many reasons. . . . The model minority myth emerged in the 1950s and 1960s as a white backlash to the black civil rights movement and was used to say, "If the black population acted like the Asian population they could achieve economic success without criticizing the white population." In doing so, the model minority myth covers up the existence of institutional racism and validates U.S. hegemonic ideologies such as color-blindness and meritocracy.[24]

The use of Asian Americans against black Americans is not just a myth. A recent case of Asian American students suing to end affirmative action was exacerbated by a white man, Edward Blum. Blum was the activist who funded and supported the Supreme Court case against University of Texas, on behalf of a young white woman, to end affirmative action. In 2016, this case failed as the Justices determined that "the race-conscious admissions program in use by the University of Texas at Austin when Abigail Fisher applied to the school in 2008 is lawful under the Equal Protection Clause."[25] Blum's aim is to end affirmative action with a focus on the black-white binary. He has now moved on to Asian Americans. "Anti-affirmative action activist Edward Blum has specifically attempted to recruit Asian American plaintiffs, using ads with photographs of Asian American students . . . The argument that affirmative action harms Asian American people is simply inaccurate. And worse, the argument is strategic rather than motivated by real concern for the well-being of Asian Americans."[26]

I asked Dr. Esaki how to interpret this anti–affirmative action lawsuit.

> The Harvard "issue" is that there are rich Asian Americans who don't feel the full brunt of racism with their social status, safe neighborhoods, and supportive Asian friends. They argue that affirmative action has hurt them, like white folk argue. They will cite their numbers and education and whatever, and see other minorities getting in and blame them for not getting in. A parallel moment is the removal of affirmative action in California schools, which has led to the dramatic increase in Asian American admittance and decrease of African American and Latino students.[27]

There have been attempts by some Americans to structure Asian peoples, with all their diversity and complexity, into a frame that fits a black-white binary, even as it is made clear to them that they are not white. Discrimination happens to Asian people; oppression happens subtly as the model minority myth is employed against them. "For Asian Americans, microaggressive comments like, 'Where are you from?' and 'You speak English well,' exemplify subtle or indirect racial slights."[28] In many ways, it is clear that "Asian American" is one of the newer racial groupings in the United States, even though there is a long history of different groups' contributions to the nation.

Continued Oppression, Activism, and Identities

The Asian American Movement (AAM) was among the first defined organized efforts for social justice that cut across different national origin groups. "The AAM was the vehicle that brought Asian American communities into the mainstream of civic life by demanding access, equity, and equality in all facets of society. . . . The AAM was grounded in a vision for structural change and was not primarily an assertion for identity."[29] The movement was most active in the 1960s through the 1980s; Yuji Ichioka, mentioned above, came from this movement. This time in American history—the 1960s to the 1980s—was a period in which multiple groups were claiming social justice for many issues in need of redress. The Civil Rights Movement eventually brought about the Civil Rights Act and the Voting Rights Act. The second-wave feminist movement pushed against inequalities and injustices experienced by women. Other groups such as the Black Panthers and Students for a Democratic Society pushed for other rights, including economic rights, for American communities. But Asian people were not just responding to trends; two incidents help to frame the development of an Asian American identity.

The greater Detroit, Michigan, area was, for many decades, a one-industry town: auto manufacturing. Most of the workers were unionized. In the 1970s, the Japanese automaker began breaking into the U.S. market. To avoid tariffs, the company built a couple of plants in the States that established new plant management styles, without unionized labor. The success of

Toyota began to cut into sales and jobs and American workers' resentment grew.

> The anger directed toward "little yellow people," in the phrase of Congressman John Dingell, who represented part of the region then and now, held them responsible for the genuine concerns about layoffs and downward mobility. Asians were blamed for a set of much more complex problems, including corporate leadership that had refused to consider fuel-efficient cars, consumer habits that took for granted the abundance of imported oil, lack of universal health care that imposed the insurance costs on employers, the failure to diversify the economic base of a metropolitan area, and cultural expectations about wages that could not continue to be met in the face of global competition, among other factors. Asians, and by extension, Asian Americans, were resented, because, it was believed, even as everyone else suffered, "those people" continued to do well.[30]

In June 1982, Ronald Ebens and Michael Nitz chased down Vincent Chin, of Chinese descent, and beat him to death with a baseball bat. "The two plead guilty to manslaughter in 1983. Neither Ebens nor Nitz served time in prison, but were sentenced to three years of probation. Ebens received a fine of $3,000 and $780 in court costs."[31]

Vincent Chin had nothing to do with the failure of auto companies or the lack of employment for the two white men, Ebens and Nitz; their entitlement to jobs superseded Chin's entitlement to life. The fear of job loss to an Other triggered racism. In 1882, Congress took up the cause and passed the Chinese Exclusion Act. And one hundred years later, the racism remained and two men acted: "The assault also seemed to confirm the charge 'you all look alike' that had rendered the Far East the source of a faceless horde since the advent of Yellow Peril."[32]

Vincent Chin's brutal murder and the murderers' lack of punishment mobilized Asian Americans across the country, beginning in Detroit. "The tragic death—and subsequent lenient punishment (probation and a $3,000 fine)—outraged Asian Americans in Detroit. They organized, forming new coalitions and the civil rights group American Citizens for Justice, sparking an Asian-American civil rights movement that continues today."[33]

Nearly ten years later, another attack occurred, this time by black Americans against Koreans. During the Rodney King riots in Los Angeles, black community members began looting and burning stores in Koreatown "for the shooting death of Latasha Harlins by a Korean shop owner." The violence and destruction were exacerbated by the police department's lack of response. "By the second day the rioters had advanced on Koreatown and still the police would not respond. They left the Koreans to fend for themselves while they defended more affluent white neighborhoods. Due to the police not responding the firefighters stopped responding as well because they kept getting shot at when they tried to put out the fires."[34] The event altered reality for many Korean Americans. One professor, Edward Taehan Chang, stated, "Korean immigrants, many who arrived in the late 1970s and early 1980s, learned economic success alone will not guarantee their place in America. What was an immigrant Korean identity began to shift. The Korean-American identity was born."[35] The riots were not merely impactful for black American communities; but Korean Americans were also remade.

There are some important lessons to be gleaned from this event for human rights from below, as will be seen later in this chapter. But in a reflection on the events of the riots, Laura Jeon, president of the Korean American Federation of Los Angeles, stated in April 2017, "Twenty-five years ago, Koreatown was in chaos, its buildings charred and its community in ruins," Jeon told the crowd. "If the Korean community and the African American community had been communicating back in 1992, the pain, agony, anger felt by both communities might have been avoided."[36]

One outcome in the face of oppressions and the search for identity was the creation of Asian American fraternities and sororities on American college campuses. Pledges study Vincent Chin's murder and the Los Angeles riots as well as anti-Asian racism and aspects of culture.

> Of the 18 Asian-American fraternities and sororities recognized by the National Asian Pacific Islander Desi American Panhellenic Association, 16 were founded between 1990 and 2000. Their mission statements promise the "making of successful leaders," as well as a commitment to service and "community awareness." The messages from the fraternities and sororities are remarkably similar—unity to achieve unexpected success, brotherhood and sisterhood devoted to establishing a professional network of high-functioning alumni. Initiations tend to promote a vague vision of Pan-Asian identity that reflects the history of Asian-American scholarship and activism, but whose urgency has been hollowed out by years of apathy.[37]

Yet there is one person who should be mentioned here, "breaking the bamboo ceiling to become a genuine household name": Jeremy Lin. His time with the National Basketball Association began with the New York Knicks in 2012; in 2018, he plays with the Brooklyn Nets; and has engendered "Linsanity" among his fans. Ellen Wu stated that, from the beginning of his professional career, "pundits and fans alike . . . reflect[ed] on their assumptions about Asian American masculinity," offering Asian Americans a glimpse of "the possibilities of a different kind of being in American life, acknowledging race yet leaving behind the confines of the yellow peril–model minority binary."[38]

Dr. Brett Esaki's words reflect the realities of these discussions: "There are many Asian American identities, and they divide along the lines previously mentioned."[39] This brief overview of racial constructions and political dimensions leads to questions about religions.

RELIGIOUS ORIENTALISMS?

The race-politics-religion intersection happens with a distinctive inflection for Asian American people. There is diversity among and within the many national origin communities. Additionally, there is decided diversity among religions and spiritualities practiced and embraced by Asian Americans from various countries and regions of the world. Discussing the "ancient cultures, philosophies, and religions" of Asia, one author stated, "This diversity of communities testifies to Asia's legacy as the birthplace of the ancient great religions of the world, including Hinduism, Buddhism, and Jainism in South Asia, Confucianism and Daoism in East Asia, Zoroastrianism in Central Asia, and Judaism, Christianity, and Islam in West Asia."[40]

That religious diversity is part of the experiences of religions of Asians in America. The Pew Research Center identified religious affiliations of the six largest groups of Asians in America:

- Chinese, 23.2 percent of total Asians in America population: the majority are religiously unaffiliated;
- Filipino, 19.7 percent of total Asians in America population—most are Catholic;
- Indian, 18 percent of total Asians in America population—about half are Hindu;
- Vietnamese, 10 percent of population—most are Buddhist;
- Korean, 9.9 percent of population—most are Protestant;
- Japanese, 7.5 of population—religious affiliation divided between Christian, Buddhist, and unaffiliated.[41]

This is a much more complex portrait of religious life than most Americans think of with Asian groups.

Dr. Esaki's research provides even greater detail than the above Pew numbers. He defines more fully the diversity of religious belief within Japanese American cultures in his writings.

> Japanese Americans preserved Japanese religions of Shinto, Confucianism, and Buddhism and hybridized them into other religions, including Christianity and contemporary American spirituality. In these efforts of preservation and hybridization, Japanese Americans frequently invigorated a sense of interconnectedness with the spirits of land, community, and family. In some cases, Japanese Americans explicitly linked this feeling of interconnectedness, mutu-

al responsibility, and spiritual survival to Native American religions and other indigenous religions. [42]

Esaki credits this religious framework as "lessons of spiritual survival [for] future generations of Japanese Americans."

The inability to oversimplify Asian meanings into one, easily accessed thing is evident in this one excerpt of a much longer study. The desire to apply these understandings of Japanese American religious thought to other Asian groups is quickly undercut by considering another scholar, theologian Anne Joh. Dr. Joh is Christian and draws from her Korean American religious concepts in order to define a postcolonial, feminist, liberation theology. She uses the concept of *han*, stated by another scholar, as "a sense of unresolved resentment against injustices suffered, a sense of helplessness because of the overwhelming odds against one's feeling of total abandonment, a feeling of acute pain and sorrow in one's gut and bowels."[43]

The concept of *han* has been explored by a variety of Korean American theologians, but Dr. Joh adds the concept of *jeong*; both these terms, she warns, "resist easy translation into Western vernacular."

> *Jeong* embodies the invisible traces of compassion in relationships and is most often recognized when we perceive our very own self, conscious and unconscious, in the mirrored reflection of the other. *Jeong* is a Korean way of conceiving an often complex constellation of relationality of the self with the other that is deeply associated with compassion, love, vulnerability, and acceptance of heterogeneity as essential to life. [44]

These two very short examples by Esaki and Joh demonstrate how any study of "Asian" religions cannot be reduced to simple terms. Further, the diversity of religious thinking is not immediately related to Western religious conceptualizations. The religious concepts that Esaki and Joh have highlighted provide some insight into differences among diverse Asian groups.

Americans, however, have barely grappled with these complexities. While the religious diversity may aid in maintenance of cultural identities, when American versions of Buddhism or Hinduism are born, they often reflect American ideas about what religion is or is not. There might be more evangelistic zeal, more inclusion of psychological practices, or a greater focus on specific goals, such as world peace. Because Americans understand "religion" so narrowly—it must look like *this* and do *this* or it is not religion—aspects of Asian religious systems, such as Confucianism or Daoism, are considered mere philosophies. This is an ongoing problem in approaching the study of religions[45] and Americans are often left with popularized versions of religions, captured in New Age beliefs.

Traditional Chinese, Japanese, or Indian religious beliefs are occasionally co-opted into American New Age beliefs. As some Native American religious practices have been commodified, in like manner, some Asian-derived concepts are taken out of the contexts that give specific religions their meanings. One of the earliest books to bring Eastern belief into a Western frame while achieving commercial success was Robert Pirsig's *Zen and the Art of Motorcycle Maintenance*.[46] There are also practices that have become popularized. For instance, Chinese astrology is readily available online at astrology.com, a website that also provides horoscopes, psychic readings, and tarot card interpretations.

The infusion of New Age/Asian-style religious thought into the United States does not account for different understandings of the body, mind, and spirit. Western thought divides body from spirit as two separate entities. The sacred and secular are sharply divided. The yin-yang symbol from China is an Eastern image that indicates the difference, as each "side" holds elements of the other. The human body in the West is given medical treatment based on symptoms and illnesses; the Eastern image of the body is much more complex. Types of Eastern-derived treatment include acupuncture, moxibustion, various forms of herbal medicine, and kampo.[47] The differences in understanding the body indicate that something is missing when parts of Asian religious orientation are ripped out to incorporate into various Western religious or medical practices.

For instance, mindfulness has been dropped into various settings without the Buddhist contexts. "The evolution of MM (Mindfulness Meditation) as an operationally defined and empirically tested therapeutic activity began by intentionally separating meditational practices from its religious and spiritual moorings. . . . This unsystematic disembedding of method from the cultural worldview from which it is drawn is an issue for some Buddhist practitioners."[48] But it is more than just disembedding. Like the misappropriation of Native American spirituality and practice, the use of mindfulness is big business. "Mindfulness training is a $1 billion plus business in the United States alone and growing robustly."[49]

This is one example of an out-of-context, commodified use of an Eastern religious concept. These simplistic uses cannot reduce people from Asia into simplistic American categories. These cannot improve cultural understandings.

Sociologist Jung Ha Kim analyzed the appropriation of Asian religious and spiritual thought and practice into forms for Western consumption. First, in contrast to the rugged individualism of the West, the East understands the human as interdependent. "Thus conducting rituals of ancestral veneration and making pilgrimages to shrines and temples, for example, are matters pertaining to community and not to individuals."[50] Second, as indicated in the above discussion of mindfulness, communal aspects of meditation become private events, focused on the self. Additionally, she mentions that the use of Asian visual art seems to give "ample evidence that the spiritual ethos of American artists is much informed by Asian traditions."[51] She concludes, "Appreciating the Other . . . must not be equated with appropriating the Other, and acts of consuming 'exotic' spiritual commodities must not be equated with acknowledging the spiritual traditions of the Other."[52]

But there are times that Western Christian groups go so far as to demonize Asian American religion and spirituality when concepts are judged as evil. So, yoga from India, related to Buddhism and Hinduism, became a symbol of pagans or evil for some radical Christians. I mentioned an exercise program that included yoga to a young woman and she was quickly replied, "My pastor said that's from the devil!" To avoid the evil devil, some Christians practice something called Christian yoga.[53] One website tries to promote areligious yoga and, therefore, denies any connection to Hinduism or Buddhism: "Yoga is not a religion. It is nonsectarian, but contains the ability to deepen anyone's faith."[54]

Commodified religious thought or demonized belief and practice have not strengthened communication between white Americans and Asian people. Perhaps there is hope: a discussion of human rights brings a critical focus to discussions of race, politics, and religion in an Asian American key.

HUMAN RIGHTS

As the complex webbing of identities of Asian peoples in America demonstrates, the construction of "Asian America" is simplistic and one-dimensional. The twenty-first century is not the seventeenth; what was done to captured Africans to redefine their names, to capture their cultures, is not possible now. We live in more sophisticated times: television with programming in different languages from different countries; phones and Internet; transportation speed and availability; and mail-delivery systems all provide ways for people who immigrate to the United States to stay in touch with "home" if they so choose. Africans brought to this country had to "exchange their country marks"[55] to brilliantly craft identities that retained their humanity in spite of people who were trying to define it away. Today, Asian people who immigrated to the United States, no matter the time period or income level, can still retain their stories of origin and touch back to, or outright reject, known persons and places. There is reason for their identities to be inspirational, acknowledging race but leaving behind racism and stereotypes, as Ellen Wu asserts in this vision statement,

> There is much hope to be found in these multifaceted undertakings. In all, they remind us that Asian American identity is neither predictable nor fixed. They can press us to "imagine otherwise." They spotlight, too, the centrality of Asian American initiative in defining Asian America—and America and beyond. . . . We can read these acts, ranging from humble to audacious, as

repudiations of the racisms that rob individuals of their full humanity. Such refusals are important steps toward the destruction of a racial and geopolitical order anchored by inequality and exploitation, and the rebuilding of relationships that hold dear visions of a humane and just global community.[56]

Human rights from below, for Asian Americans, will have different inflections than for other racial and religious groups. Human rights cannot be simply addressed, say, by removing affirmative action requirements from college admissions. There is more to learn. The failure of attempts to compress the diversity of Asians into Asian Americans provides an opportunity to understand some dimensions of creating human rights at local levels.

Human rights take on different meanings when Asian values are taken into account. While some Asian countries, such as China or Myanmar, are critiqued for not upholding human rights, there are still values that inform Asian conceptions of being human:

> Underlying some of the Asian voices is clearly the genuine concern that a liberal individualistic ethos in conjunction with a legalistic, aggressive and consumerist attitude does not meet traditional values of Asian societies, i.e. social harmony, respect for family and authorities, and in particular, emphasis on duty and responsibility rather than on rights that can be claimed. . . . [B]oth sides, the representatives of "Asian values" and the defenders of "Western liberalism," could learn from each other and in a sense, complement each other, although not on the same level exactly—i.e. not on the legal level of those minimal protective rights which are meant to guard the freedom of the individual from powerful communities and institutions.[57]

I have three examples of the possibilities of working together. The first is connected with Dr. Martin Luther King and nonviolence, inspired directly by Mohandas K. Gandhi. The methods are still taught through the King Center in Atlanta, Georgia.

> An ardent student of the teachings of Mohandas K. Gandhi, Dr. King was much impressed with the Mahatma's befriending of his adversaries, most of whom professed profound admiration for Gandhi's courage and intellect. Dr. King believed that the age-old tradition of hating one's opponents was not only immoral, but bad strategy which perpetuated the cycle of revenge and retaliation. Only nonviolence, he believed, had the power to break the cycle of retributive violence and create lasting peace through reconciliation.[58]

Grace Lee Boggs (1915–2015) was an activist in Detroit whom I knew. Grace Lee was a Chinese American, from a successful family on the East Coast. After she married an African American auto worker, her family disowned her. Her years of activism influenced many; she remained committed to improving Detroit. Her influence is still found in her words:

Just as we need to reinvent democracy, now is the time for us to reimagine work and reimagine life. The new paradigm we must establish is about creating systems that bring out the best in each of us, instead of trying to harness the greed and selfishness of which we are capable. It is about a new balance of individual, family, community, work, and play that makes us better humans. . . . [W]e have the power within ourselves to create the world anew.[59]

Here is a humanistic mindfulness built into an activist's life. I will return to some of Grace Lee's words in the final chapter, because she pointed the way to human rights from below.

The final example revisits the Korean American and African American communities following the violence of the L.A. riots, mentioned above. If the Korean American community was born from the ashes of the riots, new work at community building with African Americans also happened. Korean David Ryu began working with African American Nathan Redfern at a dispute resolution center following the riots. "Later, they worked on a citizenship project, Ryu teaching classes in English as a second language and Redfern giving mock citizenship exams at the Korea American Coalition,"[60] pragmatically removing barriers to communication between Korean Americans and African Americans.

In April 2017, a ceremony marking twenty-five years since the riots brought black American and Korean Americans together to remember.

"Twenty-five years ago, Koreatown was in chaos, its buildings charred and its community in ruins," Jeon told the crowd. "If the Korean community and the African American community had been communicating back in 1992, the pain, agony, anger felt by both communities might have been avoided." The Rev. Barbara Brooks, associate minister at First AME Church, said remembering the civil unrest together serves as a vehicle to better relations and fight "complacency." "It's like when you have a goal of losing 50 pounds, and when you reach your goal you say, 'OK, I don't have to do this anymore,'" Brooks said. "But to maintain what you've lost, you've got to do something different." For the African American and Korean communities, Brooks said, that "something different" is teamwork. Kieja Kim, president of the Victor Valley Korean American Assn., wasn't in Los Angeles during the riots, but she came Saturday to show solidarity and support. "Community relationships are important," said Kim, 60. "We aren't different. Black, Korean, Asian—we're human."[61]

NOTES

1. Edward Said, *Orientalism* (New York: Vintage Books, 1979), 202–3.
2. Said, *Orientalism*, 203.
3. Gayatri Chakravorty Spivak, *Other Asias* (Malden, MA: Blackwell Publishing, 2008), 236.

4. Jay Caspian Kang, "What a Fraternity Hazing Death Revealed about the Painful Search for an Asian-American Identity," *New York Times Magazine*, August 9, 2017, 34.

5. Based on this author's work, "Asia" here includes: China, Hong Kong, India, Iran, Israel, Japan, Jordan, Korea, Philippines, Syria, Taiwan, Turkey, Vietnam, and other countries in Asia.

6. Ines M. Miyares, "Creating Contemporary Ethnic Geographies: A Review of Immigration Law," in *Contemporary Ethnic Geographies*, 2nd ed., ed. Christopher A. Airriess (Lanham, MD: Rowman & Littlefield, 2016), 34.

7. Miyares, "Creating Contemporary Ethnic Geographies," 38.

8. Mae M. Ngai, "The Architecture of Race in American Immigration Law: A Reexamination of the Immigration Act of 1924," *The Journal of American History* 86, no. 1 (June 1999): 80.

9. Paul Taylor, ed., *The Rise of Asian Americans*, Pew Research Center, April 4, 2013, v, http://www.pewsocialtrends.org/files/2013/04/Asian-Americans-new-full-report-04-2013.pdf.

10. Miyares, "Creating Contemporary Ethnic Geographies," 51.

11. Sohyun An, "AsianCrit Perspective on Social Studies," *The Journal of Social Studies Research* 41, no. 2 (2017), 135–36.

12. Nami Kim, "The 'Indigestible' Asian: The Unifying Term 'Asian' in Theological Discourse," in *Off the Menu: Asia and Asian North American Women's Religion and Theology*, eds. Rita Nakashima Brock et al. (Louisville, KY: Westminster John Knox Press, 2007), 28.

13. From the "Asian American History Timeline," https://www.us-immigration.com/asian-american-history-timeline/.

14. T. A. Frail, "The Injustice of Japanese-American Internment Camps Resonates Strongly to This Day," *Smithsonian Magazine*, January 2017, https://www.smithsonianmag.com/history/injustice-japanese-americans-internment-camps-resonates-strongly-180961422/.

15. Qin Zhang, "The Mitigating Effects of Intergroup Contact on Negative Stereotypes, Perceived Threats, and Harmful Discriminatory Behavior toward Asian American," *Communication Research Reports* 33, no. 1 (January–March 2016): 3.

16. K. Connie Kang, "Yuji Ichioka, 66: Led Way in Studying Lives of Asian Americans, Obituary, *Los Angeles Times*, September 7, 2002, http://articles.latimes.com/2002/sep/07/local/me-yuji7.

17. Taylor, *The Rise of Asian Americans*.

18. Peter N. Kiang, "Understanding Our Perceptions of Asian Americans," Asian Society, Center for Global Education, http://asiasociety.org/education/understanding-our-perceptions-asian-Americans.

19. Brett J. Esaki, conversation with author, August 2017.

20. Esaki, conversation with author, August 2017.

21. Frank H. Wu, "Embracing Mistaken Identity: How the Vincent Chin Case Unified Asian Americans," *Harvard Journal of Asian American Policy Review* 19 (2010): 18.

22. An, "AsianCrit Perspective on Social Studies," 133.

23. Lee Bebout, *Whiteness on the Border: The U.S. Racial Imagination in Brown and White* (New York: NYU Press, 2016), 7–8.

24. An, "AsianCrit Perspective on Social Studies," 133.

25. "Fisher v. University of Texas at Austin," SCOTUSblog, http://www.scotusblog.com/case-files/cases/fisher-v-university-of-texas-at-austin-2/.

26. Nancy Leong and Erwin Chemerinsky, Aug 3 2017, "Don't Use Asian Americans to Justify Anti-Affirmative Action Politics," *Washington Post*, https://www.washingtonpost.com/news/posteverything/wp/2017/08/03/dont-use-asian-americans-to-justify-anti-affirmative-action-politics/.

27. Esaki, conversation with author, August 2017.

28. Alisia G. T. T. Tran and Richard M. Lee, "You Speak English Well! Asian Americans' Reactions to an Exceptionalizing Stereotype," *Journal of Counseling Psychology* 61, no. 1 (2014): 485.

29. Michael Liu, Tracy A. M. Lai, and Kim Geron, *The Snake Dance of Asian American Activism: Community, Vision, and Power* (Lanham, MD: Lexington Books, 2008), xv–xvi.

30. Wu, "Embracing Mistaken Identity," 20.

31. Louis Aguilar, "Estate of Vincent Chin Seeks Millions from His Killer," *Detroit News*, June 24, 2017, http://www.detroitnews.com/story/news/local/oakland-county/2017/06/24/vincent-chin-th-anniversary/103167672/.

32. Wu, "Embracing Mistaken Identity," 20.

33. Niraj Warikoo, "Vincent Chin Murder 35 Years Later: History Repeating Itself, *Detroit Free Press*, June 23, 2017, http://www.freep.com/story/news/2017/06/24/murder-vincent-chin-35-years-ago-remembered-asian-americans/420354001/.

34. Gikorea, "Attacks on Korean Shop Owners Featured Heavily in Smithsonian Documentary about the 1992 LA Riots," ROK Drop: Korea from North to South, May 10, 2017, http://www.rokdrop.net/2017/05/attacks-on-korean-shop-owners-featured-heavily-in-smithsonian-documentary-about-the-1992-la-riots/.

35. Gikorea, "Attacks on Korean Shop Owners Featured Heavily."

36. Sarah Parvini and Victoria Kim, "25 Years after Racial Tensions Erupted, Black and Korean Communities Reflect on L.A. Riots," *Los Angeles Times*, April 29, 2017, http://www.latimes.com/local/lanow/la-me-ln-la-riots-unity-meeting-20170429-story.html.

37. Kang, "What a Fraternity Hazing Death Revealed," 34.

38. Ellen D. Wu, *The Color of Success: Asian Americans and the Origins of the Model Minority* (Princeton, NJ: Princeton University Press, 2013), 257–58.

39. Esaki, conversation with author, August 2017.

40. Jonathan Y. Tan, "Dynamics of Interfaith Collaborations in Postcolonial Asia: Prospects and Opportunities," in *Postcolonial Practice of Ministry, Leadership, Liturgy, and Interfaith Engagement*, eds. Kwok Pui-lan and Stephen Burns (Lanham, MD: Lexington Books, 2016), 167.

41. Taylor, *The Rise of Asian Americans*, 7–8.

42. Brett J. Esaki, *Enfolding Silence: The Transformation of Japanese American Religion and Art under Oppression* (New York: Oxford University Press, 2016), 208.

43. The definition of *han* by Han Wan Sang, cited in Wohnee Anne Joh, *Heart of the Cross: A Postcolonial Christology* (Louisville, KY: Westminster John Knox Press, 2006), xxi.

44. Joh, *Heart of the Cross*, xxi.

45. The History of Religions, Chicago School at the University of Chicago, has addressed aspects of the limits of how we study and therefore understand religions. One author is Charles H. Long, *Significations: Signs, Symbols, and Images in the Interpretation of Religion* (Milwaukee: Fortress Press, 1986); another is Mircea Eliade, *The Sacred and the Profane* (New York: Harcourt, 1987).

46. Robert M. Pirsig, *Zen and the Art of Motorcycle Maintenance* (New York: Bantam Books, 1975).

47. There are extensive studies of these health practices in the United States. The Society for Medical Anthropology, http://www.medanthro.net/about/about-medical-anthropology/, is a professional organization for those who study different cultures' healing and medicine practices. In addition, complementary and alternative medicine is offered at some existing hospitals, such as the Mayo Clinic, http://www.mayoclinic.org/healthy-lifestyle/consumer-health/in-depth/alternative-medicine/art-20045267.

48. Stephen P. Stratton, "Mindfulness and Contemplation: Secular and Religious Traditions in Western Context," *Counseling and Values* 60 (April 2015): 102–3.

49. Kevin D. Williamson, "'Mindfulness': Corporate America's Strange New Gospel," *National Review*, January 1, 2018, http://www.nationalreview.com/article/455026/mindfulness-fad-corporate-america-buddhism-without-buddha.

50. Jung Ha Kim, "Spiritual Buffet: The Changing Diet of America," in eds. Brock et al., *Off the Menu*, 82.

51. Kim, "Spiritual Buffet," 83.

52. Kim, "Spiritual Buffet," 84.

53. For example, Brooke Boon, *Holy Yoga* (New York: FaithWords, 2007); Laurette Willis, *PraiseMoves: The Christian Alternative to Yoga* (Eugene, OR: Harvest House Publishers, 2006), DVD.

54. Michelle Thielen, "Christian Yoga," *Seattle Yoga News*, https://yogafaith.org/the-christian-yoga-myth/.

55. Michael A. Gomez, *Exchanging Our Country Marks: The Transformation of African Identities in the Colonial and Antebellum South* (Durham: University of North Carolina Press, 1998) traces the development of an African American identity from the many tribal affiliations brought to this country.

56. Wu, *The Color of Success*, 258.

57. Perry Schmidt-Leukel, "Buddhism and the Idea of Human Rights: Resonances and Dissonances," in *Buddhist Approaches to Human Rights*, eds. Carmen Meinert and Hans-Bernd Zollner (New Brunswick, NJ: Transaction Publisher, 2010), 59.

58. Included in philosophy statement, The King Center, Peachtree Street, Atlanta, GA, "The King Philosophy," The King Center, http://www.thekingcenter.org/king-philosophy.

59. Grace Lee Boggs, preface to the paperback edition, *The Next American Revolution: Sustainable Activism for the Twenty-First Century* (Berkeley: University of California Press, 2012), xxi and xxiii.

60. Parvini and Kim, "25 Years after Racial Tensions Erupted."

61. Parvini and Kim, "25 Years after Racial Tensions Erupted."

Chapter Seven

Muslims, The Newest/Old Others

The racial groups discussed so far—white, Native, black, Latinas/Latinos, and Asian-origin Americans—have an extended, if uncomfortable, history in the United States. As disjointed as it may seem, it is the history and character of America. The next group, Muslims, has had an overlooked presence in the land since colonial times; yet "Muslim" is a more contemporary construction, illustrating processes of creating Othered citizens.

There is a diversity of Muslims, as there is a diversity of Christians. Muslim Americans may reflect different national origins and different races. There are different strands of Islam—including Sunni, Shia, Sufi, Nation of Islam—that reflect nations, regions, and cultures.

Today, when the words "Muslim" and "Islam" are mentioned, often influenced by media and conspiracy theories, too often the word "terrorist" follows. The general American public may not recognize the diversity of those who profess Islam, thinking instead only of a few Middle Easterners, hearkening to the events of 9/11, that are seared into the American consciousness. The religion itself is misconstrued with simplistic understandings; words like "Sharia" and "jihad" are mistranslated as "we are coming to blow you up." From this fear of an imposition of Sharia law, the legislatures of several states have passed anti-Sharia laws.[1]

As mentioned in chapter 6, the Orientalized construction of Asian identities included Muslims from Middle Eastern countries. This construction was another aspect of Orientalism, and these "Muslim" images were powerful. Two authors discuss the visual representation of Muslims, noting that, from 1800 to 1950, more than 60,000 books were published by Western authors. "The key theme of these books was the depiction of colonized Arabs/Muslims as uncivilized and inferior in dire need of the progress proffered to them by the superior colonizers. It is in this political context that images of veiled Muslim women and women in harems appeared as a source of captivation and fantasy for western writers."[2] These constructions from the perspective of the West's colonial adventurism did not really die away but lingered, traveling to the shores of the United States.

Unlike the European Orientalism that grouped all Easterners together, Muslim-in-America has become its own grouping over time, focusing on the religion itself, to construct an imagined group. There are three periods of Muslims in America, sketched in brief below. The first two periods trace a path that leads to the construction of the third, the newest version of Othered Muslims. This path points to the development of intra–Muslim American divisions with their own race-politics-religion divisions. While those inner group arguments occur, the wider American political scene is littered with constructions of a Muslim race that overlaps again with an American image of religion.

BLACK AMERICAN MUSLIMS

There have been Muslims in the Americas since colonial times as enslaved Africans were brought to the colonies for forced labor. C. Eric Lincoln wrote, "Among the millions of Blacks who were made involuntary immigrants under the aegis of slavery, there were inevitable numbers of Muslims from the Islamic kingdoms of the West Coast of Africa. How many thousands (or perhaps tens of thousands) we shall never know. . . . The slave trade required and maintained a determined myopia regarding the religious interests of its hapless human commodities."[3]

Today much more is being uncovered about these early Muslims. For instance, in 1802 a plantation owner brought an enslaved Bilali Muhammad to Sapelo Island, Georgia. Muhammad was a Fulani, from Timbo in Futa-Jallon, or what today is Guinea. Known as Ben Ali, "He became Spalding's slave driver or overseer, and again, because of Sapelo Island's isolation, Bilali Muhammad, his family, and other Muslim slaves on Sapelo Island were able to freely practice their faith and its traditions. In the 1820s, Bilali Muhammad hand-wrote a 13-page Arabic text of Islamic laws and traditions. That text is now in the archives of the University of Georgia."[4]

The Islam practiced by the enslaved Africans was not exactly the same as the Arabic versions we might think of today. Rudolph Ware has provided significant information on how West African Muslims studied Islam.

> [Their] approach to schooling that I encountered in the testimonies of former Qur'an school students was a bodily approach. Islamic knowledge was being transmitted as much through bodily practices as mere words. This focus on bodily transmission of religious ideas expresses an understanding of knowledge as a thing that inheres in the body. What it means "to know" in the

context of Senegambian Qur'an schooling differed dramatically from what it meant for contemporary Westerners. Knowing was produced as much by the limbs as by the mind. . . . The people were the books, just as the Prophet was the Walking Qur'an.[5]

Because they understood themselves as holy bearers of the Qur'an, there was enhanced resistance to enslavement. Bilali Muhammad clearly straddled a line in being an overseer and faithful to his religious beliefs. It helped that Sapelo Island in Georgia is isolated, part of the chain of current Gullah and Geechee Americans.

Much of that enslaved Muslim lineage is lost or obscured. However, a black American Muslim presence surfaces again in the early 1900s. Timothy Drew was an itinerant peddler who found a way to study Islam. In the 1920s, he founded the first Moorish Science Temple in Newark, New Jersey. He was called Noble Drew Ali and considered an American prophet. He found the failure of the United States, which had ended enslavement but not subjugation of black people, proof that this country was not their home and Christianity was not their religion. "The new faith, with its lapel buttons, red fezzes, and identification cards, opened up a whole unexplored and fascinating perspective on 'the black race in Babylon' for black youth, new books to read, a new 'scientific view' to conjure with, and a new lifestyle in the drab existence of the great industrial centers of the nation."[6] Religion, race, and politics were constructed into his belief system, as the following quote attributed to Ali demonstrates: "The Nationality of the Moors was taken away from them in 1774 and the word negro, black, and colored was given to the Asiatics of America who were of Moorish descent, because they honored not the principles of their mother and father, and strayed after the gods of Europe of whom they knew nothing."[7]

In 1934, Elijah Poole, with the religious name Honorable Elijah Mohammed, became leader of the Black Muslims. Mohammed presented a view of Islam that attracted black Americans to the Nation of Islam (NOI): "His 'people' were those who were most battered by racism and stifled by convention, and whose experience of the white man's 'invincibility' made the acceptance of Black inferiority seem as reasonable as it was pervasive."[8] Targeting his message for African Americans, particularly the poor and the prisoner, Mohammed, the "Messenger of Allah," built an institution that was the primary face of Islam in the United States for decades.

The NOI made strides in black urban communities and impacted black Americans' self-identities. The NOI spoke directly to African American experiences, conceptualizing why things were the way they were; simply put, black people themselves were not to be blamed for their lives' conditions. The NOI provided views of black life that countered the negative views held by white Americans. However, they were intentional in separating themselves from what they understood as the negative influences of white American culture. Their diets reflected both Islamic restrictions such as not eating pork as well as restrictions against "slave" food such as watermelon. Islamic determinations for women's dress, specifically modesty, were followed, but they applied an American spin on the colors and beauty of fabrics used. Black communities benefited from their businesses, such as grocery stores that sold fresh fruits and vegetables. Black prisoners were converted and taken into homes after their sentences were complete; they were given duties and were rehabilitated as black Muslims. Well-dressed black men were often found selling their newspapers, *The Final Call*, on street corners. Their activities attracted the attention of the FBI, and the NOI was under suspicion, as were the members of the Moorish Science Temples.

In the early 1960s, the FBI circulated their judgment of the NOI, stating that they claimed to adhere to "the religious principles of Islam . . . and the spiritual and physical uplift of the Negroes . . . [however the] constant emphasis on the vindictive doctrines of the cult results in the propagation of hatred of the white race."[9] Setting up future problems, the FBI, the media, and academics declared that "The real Muslims of America . . . were the immigrant Muslims. . . . Their immigrant Islam, in contrast with African American Islam, was viewed as a sign by some in the 1950s as a healthy expression of American ethnic identity . . . as long as they assimilated to other American values." Here, in the law enforcement's judgment of black Muslims, the preference for immigrant Muslims, and the subsequent establishment of those Middle Eastern Muslims as "ethnic whites," the foundation was laid for Muslims from the United States to be pitted against those from other countries.

One central difference between NOI and the "real" or immigrant Muslims was whether or not Islam could or should attend to issues of race, as did African American Muslims. Two notable black American Muslims who demonstrated the continued awareness of and commitment to justice for all black Americans, whether or not they were Muslims, were Malcolm X and Muhammad Ali.

Malcolm X was appointed to a leadership role in the NOI by Elijah Muhammad. He was a controversial figure during his lifetime, holding out a seeming alternative to the nonviolence of Dr. Martin Luther King, Jr., an alternative that included violence as indicated by a phrase he uttered—"by any means necessary." In a July 1964 speech, Malcolm X stated, "My fight is two-fold, my burden is double, my responsibilities multiple . . . material as well as spiritual, political as well as religious, racial as well as non-racial."[10] In a photo, Malcolm was seen holding a gun and peering out of a curtained window; the photo seemed to prove his proclivity for violence. He was actually in the process of protecting his family against the NOI: he had broken away from the NOI, left his leadership position, and become Sunni

Muslim. Malcolm X was assassinated in 1965 by members of the NOI. At the time of his death, he was viewed negatively among some Americans. Yet, James Cone pointed to the resurgence of appreciation for Malcolm X that many young African Americans express, over against a lessened appreciation for Martin Luther King. While older black Americans still revere King, younger black people find that "Malcolm represents an abrasive, 'in-your-face' assertion of blackness, a 'don't mess with me' attitude. Young blacks love Malcolm's courage to speak the truth that whites did not want to hear. They love his righteous and fearless anger, his eloquence, wit, and self-confidence. Malcolm said in public what most blacks felt but were afraid to say except in private among themselves."[11] These ideas do not reference Malcolm X's religion, Islam, as a source for their admiration.

Muhammad Ali was initially a member of the NOI, but eventually became Sunni Muslim as did Malcolm X. Unlike Malcolm, though, he was a more welcome public figure. He had been a boxer who was the heavyweight champion of the world when he converted to Islam.

> The US government . . . sought to blunt his rising popularity by any means available. . . . The US Army drafted him. In 1966, at the height of the military conflict in Vietnam, Ali proclaimed that he was willing to give up his boxing crown and go to jail rather than be inducted. He said he was a conscientious objector whose religion prohibited the killing of innocents. Casting the Vietnam War as a racist and immoral conflict, Ali also stated that the US participation was hypocritical . . . [falsely] defending freedom abroad when [the United States] had its own problems with racial equality at home. In 1967, he was convicted of draft evasion and stripped of his boxing title.[12]

Ali was a larger-than-life figure who may have presented an attractive portrait of Muslims, black or otherwise. He spoke to issues of peace, as he retained connections with black communities. Even as he was in court fighting his conviction (which was overturned in 1971), the story of Muslims in America changed again. The connections between religion, race, and politics take a slightly different turn in the next historical phase.

AFTER THE HART-CELLER ACT, 1965

Congress passed the Johnson Reed Act in 1924 to curb immigration. A quota system, based on national origins, mandated that northern Europeans were given nearly three-fourths of all immigrant slots. Eastern Europe, Asia, and Africa were given portions of slots from the remaining one-fourth of annual slots given to immigrants. The determinations of who's in and who's out were made by a Quota Board. This board worked from an unspoken mission that the white race be the determinative factor in American identity; the "science" of eugenics fueled this mission. Narrowly understanding "white" to be from Western European countries, Eastern Europeans were less desirable. The surface argument for immigration restrictions was that the Western Europeans had the greatest assimilability into the United States' system and citizenship. The Board set the numbers of all possible immigrants based on the United States census; but these quotas included minimal numbers of, or completely excluded, black people from African countries or the Caribbean, Chinese and South Asian people, as well as Hawaiians and Puerto Ricans. These racial or ethnic designations were included on census forms of the past so the exclusion of this data was quite deliberate. In other words, everybody else was rendered invisible, even taking into account census enumeration. Certainly, people from Arabic countries were deemed unacceptable under this quota system. Under the surface of the 1924 act, seldom stated but a motivation: the white identity of the country was to be maintained. [13]

In 1968, President Lyndon Johnson helped usher the Hart-Celler Act to passage. Ending the quota system as anti-American, in the spirit of an era that sought racial justice, the act changed the immigration laws: "Especially by prioritizing family reunification, it also stimulated rapid growth of immigration numbers. Once immigrants had naturalized, they were able to sponsor relatives in their native lands in an ever-lengthening migratory process called chain migration. That unintended consequence is Hart-Celler's enduring legacy."[14] President Johnson, in some respects, had false hopes for the legislation. Edward E. Curtis reported that Johnson signed the act into law "on October 3, 1965. . . . Speaking from Liberty Island in New York, President Johnson stressed that the new legislation was not 'revolutionary.' He claimed that it would 'not restructure our daily lives.'"[15]

But the law was revolutionary and did change the complexion of the nation. Hart-Celler, within several years, changed the flow of immigrants from other countries beyond Western Europe into the United States. Ultimately, the act increased the diversity of races, nationalities, and cultures within the United States. And the United States is a country that has yet to deal with issues of diversity or races, nationalities, and cultures. Increases in Middle Eastern Muslim immigration also changed. In 2002, the Center for Immigration Studies estimated that Middle Eastern immigrants had grown "seven-fold, from fewer than 200,000 in 1970 to nearly 1.5 million in 2000." It was estimated that "73 percent (1.1 million) of all Middle Eastern immigrants were Muslim."[16]

One other change occurred after 1968 that is important for understanding Muslims in the United States in the early twenty-first century. In 1975, Elijah Mohammed died. His son, Wallace D. Mohammed, moved the majority of Nation of Islam into the orthodoxy of Sunni Islam within a year. Malcolm X and Muhammad Ali had already found their way to this form of Islam after making personal pilgrimages to Mecca. Islam was not as narrow as the

Nation of Islam portrayed it; yet it could not be separated from black American struggles for justice. Malcolm X angered Elijah Mohammed with his departure from the NOI. So, it was not until Elijah Mohammed's death that his son could envision the religious lives of the organization in new ways. Yet, some of the NOI refused to move with the son; they continued under the leadership of Louis Farrakhan. The African American Muslim community has its own diversity.

MIDDLE EASTERN MUSLIMS IN AMERICA

As Muslim immigrants, the FBI's "real" Muslims, entered the country, several lines of miscommunication were established. The American-born, black Muslims were outnumbered as waves of Arab immigrants brought a different face of Islam to the United States. Edward E. Curtis stated, "The new immigrants and foreign students taught second and third-generation Muslims how to perform their prayers in Arabic, often teaching them phonetically. They also translated literature about Islam into English and offered lectures on Islamic religious traditions. . . . Newly arrived immigrants would play an important role in sparking various religious awakenings among Muslim Americans."[17]

This influx of immigrants established Middle Eastern enclaves in some areas of the country. One was in Dearborn, Michigan. Dearborn is near the city of Detroit, which has historically large African American Muslim populations, both Nation of Islam and of the American Society of Muslims. Dearborn historically kept black Americans from purchasing homes, with a reputation that it was known as a bad town for black people to be in when the sun went down. In the 1980s, I spoke with a white woman who had lived in Dearborn her entire life. Middle Eastern people, both Muslim and Christian, had been able to purchase homes there, as they had been designated white ethnic; but they had not had a comfortable time with the white residents. The expectations of the immigration laws, despite the liberal feel to Hart-Celler, were assimilation to American culture and, addressing me, the woman stated, "If we'd know what *they* were like, we'd have let *you* move in."

With the influx of Middle Eastern immigrants, the face of Islam in America began to change.

> They increasingly turned to religion to define their identity. The use of U.S. power abroad transformed Muslim American consciousness at home. . . . For some, the religious awakening of the late twentieth century inspired the hope that the Muslim community in the United States would become a beacon for the rest of the Islamic world, modeling what Islam could be if lived with verve and commitment. Though it was highly diverse in form and content, the revival also united Muslim Americans in the belief that their destiny was shared.[18]

Curtis here presents one side of a discussion about Middle Eastern Muslims and American Muslims; his view is mostly positive for "united" Muslim Americans with shared destinies. However, the varieties of Muslim in America militate against easy, collapsible discussions of Muslim Americans. As another author challenges, what are "the ways in which Islam—as interpreted and practiced by participants—"[19] actually constructs contemporary meanings of being Muslim in America? We are not yet able to answer how diversity among Muslim Americans, native-born or immigrant, is understood among members.

Perhaps because the "Muslims" are the newest Others in the American imaginary, it is easier to tease out some of the differences with which these diverse people are themselves constructing identities and are responding to the overlap of race and politics from within their religious views. The group dynamics are not simple or static but are in process of forming and re-forming.

With the dominance of immigrant Muslims, in some instances, smaller groups of African American Muslims wonder if their mosques will have the membership to continue. While those African American Muslims in urban areas, such as Chicago or Detroit, may have had stronger and more vibrant mosques, some traveled to rural settings and are struggling to survive. Abdul Hakim Shareef is eighty-six and, thirty years earlier, began a small mosque—New Medinah—outside of Hattiesburg, Mississippi. "The dream was to be able to feed themselves, educate themselves and live an Islamic life in a community all their own." However, his grandchildren moved away, the community does not attract new members and it is shrinking. "For many black American Muslims today, the legacies of the Nation of Islam and W. D. Mohammed are 'not relevant anymore,' said Nicquan Church, 40, of Philadelphia, who attends a Salafist mosque, a strict Orthodox sect of Sunni Islam. American blacks who are Muslim now constitute a diverse population of different sects, ideologies, cultures and national heritages."[20] This may be an isolated case but it is a cause for worry about the future of diversity and outreach among American Muslims.

If there is some loss in the numbers of African American Muslims, it is not helped by the lack of warm welcome they receive from the immigrant Muslim mosques. In fact, they may experience racism within these settings. Zeba Khan stated, "African-American Muslims in particular are segregated out of mosques dominated by South Asian– and Arab-American Muslims. Referring to black Muslims as *abed*, or 'slave,' is commonplace among some Muslim communities, and many South Asian– and Arab-American families discourage if not outright forbid their children to marry them."[21]

This is painful considering the history of black Americans. Yet such rejection by immigrant populations is part of black American experiences. It is not new but exposes experiences of other immigrant groups' derision of black Americans. It is not reasonable, yet rejecting black Americans as inadequate indicates the impact of the sustained anti-black campaign on which the binary definition of race—white-over-black—is built. These experiences provided the emotional fuel that ignited the L.A. riots of black Americans against Korean Americans, discussed in chapter 6.

Zeba Khan emphasized that American Muslims are distinctive in their racial diversity, "the most racially diverse religious group in the country, yet there is a long history of intrafaith racism against black Muslims. The roots of this racism are multifaceted. Immigrants from South Asia come to the U.S. with a host of cultural beliefs and remnants of colonial thinking that place a premium on lighter skin."[22]

Clearly, there was a sharp distance between African Americans, regardless of religious belief, and Middle Eastern immigrants. This distance may reflect what another author, Sherman Jackson, terms "Black Orientalism." As Edward Said discussed how white people viewed people from Asian countries, including Muslims, Sherman Jackson discusses how, incorrectly, black scholars might develop and reflect negative ideas about Middle Eastern Muslims. Broadly stated, (a) the insistence on Arabic language, dress, and direction toward which prayer is turned forces something external to their culture on black Americans; (b) Arabs destroyed the ancient kingdom of Nubia (on the African continent) because the population was black, as well as the color complexes of black Muslims on East Coast of Africa; and (c) racism and anti-black racism are the results of Islamic belief.[23] Jackson draws these out to refute them. But the reality is that black communities in the United States had developed from a historical lineage that included African Muslims and that, with the positioning of Middle Eastern immigrants as white, a race, politics, and religion intersection was built into Islam in America. These distinctions were exacerbated after the tragedies of 9/11.

9/11 AND MUSLIM IDENTITIES IN THE UNITED STATES

September 11, 2001: Four groups of terrorists hijacked four planes. One flew into the Pentagon in Virginia; two flew into World Trade Center towers in New York City; one was headed to Washington, DC, but was aborted by the actions of passengers. These were the most significant attacks on U.S. soil and were engineered by al-Qaeda, with direction and support from Osama bin Laden, working from Afghanistan. The description of the 9/11 report encapsulates a variety of dimensions of the groups of terrorists.

> It was carried out by a tiny group of people, not enough to man a full platoon. Measured on a governmental scale, the resources behind it were trivial. The group itself was dispatched by an organization based in one of the poorest, most remote, and least industrialized countries on earth. This organization

recruited a mixture of young fanatics and highly educated zealots who could not find suitable places in their home societies or were driven from them. . . . America stood out as an object for admiration, envy, and blame. This created a kind of cultural asymmetry. To us, Afghanistan seemed very far away. To members of al Qaeda, America seemed very close. In a sense, they were more globalized than we were. [24]

I lived in Detroit, Michigan, at the time, not far from the Dearborn area that had the largest population of Middle Eastern immigrants in the United States. The businesses in the city, colleges in the entire area, and especially the airport, were closed, opening sporadically. Helicopters from nearby military bases flew overhead.

In the confusion after the attacks, both President George Bush and the 9/11 Commission stated that all of Islam was not to be blamed. This was clear in the Commission's report:

> Islam is not the enemy. It is not synonymous with terror. Nor does Islam teach terror. America and its friends oppose a perversion of Islam, not the great world faith itself. Lives guided by religious faith, including literal beliefs in holy scriptures, are common to every religion, and represent no threat to us. Other religions have experienced violent internal struggles. With so many diverse adherents, every major religion will spawn violent zealots. Yet understanding and tolerance among people of different faiths can and must prevail. [25]

Despite these words, centering on Muslim communities in Dearborn began immediately after the 9/11 attacks. "Within hours of the 9/11 attacks, hundreds of journalists and investigators were on the ground in Detroit, looking for stories, suspects, and informants. The first terror-related arrests were made in Dearborn on September 17, 2001; by early 2002, Dearborn (not New York) was the first American city to have a local office of Homeland Security." [26]

The religion of Islam, with no distinctions between different branches or national boundaries, was given the face of Middle Easterners and a unique form of racialization began: Islamophobia. Islamophobia was not an accidental, irrational fear that grew among the American public, despite the events of 9/11. From 9/11, the image of Muslims became that of immigrants. From that time, the impact of the Hart-Celler Act on the growth of immigration from the Mideast was understood, providing a building support for ending immigration of brown and black people, particularly of Muslims.

In 2015, Syrian refugees were fleeing the brutal political regime in Syria. The United Nations members agreed to allow several thousand into their countries; a few Syrian refugees in Paris committed a terrorist massacre. One American pundit argued for not allowing Syrian refugees into the United States. "Nervous about Syrian refugees in the wake of the Paris massacre?

How dare you! Would you turn away Jews fleeing Hitler? . . . But that's not the story of Syria. . . . The majority of Syrians espouse some form of Sunni fundamentalist religious belief, a fundamentalism that Western societies asked to open their doors are entitled to find disquieting."[27] The author is arguing for revision of current immigration laws, but his selection of the most violent images of Muslims does not encourage rational, level-headed discussion. For instance, he also identifies Muslims from Somalia as sources for terrorist activity for a variety of reasons, including religion.

> As of 2014, about 5,950 of the state's [of Minnesota's] Somali population received cash assistance; 17,000 receive food assistance as of 2014. . . . Struggling with the transition from semi-nomadic-herder society to postindustrial urban life, young Somalis in the West are tempted by criminal activity. . . . Other young Somalis turn to political and religious violence. An estimated 50 American Somalis returned to fight for al Shabab [a radical, fundamentalist Muslim group based in East Africa], committing some of the most heinous acts of that insurgency.[28]

In other words, the Muslims he discusses are poor, of a different culture, and unable to assimilate into the mainstream of the United States' economic and educational systems. Unstated in this essay is that, of the Muslim immigrant groups, these poor Somalis are from the continent of Africa and are dark-skinned. The author never asks if racism is part of their struggle.

FEEDING FEAR

Since 9/11, the fear of Islam was nurtured, creating a revised Other, the Muslim terrorist. The religion itself was blamed for *all* of the events of 9/11 and the political climate has fed the fear. "Politicians have claimed that 85% of mosques are controlled by Islamic extremists [Rep. Peter King, NY] and that Islam is a political system, not a religion [Jody Hice, GOP congressional candidate, GA, 2011]. . . . They have threatened to 'Arrest every Muslim' [Rep. Saxby Chambliss, GA] . . . and called Islam a 'cancer in our nation that needs to be cut out.' [Rep. John Bennett, OK]"[29] (Names added by author.) The hatred was given more fuel from certain Christian groups and believers.

Businessman and later politician Herman Cain was interviewed by *Christianity Today* in March 2011. "Based upon the little knowledge that I have of the Muslim religion," Cain said, "they have an objective to convert all infidels or kill them." He was not alone in his bias. Religious leaders added to the frenzy of politicians. An example was "the Oak Initiative—a coalition of evangelical and Pentecostal clergy founded to be 'salt and light' in the time of America's crisis and 'the greatest threat to its continued existence.'"[30]

Following the shock of the events of 9/11, the steady barrage of religious and political hatred constructed *raced* Muslims. The messages of hatred sowed deep distrust of all Muslims. With the distrust grew the belief, aided by advice from nationalist or governmental groups, that *those* people needed to be watched. The Department of Homeland Security was developed through research of the *9/11 Commission Report* and included coordination of governmental agencies. But the department also promotes surveillance by citizens.

> "New technology" to survey those who are considered a terrorist threat, national and local government bodies are also encouraging ordinary, non-authoritative citizens to carry out direct surveillance. . . . At the national level, the Department of Homeland Security (DHS) website asserts that "all Americans should continue to be vigilant, take notice of their surroundings and report suspicious items or activities to local authorities immediately." . . . These campaigns illustrate that the encouragement of direct, visual surveillance by ordinary people is a significant facet of the counter-terrorist strategy in the USA. . . . [Such surveillance] maintain[s] the boundaries of the community, where the very action of surveilling enacts a performative membership in the community and those who are "being watched" are reiteratively racialized as Other.[31]

The growth of Islamophobia is often tangled into 9/11 and terrorism. The *Report* specified the groups and persons who wish to attach the United States and their reasons. The distinction between international actors and American citizens or legal immigrants is often not drawn by Islamophobes. All Muslims (who can be identified) are considered threats.

> Islam has an impact on converts' perceived racial status. In some instances, racializing experiences proved traumatic. Victoria, who wears a headscarf, painfully recalled being badly insulted in the street: "I have had the nasty comments. I have been called. . . . This has been really bad but 'Sand nigger.' Yeah. Someone yelled it out of the car window." As a white person, Victoria had never been exposed to such a racial slur in the past. She was embarrassed to even pronounce the word.[32]

One author refers to Islamophobia as an "industry." "The Islamic bogeyman represents the newest chapter in America's long history of monster stories. Given the vast displays of violence committed by Muslim extremists, such an emergence only seemed inevitable. . . . [T]he Islamic threat has been seized upon by a cadre of individuals—an industry of Islamophobia—that use lurid imagery, emotive language, charged stereotypes, and repetition to exacerbate fears of a larger-than-life, ever-lurking Muslim presence."[33] Monetizing Muslims through fear involves creating the need for more private prisons that warehouse immigrants for deportation, more jobs for immigration agents, more opportunities for mercenaries, and the sale of guns and survivalist equipment for other Americans' self-protection. "One of the especially troubling aspects of institutionalized Islamophobia has been in the area of police training, especially given the vast amounts of funding diverted to the new security regime. . . . Vast new powers of spying, jailing, and interrogation (including 'enhanced techniques' often considered to be torture) were being regularly employed, largely against Muslims."[34]

The intersection of religion, politics, and race is exemplified by the ongoing attention that Dearborn, Michigan, receives from Islamophobes. "A pilgrimage to Dearborn has become a rite of passage for opponents of Islam in America. They descend, like seasonal birds, on the annual Dearborn Arab International Festival, where they wander among tens of thousands of Arab and Muslim revelers, passing out proselytizing leaflets, engaging passerby in religious dispute, and occasionally being arrested for disturbance of the peace. . . . All of this is happening at a street fair, where families wait in line for their children to buy cotton candy and take rides.[35]

There are some among politicians and religious leaders who attempt to give a fairer, less terrifying portrait of Muslims. Yet, they have the fragrance of the old Orientalist, colonizing constructions that gave power to the idea that Muslim savages needed the control and saving of the West—in particular, in this newest version, saving by the United States. The First Lady, Laura Bush, specified why the Taliban in Afghanistan were to be condemned. "Only the terrorists and the Taliban forbid education to women," she said. "Only the terrorists and the Taliban threaten to pull out women's fingernails for wearing nail polish."[36] Brutality against women sounds like harem speak and, too often, Mrs. Bush's distinction of Afghani Taliban gets translated in the United States' Islamophobia: "Do you see how *they* treat *their* women?"

In like manner, news editors or movie producers attempt fairer portrayals of Muslims; yet, these often fail by showing Muslims as victimized by Islam, which could be considered a form of anti-racist racism.

> Seemingly sensitive to negative stereotyping, common positive portrayals of Muslims depicted by the current Western authors or filmmakers and television producers are limited only to a patriotic Muslim-American, a Muslim who is keen to help the United States in its war with terrorism, an innocent Muslim-American who is the victim of post-9/11 hate crimes, or a Muslim that loves the culture of the West. Another post-9/11 strategy in representing the Eastern Muslim is using the Muslims themselves to narrate their stories of victimhood in their Islamic society so that they persuade people in the West that the Middle East and its people, especially women, are in need of the Westerners for liberation. This genre of literature is cogent enough to make the readers want to put themselves in the victims' shoes. The sudden increase in publication of Muslim memoirs by and about Muslim women after the events of 9/11 can be best described as a strategy to justify the "war on terror."[37]

There are direct results on the lives of the now-raced Muslims. "They experience a differential structural positioning vis-à-vis other groups within the United States that impacts upon their life chances. Specifically, these racialized groups may have reduced access to mobility both within and between nations, and may experience reduced access to public space and/or employment opportunities."[38]

Four of the faces that Iris Marion Young identified as oppression are in the stories of Muslims in America today: marginalization, powerlessness, cultural imperialism, and of course, violence. The Southern Poverty Law Center tracks hate crimes in the United States. There were thirty-four reported hate crimes against Muslims in 2015, but 101 in 2017. This is a 197 percent increase.

> Anti-Muslim hate has been expanding rapidly for more than two years now, driven by radical Islamist attacks including the June mass murder of 49 people at an Orlando, Fla., gay nightclub, the unrelenting propaganda of a growing circle of well-paid ideologues. . . . The Muslim-bashing had consequences. Last October, three members of a militia-like group called the Crusaders were arrested and charged with plotting to blow up an apartment complex in Kansas where 120 Somali Muslim immigrants live. The attack was reportedly set for Nov. 9, the day after Election Day.[39]

These reports of incidents and the counter fears of terrorist attack are applied differently to Muslims than Christians. With Muslim "terrorists," attacks are expected. Yet while the number of Christian extremists has been growing in recent years,[40] *all* Christians are not vilified. Most Americans do not confuse these extremists with the Christian religion, unlike the collapse of terrorism into all of Islam: "Three-quarters (75%) of Americans say that self-identified Christians who commit acts of violence in the name of Christianity are not really Christian. In contrast, only half (50%) of the public say that self-proclaimed Muslims who commit acts of violence in the name of Islam are not really Muslim."[41] It seems to be a positive statement that 50 percent of Americans believe that those who claim to be Islamic terrorists are not really Muslim. But on the glass-half-full side, the rest of Americans are willing to fly into fear. There is a certain sorrow in stating how successful these campaigns of Islamophobia have been. Public safety is not assured; instead, possibilities of building community are eroded.

But there is a glass-half-full to be viewed in these situations. The anger and violence against the racialized Muslim Others has resulted in multiple human-rights-from-below efforts. As the construction of Muslim Others in the United States is distinctive from other groups, so will a focus on human rights have differently defined shapes that cross several areas: immigration, activism, and race.

HUMAN RIGHTS AND A WAY FORWARD

The fear of Muslims coupled with fears of Central Americans coming across U.S. borders have led to a political fear of brown people. Beneath this is an unspoken fear that, demographically, America will no longer be a majority white, Christian country in twenty to forty years. These combinations of fears have turned into severe anti-immigration efforts, politically and socially. New bans against the arrival of Muslim immigrants or refugees have been out—put in place or proposed. The reactions against such bans included lawyers as well as religious leaders.

On January 28, 2017, the International Refugee Assistance Project mobilized volunteer lawyers to go to international airports and assist immigrants arriving in the United States who would have been in flight when the ban was issued. "The lawyers who heeded the call were at about a dozen airports around the country. Others who heard about the effort through colleagues or the news media went to airports on their own to pitch in."[42] While the ban was reversed in court, the confusion about who was to enter the country impacted the lives of travelers. The actions of these lawyers upheld some people's rights: most who were flying into the country had already received visas. A deeper question is inherent in the ban of immigrants: is immigration a human right? Under what circumstances? What should countries do? Part of the motivation for revoking travel rights to the United States is nativism, which seeks to insulate this country's population through closing borders and avoiding greater diversity. The United Nations charters and treaties have addressed aspects of these questions, including accepting refugees.

Some evangelical religious leaders were outspoken against the ban, motivated by their religious beliefs about justice and welcoming the stranger. The U.S. government's Muslim ban in January 2017 provoked a clear response:

> "We have the opportunity to rescue, help, and bless some of the world's most oppressed and vulnerable families. . . .The question for the American Christian is: Will we speak out on behalf of those who are running from the very terror that we are rightly trying to put an end to?" [National Association of Evangelicals President Leith Anderson] asked. "People who are running from Mosul and Aleppo and a thousand other places on fire? Would we be willing to accept giving up a 1 in 3 billion chance of our safety in order to make room for them?" he continued. "Or would we say, 'I am not willing to give up even the smallest fraction of my safety to welcome people who have been vetted very carefully, who have been proven as a remarkable population of people. Will I not make room for them?'"[43]

To achieve human rights is not an exercise in theory. The pushback against an immigration ban by lawyers and religious leaders are important efforts. Raced Muslims are feared for their own religion and are therefore caught in political machinery. Some Muslims themselves learn to push back in courts to uphold civil rights. This book began by claiming that civil rights were not enough; but they are not to be ignored, as standing against oppressions. "What is certain, however, is that American Muslims can no longer afford the image that they are isolationists and removed from everyday civil rights struggles. . . . American Muslims appear more prepared than ever to fight for these rights in court. . . . Just like so many immigrants and religious minorities before them, American Muslims are asserting themselves in an important part of American society, one civil rights case at a time."[44] Such activism for civil or legal rights gives rise to hopes that human rights, with the recognition of shared humanity, can be achieved as well.

Linda Sarsour, a Palestinian American, began as director of the Arab American Association of New York following the 9/11 attacks. She speaks against Islamophobia, and her activism includes speaking against all injustices. Her public roles often bring her criticism, as did a speech she gave at the Islamic Society of North America's conference in July 2017. Her speech was criticized by right-wing news outlets such as Breitbart News as calling for a jihad or holy war against the president of the United States.[45] She responded to the critics,

> I sent not a call to violence, but a call to speak truth to power and to commit to the struggle for racial and economic justice. I was speaking to an all-Muslim audience; as an American, I should be free to share and discuss scripture and teachings of my beloved Prophet. My statements were clear, and my activism track record is even clearer: My work has always been rooted in nonviolence as espoused by the Rev. Martin Luther King Jr. . . . Every day, I speak about women's issues, indigenous rights, the necessity to fight for black lives and against the Muslim and refugee bans. I believe wholeheartedly that we must fight injustice and inequality—through marches and direct actions, through policy changes, and through our own voices permeating media spaces. My views are not unique or special, and many activists around the country express them as well.[46]

As Sarsour states, she is an activist for racial and economic justice, taking a wider social view than of only Muslim American justice issues.

The issue of race also becomes a source of conversation within Muslim communities. Su'ad Abdul Khabeer is a black/Latina Muslim woman—a Muslim from birth, not a convert. To the racial conversation, she brings a new perspective that she terms "Muslim Cool." Her love of hip hop and of that generation informed and infused her sense of religion: "I was Black and Muslim, being raised in a household with cultural nationalist leanings, and the music and culture of hip hop were replete with Islamic references and pro-Black and pan-African messages."[47] Muslim cool is then "about self-making . . . about the way in which young Muslims see, experience, and interpret themselves in the world. Muslim Cool constructs and 'shores up' social identity as a religious performativity that is raced and gendered . . . [with] Blackness as a blueprint for the Muslim self."[48] This is a different way of thinking about being Muslim, bringing together the history and the current reality of being Muslim in America reflected in Linda Sarsour's words. Such integration looks toward a more fully human future.

As Zeba Khan stated, Muslims in the United States have already begun new forms of activism that bring communities together, with Islam as the point of integration:

> The Quran commands Muslims to "stand out firmly for justice" even if it that means going "against yourselves or your parents or your kin." Holding Muslim organizations such as the Islamic Society of North America accountable on issues of race is an important aspect of living out that command, as is the work of new organizations such as Muslims for Ferguson or Muslims Make It Plain. But South Asian– and Arab-American Muslims must also take a hard look at the overt and subtle forms of racism and bias in their communities and mosques. New grass-roots organizations such as the Muslim Anti-Racist Collaborative, a nonprofit that provides anti-racism education to American Muslim communities, are modeling how American Muslim institutions and communities can best do that.[49]

These instances shape human rights from below, from the perspectives of Muslims, and reflect other ways that greater work for justice is happening. The history and presence of Muslim Americans reflect how the route to human rights is in knowing and accepting one's own identity. It is not identity politics; it is resisting the identity with which different groups want to burden Othered communities. These identities are not in conflict with being American, as Feisal Abdul Rauf stated.

> In America, we *protect* different expressions of faith. We assemble in our various houses of worship to pray, to chant, to sing, to recite scripture, or simply to come together and draw strength as a community. . . . For me, Islam and America are organically bound together. This is not my story alone. The American way of life has helped many Muslims make a conscious decision to embrace their faith. That choice is precious. And that is why America is precious.[50]

His words echo the Declaration of Independence but bring new meaning for these times: life, liberty, and the pursuit of happiness. An American Muslim Cool.

NOTES

1. "Since 2010, 201 anti-Sharia law bills have been introduced in 43 states. In 2017 alone, 14 states introduced an anti-Sharia law bill, with Texas and Arkansas enacting the legislation." Swathi Shanmugasundaram, "Anti-Sharia Law Bills in the United States," Hatewatch Staff, Southern Poverty Law Center, February 8, 2018, https://www.splcenter.org/hatewatch/2018/02/05/anti-sharia-law-bills-united-states.

2. Esmaeil Zeiny and Noraini Md Yusof, "The Said and Not-Said: New Grammar of Visual Representation," *GEMA Online® Journal of Language Studies* 16, no. 1 (February 2016): 130.

3. C. Eric Lincoln, "The Muslim Mission in the Context of American Social History," in *African American Religious Studies: An Interdisciplinary Anthology*, ed. Gayraud Wilmore (Durham, NC: Duke University Press, 1989), 341–42.

4. Hog Hammock Public Library, "Bilali Muhammad: An American Story, Sapelo Island, GA," http://sapelobilali.blogspot.com/2013/04/sapelo-islands-bilali-muhammad.html.

5. Rudolph T. Ware III, *The Walking Qur'an: Islamic Education, Embodied Knowledge, and History in West Africa* (Chapel Hill: The University of North Carolina Press, 2014), 49.

6. Gayraud S. Wilmore, *Black Religion and Black Radicalism: An Interpretation of the Religious History of Afro-American People*, 2nd ed. (Maryknoll, NY: Orbis Books, 1983), 160.

7. "We Greet You in Islam," Moorish Science Temple of America, https://www.msta1928.org/.

8. C. Eric Lincoln, "The Muslim Mission in the Context of American Social History," 346.

9. Central Research Section, Federal Bureau of Investigation, "The Nation of Islam: Anti-white, All-Negro Cult in the United States," (October 1960): vi, cited in Edward E. Curtis IV, "The Black Muslim Scare of the Twentieth Century: The History of State Islamophobia and Its Post-9/11 Variations," in *Islamophobia in America*, ed. Carl W. Ernst (New York: Palgrave Macmillan, 2013), 96.

10. Cited in Edward E. Curtis IV, *Muslims in America: A Short History* (New York: Oxford University Press, 2009), 46.

11. James H. Cone, *Risks of Faith: The Emergence of a Black Theology of Liberation, 1968–1998* (Boston: Beacon Press, 1999), 98.

12. Curtis, "The Black Muslim Scare of the Twentieth Century," 97.

13. Mae M. Ngai, "The Architecture of Race in American Immigration Law: A Reexamination of the Immigration Act of 1924," *Journal of American History* (June 1999): 72.

14. Jerry Kammer, "The Hart-Celler Immigration Act of 1965," Center for Immigration Studies, September 30, 2015, https://cis.org/HartCeller-Immigration-Act-1965.

15. Curtis, *Muslims in America*, 50.

16. Steven A. Camarota, "Immigrants from the Middle East: A Profile of the Foreign-born Population from Pakistan to Morocco," Center for Immigration Studies, August 1, 2002, https://cis.org/Immigrants-Middle-East.

17. Curtis, *Muslims in America*, 48.

18. Curtis, *Muslims in America*, 48.

19. Abbas Barzegar, "Discourse, Identity, and Community: Problems and Prospects in the Study of Islam in America," *The Muslim World* 101 (July 2011): 514.

20. Abigail Hauslohner, "In Mississippi, Aging Muslim Community Worries about Its Future," *Washington Post*, July 19, 2017, https://www.washingtonpost.com/national/in-mississippi-aging-muslim-community-worries-about-its-future/2017/07/19/9b609662-6346-11e7-8adc-fea80e32bf47_story.html?utm_term=.5f8e0bf71e1b.

21. Zeba Khan, "American Muslims Have a Race Problem," *Al Jazeera America*, June 16, 2015, http://america.aljazeera.com/opinions/2015/6/american-muslims-have-a-race-problem.html.

22. Khan, "American Muslims Have a Race Problem." Khan noted that some of the Middle Eastern immigrants have histories that include involvement in various slave trades.

23. Sherman A. Jackson, *Islam and the Blackamerican* (New York: Oxford University Press, 2005). Jackson draws (a) from the Afrocentrist ideas of Molefi Asante, 110; (b) from

arguments of Henry Louis Gates, 116; and (c) from the arguments of Richard Brent Turner, 122.

24. Thomas H. Kean, ed., *The 9/11 Commission Report*, National Commission on Terrorist Attacks Upon the United States, August, 2004, 339–40, https://9-11commission.gov/report/.

25. Kean, *The 9/11 Commission Report*, 363.

26. Andrew J. Shyrock, "Attack of the Islamophobes: Religious War (and Peace) in Arab/Muslim Detroit," in Ernst, *Islamophobia in America*, 140.

27. David Frum, "America's Immigration Challenge," *The Atlantic*, December 11, 2015, https://www.theatlantic.com/politics/archive/2015/12/refugees/419976/.

28. Frum, "America's Immigration Challenge."

29. Daniel Burke, "The Secret Costs of Islamophobia," CNN, November 8, 2016, http://www.cnn.com/2016/09/23/us/islamerica-secret-costs-islamophobia/index.html

30. David D. Belt, "Anti-Islam Discourse in the United States in the Decade after 9/11: The Role of Social Conservatives and Cultural Politics," *Journal of Ecumenical Studies* 51, no. 1 (Spring 2016): 211–12.

31. Rachel L. Finn, "Surveillant Staring: Race and the Everyday Surveillance of South Asian Women after 9/11," *Surveillance & Society* 8, no. 4 (2011): 415.

32. Juliette Galonnier, "The Racialization of Muslims in France and the United States: Some Insights from White Converts to Islam," *Social Compass* 62, no. 4 (2015): 575.

33. Nathan Lean, *The Islamophobia Industry: How the Right Manufactures Fear of Muslims* (London: Pluto Press, 2012), 39–40.

34. Carl W. Ernst, introduction to *Islamophobia in America*, 5.

35. Shyrock, "Attack of the Islamophobes," 151.

36. David Stout, "A Nation Challenged: The First Lady; Mrs. Bush Cites Women's Plight under Taliban," *New York Times*, November 18, 2001,http://www.nytimes.com/2001/11/18/us/a-nation-challenged-the-first-lady-mrs-bush-cites-women-s-plight-under-taliban.html?mcubz=0.

37. Zeiny and Yusof, "The Said and Not-Said," 136.

38. Finn, "Surveillant Staring," 414.

39. Mark Potok, "The Year in Hate and Extremism," The Southern Poverty Law Center, February 15, 2017, https://www.splcenter.org/fighting-hate/intelligence-report/2017/year-hate-and-extremism.

40. Ben Mathis-Lilley, "The Long List of Killings Committed by White Extremists since the Oklahoma City Bombing," *Slate*, August 14, 2017, http://www.slate.com/blogs/the_slatest/2015/06/18/white_extremist_murders_killed_at_least_60_in_u_s_since_1995.html?cq_ck=1486485587473.

41. Cox and Jones, "Nearly Half of Americans Worried That They Will Be a Victim of Terrorism."

42. Jonah Engel Bromwich, "Lawyers Mobilize at Nation's Airports after Trump's Order," *New York Times*, January 29, 2017,https://www.nytimes.com/2017/01/29/us/lawyers-trump-muslim-ban-immigration.html?mcubz=0&_r=0.

43. Kate Shellnutt, "Evangelical Experts Oppose Trump's Refugee Ban," *Christianity Today*, January 25, 2017, http://www.christianitytoday.com/news/2017/january/evangelical-experts-oppose-trump-plan-to-ban-refugees-syria.html.

44. Amany R. Hacking, "A New Dawn for Muslims: Asserting Their Civil Rights in Post-9/11 America," *Saint Louis University Law Journal* 54 (2010): 941.

45. Joel B. Pollak, "Linda Sarsour Calls for 'Jihad' against Trump Administration," Breitbart, July 6, 2017, http://www.breitbart.com/national-security/2017/07/06/linda-sarsour-calls-jihad-president-donald-trump/.

46. Linda Sarsour, "Islamophobes Are Attacking Me Because I'm Their Worst Nightmare," *Washington Post*, July 9, 2017, https://www.washingtonpost.com/opinions/linda-sarsour-no-i-did-not-call-for-violence-against-trump-heres-what-jihad-means-to-me/2017/07/09/c2acb086-64b6-11e7-9928-22d00a47778f_story.html?hpid=hp_no-name_opinion-card-f%3Ahomepage%2Fstory&utm_term=.3e8970ae007c.

47. Su'ad Abdul Khabeer, *Muslim Cool: Race, Religion, and Hip Hop in the United States* (New York: NYU Press, 2016), 21.

48. Khabeer, *Muslim Cool*, 221.

49. Khan, "American Muslims Have a Race Problem."

50. Feisal Abdul Rauf, "There Is Everything Right with Being an American Muslim," *Vital Speeches of the Day* 76, no. 11 (November 2010): 483.

Chapter Eight

Race, Politics, and Religion: Toward Human Rights at the Intersection

The previous chapters indicate the tangle of race, politics, and religion that constructs an intersection of power and privilege, as well as resistance, in the United States. That intersection is fueled and fed by the lie of white superiority. The impact of this lie was expressed by Lyndon B. Johnson in 1960 to his staffer, Bill Moyers. After seeing some signs with racially derogatory slogans, Johnson explained, "I'll tell you what's at the bottom of it. . . . If you can convince the lowest white man he's better than the best colored man, he won't notice you're picking his pocket. Hell, give him somebody to look down on, and he'll empty his pockets for you."[1] The result is structural and systemic. As ethicist Gary Dorrien emphasizes, white supremacy is reinforced by "powerful self-interested institutions, and widely denied, if not invisible to its deniers."[2]

The processes of Othering those who are not white construct groups into stereotypes whose rights can be ignored. Attempted and actual political, racial, and religious dominance by white Americans are embedded into political systems; if there were a vision of the wider common good and a will to shape justice broadly, unjust systems could be changed. Gary Dorrien lists the following to upend unjust structures: "decently progressive tax policies, living wage legislation, affirmative action programs, single-payer health coverage that extends Medicare to everyone, and a generous immigration policy."[3]

But such, while fought for by some groups, do not represent a commonly held vision—at least not in most current legislative branches. The political belief in American exceptionalism; the religious constructs of the superiority of white cultures against all others; and the binding ties of neoliberalism—all combine to construct a social milieu that is suspicious of those changes. Inhibiting the voting rights of people of color becomes a route for retaining power, for, to the privileged, liberation is indeed seen as oppression.

Political processes are layered with American myth ("melting pot") and values that are grounded in human rights (life, liberty, and the pursuit of happiness). Significantly, political processes are charged with racial content and religious content. A call to apply human rights in the United States runs into these buzz saws of race and religion. And yet, human rights from below offers a path through the tangle of seemingly intractable issues. But there are issues with which the concept of human rights must first deal.

PROBLEMS AT THE INTERSECTION WITH HUMAN RIGHTS

The first chapter began a discussion of human rights in general, turning to human rights from below as a possibility for changing some of the dynamics of the race, politics, religion intersection. But this repositioning carries its own weight, as "human rights" is not a category with a single definition.

Boaventura de Sousa Santos is a professor of sociology who challenges the ways human rights have been constructed. He traces the historical meanings of human rights and states, "The selfsame human rights discourse has had very many different meanings . . . having legitimated both revolutionary and counterrevolutionary practices. Today we cannot even be sure if present-day human rights are a legacy of the modern revolutions or of their ruins, or if they have behind them a revolutionary emancipatory energy or a counter-revolutionary energy."[4] De Sousa Santos points out another conflict in the meaning of human rights: are the rights for the *human* or for the *citizen*? "The effective, ample protection of citizenship rights has always been precarious in the large majority of countries and, further, . . . human rights have been involved mainly in situations involving the erosion of particularly serious violations of citizenship rights."[5] Basically, de Sousa Santos charges that the commonly understood idea of human rights was not about collective rights of all human beings; the emphasis was on the individual, reflecting a Western philosophical perspective.

Yet that individualistic focus is part of the change in perspective thanks to protests. "The struggles of women, indigenous peoples, African people under colonial regimes, Afro-descendants, victims of racism, gays, lesbians, and religious minorities marked the past fifty years of the recognition of collective rights, a recognition that has been always highly contested and always on the verge of being reversed."[6]

Finding ways to maintain power by *not* recognizing something as a human right is a tactic to avoid making change. The tactic is used repeatedly, whether refusing to recognize that health care is a human right, for example, or that the right to life is for the span of life, not just while in the womb; or the humanity of people who are deemed different from "my people." This tactic is sometimes called "benign neglect," but it is not kind. There is no kindness in ignoring problems, nor is justice to be enacted, and problems grow. Individually, we learn to walk quickly by the homeless person, pretending not to see. In the same way, we carefully do not challenge a friend's racist remark. Administrations find ways to put glossy paper over deep inequities, pretending to aim for resolution. Benign neglect.

Yet inaction from administrations can lead back to civil rights law as a path for resolutions that groups can pursue through courts, becoming the only option for considerations of human rights. As a society bent on individualism, we have few ways to appeal to each other. When human rights are collapsed into civil rights legal action, several things happen. The rights of the individual often are set against the community's or vice versa. When does the right to free speech become hate speech that then threatens another's security? Is the complaint against hate speech to be ignored because of free speech? Court processes are also difficult: Who has the right to bring forward a lawsuit on behalf of civil rights? Must it be a class action suit in order to be effective? Bringing a suit forward also becomes difficult when civil rights are deemed only to apply to citizens. Therefore, civil rights in terms of citizenship rights can be reduced to legalistic arguments. Immigrants under threat of deportation have limited recourse through the courts—they are not citizens. Even with a successful suit or legal change, those civil rights can always be reversed or whittled away through other legislation. All of these limits help to reinforce the race, politics, and religion power intersection. These layers of confusions are exemplified in the early twenty-first century in the matters of segregation and environmental justice.

Segregation and Human Rights

The *Brown v. Board of Education* Supreme Court decision of 1954 ended the fantasy of "separate but equal" schools. South Carolina's schools are not the only ones with such educational inequities. Using a legal loophole to secede from one and begin another school system is a tactic being used by many Southern states to resegregate. A school secession process in Pickens County, Alabama, is determined to make separate equal. "So far, however, making separate equal isn't working out very well in the segregated schools that the Justice Department oversees in Alabama and elsewhere. Alabama's data show a relatively strong correlation between segregation and failure, and between integration and success."[7] There is no law against it, and it will take the legal action of the community where it is happening to stop it.

Integration, in itself, is not necessarily listed as a human right. But political philosopher Iris Marion Young listed the four "wrongs" of segregation in her discussion of housing discrimination that apply to educational inequities:

> Segregation violates a principle of equal opportunity and thus wrongly limits freedom of housing choice. Secondly, and most importantly, processes of segregation produce and reinforce serious structures of privilege and disadvantage. The very processes that produce segregation, thirdly, also obscure the fact of their privilege from those who have it. As a result, finally, the social and special differentiation segregation produces seriously impedes political communication among segregated groups, thus making it difficult to address the wrongs of segregation through democratic political action. [8]

The impact of educational segregation limits the freedom of students who will receive poor education, reinforcing the privilege of those who attend better schools while obscuring the fact of their privilege. In the end, segregation will produce citizens with less ability to participate in democratic political action. These educational inequities are not defined as violations of human rights but dropped into the category of precariously held citizenship rights, as de Sousa Santos stated.

Environmental Justice and Human Rights

In the case of environmental justice, powerful individuals make determinations based on profits or expedience, but, with weakened voting power or civic participation, a group of people of color may find their concerns unaddressed. Determining where the waste treatment plant is built or the new highway is placed or the landfill located may be by a group in power who deem *that* land as underdeveloped or needed for the economic progress of an area. Yet that "available" land may represent home and communities, networks of human belonging. Using the levers of government, land can be acquired through declaration of eminent domain or through new zoning laws. The people who live in the area may be offered a pittance in comparison to the land's worth: this story has been told too often throughout urban and rural America.

Native Americans, for example, who are considered sovereign on their own lands, struggle with the reality that those lands hold natural resources. "Native American reservations are located on about 3% of America's oil and natural gas reserves, 15% of the coal reserves, and between 37% and 55% of the uranium reserves. Substantial quantities of bauxite and zeolites also lie beneath Indian reservations."[9] There are multiple tricky ways to get signatures of Native leaders on contracts to mine and extract resources. In addition, Native Americans are often paid less than non-Indians to extract the resources from their own lands, creating another layer of injustice. [10]

Environmental racism was the focus of the first People of Color Environmental Leadership Forum held in Washington, DC, in 1991. Of the seventeen Principles of Environmental Justice developed at that time, several specifically overlap with human rights:

> 5) Environmental Justice affirms the fundamental right to political, economic, cultural and environmental self-determination of all peoples. . . .
> 8) Environmental Justice affirms the right of all workers to a safe and healthy work environment without being forced to choose between an unsafe livelihood and unemployment. . . .
> 10) Environmental Justice considers governmental acts of environmental injustice a violation of international law, the Universal Declaration on Human Rights, and the United Nations Convention on Genocide. [11]

The Second People of Color Environmental Leadership Summit was held in 2002. One attendee stated that there has been networking among people of color but there have also been challenges and contradictions since the first summit. "These contradictions are the challenges that communities of color have always faced and which have destroyed or weakened our past movements. The contradictions were, and continue to be, race, class, and sexism."[12] This same author honestly analyzed the realities of what happened during this summit, one of the issues that repeatedly occurs with grassroots activism. What she reports represents a major challenge to any discussion of "human rights from below:" Who owns the movement? Who leads?

> At Summit II, the grassroots advocated and organized from the conference floor. It was the academics, the policy folks, and the technical assistants that many times dominated the front panels. The EJ [Environmental Justice] grassroots worked and organized for accountability from the few individuals that ultimately controlled the decision-making and the resources for Summit II. Confusion, disorganization, and division were allowed to fester without a mechanism for accountability. I am thankful to the many folks, who in the two years before the Summit, participated in the Executive Planning Committee before finally dropping out. . . . We take up the challenge to be smarter about co-optation and institutionalization. We need an ethics for our movement that speaks to a paradigm of working for our communities—and not just ourselves, our personal power, and agenda. [13]

Such difficulties, the questions of leadership and of voices heard, are currently features that must be addressed in human rights from below. I will return to questions of leadership, and possible solutions, later in the chapter.

RELIGIONS AS PROBLEMS AT THE INTERSECTION

Religions too often do not become centers to work for the kinds of structural changes Dorrien listed, shown above. Instead, too many American religions become additional territories where race and politics get played out: Whose religion? Whose religious freedom? One author contends that the reduction of Christianity to some pugilistic contest is termed "muscular Christianity":

> The conflation of virility and Christianity, and the valorization of a certain kind of machismo as the ultimate way of being "Christian" in the world, is hardly new. In fact, it derives from yet another era when social change, the development of technology, and the anxiety over a man's place in the world (and particularly a white man's place) made white Christianity a particularly reactionary force.[14]

The Universal Declaration of Human Rights states in its Article 18, "Everyone has the right to freedom of thought, conscience and religion; this right includes freedom to change his religion or belief, and freedom, either alone or in community with others and in public or private, to manifest his religion or belief in teaching, practice, worship and observance."[15] There have been attempts to bring religion and human rights into the same frame, but these efforts still have little application to the day-to-day living of the majority of Americans. In the United States, this article of the Declaration on Human Rights has been another rights issue wherein we critique other countries, looking outward rather than within. After all, the United States already commits to freedom of religion, which is guaranteed in the First Amendment of the Constitution. The implication from this data is that the United States already supports freedom of religion, therefore we have no problems. But this is not true, beginning with the problem caused by the cultural dominance of Christianity, which burdens those who do not profess the same.

This focus on freedom of religion sets up a religio-cultural conflict because it raises the question: Which Christianity is the right one? Eastern Orthodox? Anglican? Coptic? Roman Catholic? Evangelical Protestant? Mainline Protestant? Certainly, in the United States, mainline Protestantism often seems dominant, but in recent years, Evangelical Protestantism is most heavily impacting political and racial conversations, particularly when macho Christianity takes center stage.

Aiming for Religion and Human Rights, from the Top Down

While I argue that organized religion is part of the politics and race intersection, there have been efforts to build dialogues among religions in ways that parallel the United Nations Declaration of Human Rights. The attempts to build bridges among religions does reflect a concern for human rights and is to be commended. However, difficulties in applications to everyday life occur with the related work of the organization Parliament of World Religions and a document coming from that group, "Declaration Toward a Global Ethic."

The Parliament of World Religions was first held as an extension of the World Columbian Exposition in 1893 in Chicago, Illinois. The exposition's approach was to view the rest of the world as exotics, and so it was with the religious parliament. "Statistically speaking, the Parliament was dominated by English-speaking Christian representatives, who delivered 152 of 194 papers. The opportunity for the leaders from other religious traditions was limited but significant; 12 speakers represented Buddhism, 11 Judaism, 8 Hinduism, 2 Islam, 2 Parsis religion, 2 Shintoism, 2 Confucianism, 1 Taoism, and 1 Jainism. . . . Among them, Swami Vivekananda's three speeches undoubtedly drew most attention from the American public."[16] Despite the tokens-on-display character of that first parliament, the contemporary parliament defines that 1893 event as the beginning of worldwide interreligious dialogue.[17]

The 1993 parliament met again in Chicago, this time celebrating its one hundred years of growth. The parliament's focus was now more clearly defined as an interfaith movement. Hope is held as people from different parts of the world meet. But like the United Nations, by the time people meet at this global level, they are clearly not working from a grassroots level. Yet, they continue to hold to hope today as one of the parliament's programs is "Faith against Hate." The website states that the motivation comes as "Sikhs, Muslims, Jews, and other minorities are increasingly targets of hate in America. These attacks are sanctioned by a political culture that tolerates hate speech and promotes xenophobia. In 2012, the Parliament of the World's Religions recognized that hate was on the rise."[18] To address expressions of religious hatred, they began to hold listening sessions, webinars, and workshops.

In cooperation with the 1993 parliament, a small group of white men drafted a document, "Declaration Toward a Global Ethic." They felt that this work was based on the United Nations Declaration on Human Rights and thereby bridging world religions. In fact, some years earlier, the United Nations had published a document in support of religious freedom, "Declaration on the Elimination of All Forms of Intolerance and of Discrimination Based on Religion or Belief." The writers of that document promoted the idea that "freedom of religion and belief should also contribute to the attainment of the goals of world peace, social justice and friendship among peoples and to the elimination of ideologies or practices of colonialism and racial discrimination."[19]

The writers of the Global Ethic expanded on these ideas. Emphasizing the world's troubles of poverty, pain, economic inequities, and "social disarray," they begin the document with "The world is in agony."[20] The writers argue that the answer is to be found in the already-existing religious teachings of the world. In these teachings, a common ethic can be recognized. "This ethic provides no direct solution for all the immense problems of the world, but it does supply the moral foundation for a better individual and global order: A *vision* which can lead women and men away from despair, and society away from chaos."[21]

While admirable, the writers of the Global Ethic had the same problem as the developers of the United Nations: a select, self-appointed group leaves out people who are *not* participating. Do people around the world define their communities or lives as in "agony"? I am reminded of the words of Zora Neale Hurston who, as an African American woman during the 1920s and 1930s, could have conceivably defined her life as "in agony." Instead, in 1928, she wrote, "I am not tragically colored. There is no great sorrow dammed up in my soul, nor lurking behind my eyes. . . . Even in the helter-skelter skirmish that is my life, I have seen that the world is to the strong regardless of a little pigmentation more or less. No, I do not weep at the world—I am too busy sharpening my oyster knife."[22]

This one woman's resistance to a definition of herself as "tragic" does not negate the social and political problems in black and American communities. It does indicate that unanimous solutions to any community's problems occur infrequently if at all; for instance, the Civil Rights Movement was not welcomed by all black Americans. It also indicates that there are many voices to be heard in order to reach a social solution. Religious organizations' leaders have often felt that they have power and authority to make pronouncements about the world; but they are not the world. The first rule as leader in a conflict is to listen to everyone in order to finally reach resolution. The difficulty for the leader is that she or he can often quickly determine the root causes of the conflict—the neighbor who parked in the wrong place or the one who dumped garbage next door. The role of the leader is to help people make determinations for themselves, both about root causes and solutions. Human rights from below begins to rethink what is needed at local levels. It will be as messy as any conflict resolution. As people define their lives as tragic or not, they may have yet another layer of conversation needed at regional and national levels where leaders may have predetermined the local group's life and meaning.

The writers of the Global Ethic announced what the world needed and that there is a "universal" ethic. Yet this is not true. At a following conference on the Global Ethic, one of the speakers named problems the Declaration and Ethic could not address:

> Some religions do not accept freedom of religion for others. Article 18 [of the U.N. Human Rights Declaration] also declares this right includes freedom to

change one's religion or belief . . . [which is] not acceptable to a number of religions. Religious dissent from the human rights ideology concentrates on yet another basic principle; the religions of the world are not all committed to gender equality. . . . One ought to recognize the Universal Declaration and human rights are not, and were not intended to be, a complete global ethic. It is a minimal ethic. . . . The Declaration . . . say[s] nothing about brotherhood [*sic*] or love, or friendship, or other goods and other values that should be the concern of religion.[23]

Both the Declaration on the Elimination of Intolerance and the Global Ethic established experts who felt they could speak for the world. Perhaps the limited efficacy of these top-down approaches affirms the need for human rights from below.

In 2000, a background paper for a Summit at the United Nations was "Religion, World, Order and Peace." Reflecting on this document in 2010, the Nigerian religious scholar Wande Abimbola presented several challenges for the United Nations. The first challenge was calling for the establishment of an ongoing component to deal with religious conflict and intolerance, connecting religion and politics. He emphasized how indigenous religions celebrate the earth, not visible in the ongoing effects of climate change. He challenged how politics and religion combine to destroy indigenous rights.

This is an urgent issue since the shameful and violent conversion of minority peoples of the world has continued unabated. The indigenous peoples of the world remain powerless in the face of competing claims and onslaught of Christianity and Islam. Billions of dollars are being spent each year to eradicate the way of life and identities of indigenous peoples of Africa, Australia, and the Americas in the name of evangelism, which those two religions claim to be part of their holy scriptures. . . . It is sad to say that in spite of all the efforts of the UN everywhere you look in the modern world what we see is not human rights but human wrong and suffering.[24]

Along these lines, Boaventura de Sousa Santos finds Christianity itself barely able to address human rights abuses, reflecting the marriage of religion and politics. "In the Christian world, institutionalized religion made peace with the power structures of the day no matter how unjust, it hijacked the motivational strength contained in spirituality, and it turned believers into individual seekers of individual salvation in afterlife worlds."[25] On the other hand, in spirituality grounded in material realities, addressing human concerns in real time rather than theories, de Sousa Santos finds energy that can make social change.

Counterhegemonic human rights struggles are very often high-risk, sometimes life-threatening struggles against very powerful and unscrupulous enemies. They have, therefore, to be grounded on strongly motivated political will, a

will that has to be both collective and individual, since there is no collective
activism without individual activists. Without a nonconformist, rebellious, in-
surgent will, no meaningful social struggles against institutionalized injustice
and oppression can succeed.[26]

The United Nations is not alone in its top-down pursuit of religious freedom. The United States promotes and supports religious freedom through the
Commission on International Religious Freedom, which is "an independent,
bipartisan U.S. federal government commission created by the 1998 International Religious Freedom Act . . . . USCIRF uses international standards to
monitor religious freedom violations globally, and makes policy recommendations to the President, the Secretary of State, and Congress."[27] This Commission is through the State Department and releases an annual report that
designates "Countries of Particular Concern." The 2017 report designates
Russia, Burma, China, Eritrea, and others where religious freedom violations
can be clearly noted.[28] But this is without meaningful social struggle. We
Americans stand in judgment of other countries; we do not reflect about our
own shortcomings with religious freedom, as many Muslims in America can
attest.

De Sousa Santos's words about where the energy for social change arises
in contrast with how institutionalized religion has made peace with the state
raise additional questions. Was religion meant to be a creature of the state? Is
this why organized religion and human rights have difficulty meeting on the
ground in people's lives? In the same vein, is human rights in its institutional
bindings also in danger of becoming a mere creature of any given state?
Witness the 2017 responses to mostly black football players protesting by
going to one knee at the beginning of National Football League games during
the singing of the national anthem. They were protesting mistreatment of
black citizens by police departments and judicial systems, but they were
critiqued as unpatriotic for not honoring the U.S. flag. Yet, Francis Scott
Key, who penned the lyrics, was himself a supporter of enslaving Africans.[29]
The outrage over the actions of the football players indicates a national
religion—patriotism. In this case, patriotism is built on values that may or
may not align with human rights. These values become the place to begin
rethinking how to move to human rights from below in the United States.

AIMING FOR HUMAN RIGHTS FROM BELOW IN
THE TWENTY-FIRST-CENTURY UNITED STATES

Part of the race-politics-religion intersection is built on the general confusion
of the concepts of religion, human rights, and American values. Religion,
discussed in some detail in chapter 1, further becomes confused with ideas of
faith, theology, and ethics. Douglas Jacobsen and Rhonda Hustedt Jacobsen

were quoted in the introduction to this book: "America is one of the most highly religious nations in the world, and perhaps paradoxically, Americans are also, as a whole, remarkably illiterate about religion."[30] Confusing these concepts even further is the addition of patriotism to become a kind of American public religion. Patriotic, American religion is based on the belief in American values.

There is no single view of American values. American exceptionalism is one component that Kelly Brown Douglas identifies as founded within the country's history, connecting, among other ideas, whiteness, legal structures, and treatment of immigrants. "The narrative of Anglo-Saxon exceptionalism is a religious narrative, be it the narrative of civil religion or Protestant evangelicalism. Not only did the early American Anglo-Saxons believe their mission to be one of erecting God's 'city on a hill,' but they also came to believe that they essentially had divinity running through their veins."[31] This exceptionalism provides evidence, some would say, of the very greatness of the United States. The greatness is further evidenced by democracy and equality.

These ideas get woven into ideas of "my" religion and definitions of human rights. American values include "life, liberty, and pursuit of happiness." Whose life, whose freedom, and how happiness is defined become questions that can significantly change based on where the responders stand. Some people of color who have been discussed throughout this book would challenge the idea of American greatness or American exceptionalism. Others would appreciate the idea and call for the country to live up to what it claims and to provide democracy and equality for all. When these critiques are made, other Americans, especially some white Americans, can determine that there is something unpatriotic or downright evil about the ones making criticisms.

When "my" space is defined by judging "your" space, the opportunities for misunderstandings and divisiveness increase significantly. "Whose America is it?" is a question that becomes an opening for anti-democracy. The power of negative ideas and fear can be used to maintain the status quo but not promote human rights: "Notions of democracy appear to be giving way to the discourse of revenge, domestic security, stupidity, and war. The political reality that has emerged since the shattering crisis of 9/11 increasingly points to a set of narrow choices that is being dictated by jingoistic right-wing extremists."[32] Borders, walls, gated communities, redlining, and ghettoes are nonproductive for building communities but very fruitful for maintaining the current status of American societies.

The confusion may keep us divided but it may also be a springboard to aim for human rights in the United States. This statement may seem contradictory to the evidence, but when people recognize a dissonance in their lives—such as unrealized freedom; or unequal distribution of goods and services; or rights (or privileges) denied—each becomes a reason to think again and to consider activism.

CHANGES IN THE AMERICAN SOCIAL FABRIC

Intelligent activism is needed. The image of only getting into streets and marching for one or another cause is not enough. As an example, I know of a group of students who were inspired by the Black Lives Matter movement. They felt that the university they attended was not responsive to their needs and met often to decide a course of action. In the way of many protests, the students had a list of demands; they called for a meeting with the president. She agreed. Then the student leaders tried to make an appointment to meet. They selected a mutual date. The day before the planned meeting, the president called and had to cancel that meeting. They set another date three weeks later. The president called back after two weeks had passed; she had to change the meeting date again, something else had surfaced. Meanwhile the student energy dropped although nothing had changed and their demands were not addressed. The president finally met with the students. She was gracious and provided a very nice dinner. But, again, nothing has changed. The students know somehow, they were duped, but they do not know what happened. Perhaps they are discouraged from ever trying such protest for social justice again.

Change happens when people know how to make changes. To make change requires knowing how institutions work. Marching, by itself, is not enough. How do people, who experience dissonances between their lives and the country's stated ideals, make social changes happen?

Analyzing power is a necessary component of social change. Recognizing where lines of authority exist and who wields power includes recognizing the written and unspoken rules that govern the processes. To not define one's community as helpless in the face of power also requires recognizing that there are other lines of power—ones that are hidden.

> People may be unaware of their rights, their ability to speak out, and may come to see various forms of power or domination over them as "natural," or at least unchangeable, and therefore unquestioned. Poor people, for instance, may accept their circumstance as the status quo even in the face of inequalities around them, internalizing dominant explanations of poverty that tell them poverty is "their fault" rather than a systemic problem. . . . But hidden forms of power also can involve more hidden forms of action as well, in which people resist domination and control through less public ways. [33]

The students in the above story realized that there were dissonances in their lives and realized that their college could work better with their ideas to create a more just environment. They did not question the prerogative of the president to change several appointments, to put them off, basically renegotiating the terms of engagement. Part of their problem was that they, like most Americans, too often look to business models to effect social change. A business model operates on hierarchies, on power from the top, on deterministic roles. some groups are rethinking this model. The Social Impact Creation Cycle, as one example, redefines progress in reaching goals for "nonprofits, companies, and impact investors." In the past, business models were applied to nonprofit organizations. But the effectiveness of organizations trying to do good in the world might not achieve such because they do not know how. This is what the Social Impact Creation Cycle attempts to teach organizations.[34] While their focus is on improving the effectiveness of nonprofit organizations, the core idea of analyzing and understanding the cycle for creating a desired social impact can apply to any group working for social justice. This rethinking responds to the call of Martin Luther King, Jr. for an inclusive democracy:

> The principle that citizens should have "maximum feasible participation" in community planning and other decisions affecting their lives is growing. The rights of all parents—not only the wealthy—to have a significant role in educational decisions affecting their children is still another developing concept. From a variety of different directions, the strands are drawing together for a contemporary social and economic Bill of Rights to supplement the Constitution's political Bill of Rights. The new forms of rights are new methods of participation in decision-making. The concept of democracy is being pushed to deeper levels of meaning—from formal exercise of voting, still an issue in much of the United States for many Negroes, to effective participation in major decisions.[35]

Or, as stated differently by Grace Lee Boggs, "Democracy must become a normal and natural practice of our everyday activities."[36] Perhaps the core of American values is democracy. And that may be the key to defining human rights from below.

SELF-REFLECTION

Question: Do you think a person can have deep spirituality without reflection?

Barbra Fitzgerald: No. But they can be manipulated.

As one of my conversation partners pointed out, reflection is necessary. New ways of thinking about how to understand human rights demands levels of self-reflection of our individual selves as well as American society.

Ethicist Sharon Welch emphasizes the same when she states, "To participate in the beloved community with honesty and integrity demands of us that we face, without excuses, the ways in which our social order falls short of our cherished ideals. It also requires that we examine the ways in which the stories we tell ourselves—the stories of who we are, what we have suffered, and what we have achieved—may hinder the work of healing and reconciliation."[37]

Henry Giroux provides an example of such self-reflection and personal storytelling in his own movement to scholarly activism. He stated that messages from institutions during his working-class youth defined him "through his deficits, which amounted to not having the skills and capacities to do anything but become either a cop or a firefighter. . . . The message was always the same. We were incomplete, unfinished, excess, and disposable." Yet, through reflection, he came to realize that his so-called deficits were in fact strengths: "a sense of solidarity, compassion, a merging of the mind and the body, learning and willingness to take risks, embracing passion, connecting knowledge to power, and being attentive to the injuries of others while embracing a sense of social justice."[38] His words demonstrate the importance of defining values. His words resonate with these words of Martin Luther King, Jr.: "For the evils of racism, poverty and militarism to die, a new set of values must be born."[39]

Yet, birthing new values through self-reflection are discouraged by neoliberal determination to retain power through social divisions. To maintain social divisiveness, conversations are terminated, dissent is invalidated, and the Others are silenced. Coming to see diversity as a benefit and not a problem helps to birth new values and promote self-reflection because these help us see past the labels and to begin new conversations. Even as I write this, I am reminded that Americans often resist any sense they are being told what to do or with whom they should associate. Diversity and self-reflection will not change people into someone they are not; rather, they will build a deeper sense of self, community, and nation. "Reflection" and "diversity," and "integration" can seem loaded terms, as if demanding that people dismiss their own identities. Perhaps another term by Iris Marion Young is more precise: "differentiated solidarity."

SOLIDARITY QUESTIONS

Iris Marion Young discussed the shortcomings of housing segregation and used the term "differentiated solidarity" to "formulate a different ideal of social political inclusion."

> Differentiated solidarity allows for a certain degree of separation among people who seek each other out because of social or cultural affinities . . . . If not fellow feeling, what is the moral basis for such attentiveness across social distance? It is that people live together. They are together in a locale or region,

whether they like it or not. Because they are together, they are all affected and relate to the geographical and atmospheric environment. . . . They are all potentially affected by an earthquake, reduction in electrical service, or complex rush hour traffic jams. . . . Their daily activities assume dense networks of institutional relations which casually relate them in the sense that the actions of some . . . affect many others whom they do not know.[40]

She stated the realities of contemporary American society, which are already diverse despite anyone's efforts to live in a racial and political bubble of sameness. Living in a social bubble in the early twenty-first century requires a kind of violence to *not* see social changes, to ignore racial difference, and to concur with injustice—racial discrimination, unequal education, underemployment, poverty—by complacency. Differentiated solidarity provides a way to think about building alliances as people come together for common causes. As Young pointed out, very pragmatically, people live together and that is the basis for networking.

Networking is often used in terms of business connections: knowing business leaders gives broader opportunities to become employed. Networking also refers to social capital. Knowing people, how institutions work, which institutions do what: each of these help a person navigate social structures. In like manner, people are finding new ways to network on behalf of human rights. Human rights from below means that the rights in question, around which differentiated solidarity might occur, are the issues in the neighborhoods and regions.

A situation that exemplifies human rights from below and differentiated solidarity is found in the water crisis in Flint, Michigan. In 2013, at the directive of an emergency manager appointed by the governor of the state, Flint switched the source of the community's water without correcting the pipes that carried the water. The result was an extended time when community members' water was contaminated with high lead levels. Calling attention to the results were community members themselves, complaining of water that smelled bad, water that was discolored, and eventually multiple symptoms of illness that arose, especially among children. Pediatricians, medical personnel, and university researchers responded with data that disproved any statements from the governor's office that the water was just fine. In February 2017, after some of the issues had been addressed and several lawsuits had been awarded or were proceeding, the Michigan Civil Rights Commission issued its report on the systemic racism at work in the crisis. The overall report demonstrates the possibilities when people act together to resolve problems. They also specify different ways that justice can be achieved: distributive justice, procedural justice, and corrective justice. Community activism across all levels was needed; specific collaborative solutions could be found. Grace Lee Boggs pointed out the possibilities for activism and solutions when she wrote, "In these desperate times, we must come together as inventors and discoverers committed to creating ideas and practice, vision and projects to help heal civilization."[41]

Words from the conclusion of the Flint crisis report are instructive:

> Implicit bias and systemic racism teach us that race will reflect the decisions we make unless we consciously address these shortcomings. Housing, education, the environment, and emergency management are all connected, and any policy that affects one, affects the others. Drawing a clear policy line defining where one ends and the next begins is impossible. The same is true of racism, racialization, and systemic racism. They overlap and it is usually impossible to define precisely which applies and caused a particular outcome to be racially disparate. The structures, norms, policies, and practices cut across institutions, neighborhoods, and communities with cumulative and compound effects. This Commission believes that, particularly applied to government, getting too caught up in precisely defining which is at play is both distracting and counterproductive. When we know policy will bring about disparate outcomes based on the color of people's skin, it is our responsibility to address it. It is not enough to say the result is unintended.[42]

The tangle that occurs when racism collides with policy; the realities of cumulative effects; and disparate outcomes on people of color: to reach solutions is impossible if trying to isolate one section without considering the whole system. Education, leadership, and practical, communal re-visioning are other components that make human rights from below achievable possibilities.

BACK TO EDUCATION

Education can be a component in the development of human rights, from kindergarten through college. There are educators experimenting with the idea of human rights from below for K–12, geared particularly to children in poorer American communities. These educators use the term human rights from below differently but are still aiming for social justice.

> This development [human rights education] is partially in response to the legal and international focus on much of the United States' understanding of human rights. The educators who developed this work define human rights from below as "acknowledging the radical legacies of human rights movements that struggled against racism, xenophobia, oppressive regimes and colonialism." They hold up Ella Baker, Malcolm X, and Paul Robeson as models.[43]

The scholar and teacher bell hooks also developed such ideas. She contrasted teaching for freedom with those teachers who use the classroom to influence students to associate freedom with materialism. "They teach us to believe that domination is 'natural,' that it is right for the strong to rule over the weak, the powerful over the powerless."[44] Instead, she calls for a view of education that is communal and joyful and liberating. "All of us in the academy and in the culture as a whole are called to renew our minds if we are to transform educational institutions—and society—so that the way we live, teach, and work can reflect our joy in cultural diversity, our passion for justice, and our love of freedom."[45]

The students who planned to protest at their college, mentioned above, might have had some in-class teaching that held up these values. But another question related to human rights from below is about leadership. Who leads? What comprises good leadership for justice? What are the values of the group and are they shared by all? What should the college president have done as a leader? How should students have understood their abilities to lead? And, most importantly, where could either of them have learned to lead? One study of leadership and training finds this:

> A recent report on the state of leadership development programs noted that nearly 75% of respondents from a wide variety of industries and organizations view their leadership development programs as ineffective. Despite this finding, the amount of money spent to train and develop leaders has more than doubled from $7 billion in 1996 to over $15 billion in 2013. Similarly, considerable investment of time and resources in understanding the outcomes of leadership development has yielded little clarity on the link between the learning activities and the emergence of these outcomes. Insufficient consideration has been given to understanding the pathways of change in leadership development programs. The pathways or connections between activities and outcomes constitute a program's theory of change, which can be used to better understand the effectiveness of programmatic activities used to facilitate changes in individuals or groups.[46]

LEADERSHIP

The processes of leadership are not those of a dictatorship. Instead, it should empower individuals and communities. Leadership is not controlling dissent; much can be discovered through recognizing those areas of social discomfort. Human rights from below are enacted through such leadership. In different areas of the country, Grace Lee Boggs and Rev. William Barber have provided such empowering leadership.

Grace Lee Boggs spent her life as an activist in the city of Detroit. In a new preface to a reprint of one of her earlier books, Grace Lee, as she preferred to be called, reflected on why her writing was resonating with people. Perhaps, she pondered, people have moved beyond protest organizing to visionary organizing.

Maybe it's because it gives Americans in all walks of life a more people-friendly view of revolution as empowerment rather than as struggle for political power. Maybe it helps us to view revolutionaries as solutionaries, working together to solve very practical problems of daily life. . . . Maybe it gives us the new more positive view of ourselves that we've been hungry for. . . . Maybe it also helps us see ourselves as evolutionaries.[47]

Rev. William Barber has defined the movement that has been successful among organizers. While he refers to fourteen steps for effective organizing, I mention only a few here:

- Engage in indigenously led grassroots organizing across the state. There is no end run around the relational work of building trust and empowering people. . . .
- Use moral language to frame and critique public policy, regardless of who is in power. a moral movement claims higher ground in partisan debate by returning public discourse to our deepest moral and constitutional values. . . .
- Build a stage from which to lift the voices of everyday people impacted by immoral policies. . . .
- Recognize the centrality of race. . . .
- Make a serious commitment to academic and empirical analysis of policy. Nothing is worse than being loud and wrong.[48]

These are beginning points for organizing. Religious thinkers are offering other ways to direct energy for change.

TAKING RELIGION BACK

The drivers of religion with politics and race in the United States have been primarily some Christians. They have often been loud and quick to take on the mantle of the "holy." One example is Evangelical Jerry Falwell, Jr. He defended against the charge that he is abetting negative and immoral actions of the United States government, as found in Falwell's and other Christian leaders' support of leadership such as President Trump's. He responded in a tweet to these charges: "Jesus said love our neighbors as ourselves but never told Caesar how to run Rome—he never said Roman soldiers should turn the other cheek in battle or that Caesar should allow all the barbarians to be Roman citizens or that Caesar should tax the rich to help poor. That's our job."[49]

There is another example of religious leaders connecting politics and religion, ultimately working to take religion back from the Falwells and their ilk. The Barmen Declaration of 1934 was written by leading theologians of the day who protested the takeover of Christian religion and thought by fascism and Nazism. Using this work as a springboard, a contemporary group of theologians put together a document and released it November 20, 2017. It is the Boston Declaration.[50]

Using language and concepts from Christian Scripture, the Declaration has four sections: Choose Life, Lamentation, Condemnations, and Call to Action. The authors specify that they are followers of Jesus who are "are outraged by the current trends in Evangelicalism and other expressions of Christianity driven by white supremacy, often enacted through white privilege and the normalizing of oppression." Instead, they claim a "Jesus Way," beyond denominational particularity, that "calls us to act in ways that are Spirit-led and strategic in confronting evil wherever evil exists, to combat ignorance wherever ignorance has led people astray and to place our lives and our bodies on the line with whoever is being threatened, beat down, or oppressed in any way, anywhere."

This Declaration stands with the work of many other theologians and ethicists who have called out limited visions of religion. Such religiosity can certainly call us into becoming and being human together.

FROM BELOW: HUMAN RIGHTS

In the United States, problems with communications among white Americans, Native Americans, African Americans, Latino/Latina Americans, Asian Americans, and Muslims have compounded social and political divisions. Political divisions are strengthened by legal and economic barriers, established to keep power lines in place. Existing communication problems have been exacerbated by the influx of immigrants and refugees as questions arise about who is really American. There seem to be more ways to misunderstand and misrepresent with seemingly fewer opportunities for conversations. Religions offer platitudes toward humane treatment of other people but stop short if their own congregation's connection to political power is threatened. Understanding our shared humanity, because of the race, politics, and religion intersection, is difficult in America.

My conversation partners throughout this last chapter were two friends, Christie and Ernie Otter. There were arguments and areas of agreement. Christie cut through many of my concerns by defining the difference between morality and ethics. Ethics is a behavioral standard that is not changed by ideology. There may be some cultural differences but the bottom line can be reached: this is what we should do. But, recognizing that, ethics is the work of communities, at grassroots levels, rather than political or religious decrees. Morality, however, is changed by ideology, both religious and political. For that grassroots work, activism at all levels is needed, some of which I have mentioned in this book.

Miguel de la Torre discussed an academic organization that he founded: The Society for Race, Ethnicity, and Religion.[51] Scholars of color and others come together, across disciplines, to "engage, learn, and be challenged." De la Torre's words about the organization—"I want us to talk to each other!"—reflect Martin Luther King's call for the development of new sets of values.

De la Torre's work is in the academic world, but he is also an activist. Grace Lee Boggs was an activist in the community of Detroit and across the country. Reverend Barber's work crosses the country but is grounded in church communities. Each moment is one more step toward a future where humans are valued and where the race, religion, and politics intersection can be undone.

There are many others who are involved in human rights work from below. Sometimes they refer to themselves and their work as human rights, sometimes not. Highlighting just a few here:

Showing Up for Racial Justice (SURJ) "is trying to create a culture and community that people actually want to be a part of." They are located in Louisville, Kentucky. SURJ works to network different groups. Their focus: "Spurred by the courageous leadership of the movement for Black lives, and the struggles for immigrant and indigenous justice, more and more white people are coming to understand that our silence holds oppression in place, and that our liberation is bound up in ending white supremacy."[52]

The Poor People's Campaign is inspired by the 1967–1968 Campaign of Dr. Martin Luther King. As cited on their website, in 1967 at a Southern Christian Leadership Conference retreat, Dr. King stated, "I think it is necessary for us to realize that we have moved from the era of civil rights to the era of human rights. . . . In short, we have moved into an era where we are called upon to raise certain basic questions about the whole society."[53] Inspired by the historic movement, people of faith and faith leaders participate in living this vision, through questioning and nonviolent acting for justice today.[54] Their principles are closely aligned with those of the Universal Declaration of Human Rights, including these: to lift up the leadership of America's poor and disenfranchised; to move from a war economy to a peace economy; to end unjust criminalization; to end systemic racism.[55]

Finally, a group called Indivisible aims to train community activists and political leaders who can lead local actions. As their slogan states, "We're not the leaders of this movement: you are."[56] The importance of their work is that they empower people to act in political arenas, which combats feelings of communal disconnection.

Throughout the book, I have mentioned other moments where people act for rights including protection of voting rights, use of court systems to achieve communal justice, protection of immigrants, and specifying the truth of history. All of these taken together are bright spots that point to the possibilities of achieving human rights in the United States.

NOTES

1. Bill D. Moyers, "What a Real President Was Like," *Washington Post*, November 13, 1988,   https://www.washingtonpost.com/archive/opinions/1988/11/13/what-a-real-president-was-like/d483c1be-d0da-43b7-bde6-04e10106ff6c/?utm_term=.d547517f3504.

2. Gary Dorrien, *Social Ethics in the Making: Interpreting an American Tradition* (Malden, MA: Wiley-Blackwell, 2009), 680.

3. Dorrien, *Social Ethics in the Making*, 680.

4. Boaventura de Sousa Santos, *If God Were a Human Rights Activist* (Stanford, CA: Stanford University Press, 2015), 4.

5. De Sousa Santos, *If God Were a Human Rights Activist*, 5.

6. De Sousa Santos, *If God Were a Human Rights Activist*, 6.

7. Emmanuel Felton, "The Secession Movement in Education," *The Nation* 305, no. 7 (September 25/October 2, 2017): 24.

8. Iris Marion Young, *Inclusion and Democracy* (New York: Oxford University Press, 2000), 205.

9. Dorceta Taylor, *Toxic Communities: Environmental Racism, Industrial Pollution, and Residential Mobility* (New York: NYU Press, 2014), 50.

10. Taylor, *Toxic Communities*, 52.

11. "The Principles of Environmental Justice," Environmental Justice / Environmental Racism, October 1991, http://www.ejnet.org/ej/principles.pdf.

12. Sofia Martinez, "The Second National People of Color Environmental Leadership Summit: What Next?," Southwest Research and Information Center, http://www.sric.org/voices/2003/v4n1/summit.php.

13. Martinez, "The Second National People of Color Environmental Leadership Summit."

14. Tara Isabella Burton, "How One Strain of Macho Theology Leads to a Church Choir Singing 'Make America Great Again,'" *Vox*, July 4, 2017, https://www.vox.com/identities/2017/7/4/15913590/muscular-christianity-make-america-great-again-trump-hymn.

15. United Nations, "The Universal Declaration of Human Rights," December 1948, http://www.un.org/en/universal-declaration-human-rights/.

16. Boston Collaborative Encyclopedia of Western Theology, "World Parliament of Religions (1893)," http://people.bu.edu/wwildman/bce/worldparliamentofreligions1893.htm.

17. "Chicago, 1893," Parliament of World's Religions, https://parliamentofreligions.org/parliament/new-chicago-1893/new-chicago-1893.

18. "Faith against Hate," Parliament of World's Religions, https://parliamentofreligions.org/parliament/faith-against-hate/faith-against-hate.

19. "Declaration on the Elimination of All Forms of Intolerance and of Discrimination Based on Religion or Belief," November 25, 1981, http://www.un.org/documents/ga/res/36/a36r055.htm.

20. parliament of the World's Religions, "Declaration Toward a Global Ethic," September 4,   1993,   https://parliamentofreligions.org/pwr_resources/_includes/FCKcontent/File/TowardsAGlobalEthic.pdf.

21. parliament of the World's Religions, "Declaration Toward a Global Ethic."

22. Zora Neale Hurston, "How It Feels to Be Colored Me," in *I Love Myself When I Am Laughing and Then Again When I Am Looking Mean and Impressive*, ed. Alice Walker (New York: Feminist Press, 1979), 153.

23. Louis Henkin, "Panel #1 Presentation," in *The United Nations and the World's Religions, Prospects for a Global Ethic*, Proceedings of a Conference held October 7, 1994 (Cambridge, MA: Boston Research Center for the 21st Century, 1995), 14–15.

24. Wande Abimbola, "Religion, World Order and Peace, An Indigenous African Perspective," *Crosscurrents* 60, no. 3 (September 2010): 307–9.

25. De Sousa Santos, *If God Were a Human Rights Activist*, 81.

26. De Sousa Santos, *If God Were a Human Rights Activist*, 80.

27. Who We Are / What We Do," United States Commission on International Religious Freedom, http://www.uscirf.gov/about-uscirf/who-we-arewhat-we-do.

28. "USCIRF Releases 2017 Annual Report," United States Commission on International Religious Freedom, April 26, 2017, http://www.uscirf.gov/news-room/press-releases/uscirf-releases-2017-annual-report.

29. From the third stanza of Francis Scott Key's "The Star-Spangled Banner," "No refuge could save the hireling and slave / From the terror of flight or the gloom of the grave, / And the star-spangled banner in triumph doth wave / O'er the land of the free and the home of the brave." "Complete version of 'The Star-Spangled Banner,'" Maryland Historical Society collection, https://amhistory.si.edu/starspangledbanner/pdf/ssb_lyrics.pdf."Key . . . spoke publicly of Africans in America as 'a distinct and inferior race of people, which all experience proves to be the greatest evil that afflicts a community.'" Jefferson Morley, *Snow Storm in August* (New York: Anchor Books, 2013), 40.

30. Douglas Jacobsen and Rhonda Hustedt Jacobsen, *No Longer Invisible: Religion in University Education* (New York: Oxford University Press, 2012), 59.

31. Kelly Brown Douglas, *Stand Your Ground: Black Bodies and the Justice of God* (Maryknoll, NY: Orbis Books, 2015), 42.

32. Henry A. Giroux, *America's Addiction to Terrorism* (New York: Monthly Review Press, 2016), 37.

33. John Gaventa and Jethro Pettit, "Invisible Power," *Power Cube*, Institute of Development Studies, University of Sussex, UK, 2011,https://www.powercube.net/analyse-power/forms-of-power/invisible-power/.

34. Marc J. Epstein and Kristi Yuthas, *Measuring and Improving Social Impacts: A Guide to Nonprofits, Companies, and Impact Investors* (San Francisco: BK Publishers, 2014).

35. Martin Luther King, Jr, *Where Do We Go from Here: Chaos or Community?* (1968; repr., Boston: Beacon Press, 2010), 211.

36. Grace Lee Boggs, *The Next American Revolution: Sustainable Activism for the Twenty-First Century* (Berkeley: University of California Press, 2012), xv.

37. Sharon D. Welch, *Real Peace, Real Security: The Challenges of Global Citizenship* (Minneapolis: Fortress Press, 2008), 11.

38. Henry A. Giroux, *America's Addiction to Terrorism*, 239–40.

39. King , *Where Do We Go from Here*, 142.

40. Young, *Inclusion and Democracy*, 221–23.

41. Boggs, *The Next American Revolution*, xxiii.

42. Dan Levy et al., *The Flint Water Crisis: Systemic Racism through the Lens of Flint*, Michigan Civil Rights Commission, February 17, 2017, 114, http://www.michigan.gov/documents/mdcr/VFlintCrisisRep-F-Edited3-13-17_554317_7.pdf.

43. Melissa Canlas, Amy Argenal, and Monisha Bajaj, "Teaching Human Rights from Below: Towards Solidarity, Resistance and Social Justice," in *Radical Teacher* no. 103 (Fall 2015): 39.

44. bell hooks, *Teaching to Transgress: Education as the Practice of Freedom* (New York: Routledge, 1994), 28.

45. bell hooks, *Teaching to Transgress*, 34.

46. Bradley Burbaugh, Megan Seibel, and Thomas Archibald, "Using a Participatory Approach to Investigate a Leadership Program's Theory of Change," *Journal of Leadership Education* 16, no. 1 (January 2017): 191–92.

47. Boggs, *The Next American Revolution*, 11.

48. William J. Barber II, *The Third Reconstruction: How a Moral Movement Is Overcoming the Politics of Division and Fear* (Boston: Beacon Press 2016), 127–29.

49. Tara Isabella Burton, "Evangelical Jerry Falwell Jr. Defends Trump: Jesus 'Never Told Caesar How to Run Rome," *Vox*, January 26, 2018, https://www.vox.com/2018/1/26/16936010/evangelicals-jerry-falwell-trump-caesar-rome.

50. "The Boston Declaration," November 20, 2017, https://thebostondeclaration.com/.

51. Society for Race, Ethnicity, and Religion, Facebook page, https://www.facebook.com/Society-of-Race-Ethnicity-and-Religion-181068971982277/.

52. "Poor and Working Class Commitment," Showing Up for Racial Justice, April 26, 2016, http://www.showingupforracialjustice.org/pwc_commitment.

53. "Dr. King's Vision: The Poor People's Campaign of 1967–68," Poor People's Campaign, https://www.poorpeoplescampaign.org/history/.

54. "Poor People's Campaign: A National Call for Moral Revival," website, https://poorpeoplescampaign.org/.

55. "Fundamental Principles," Poor People's Campaign, https://poorpeoplescampaign.org/index.php/fundamental-principles/.

56. "Act locally," Indivisible, https://www.indivisible.org/act-locally/.

Chapter Nine

Conclusion

Toward Human Rights from Below in the United States

Throughout this book, I have explored multiple identities of Americans and multiple dimensions of oppression. I aimed to show the importance of human rights from below in the United States, sometimes in conversation with international human rights. There are major cautions in this study and both are important.

CAVEAT 1

I do not discuss every group that has been oppressed by white identity politics in the United States. For example, in chapter 2, I briefly discussed Jewish Americans, who themselves are white but suffer through anti-Semitism. However, they have been considered a race, so designated in the 1930s German regime. As the racial category of the Jews shifted, so do other raced designations of people, across time and location. In like manner, ethnicity can become a shifting, rather than a firm, terrain. These underline the point that race and ethnicity are social constructions. They are constructions that can too easily be used in service to religions or politicians.

CAVEAT 2

As I emphasized in the introduction, the discussions about different groups— white, Native, black, Asian, Latinx, and Muslim Americans and immigrants—are only openings for further discussion and study. All histories, stories, or texts are not included. But many other questions are raised: What are the dynamics within each group that create other layers of diversity? How do locales and regions differentiate each group's experience? Are there places where there is greater harmony and interaction among the different groups? Places where there are more lines of tension? What makes a difference? Which other voices are being ignored or forgotten?

NATION/COMMUNITY/DEMOCRACY

These discussions lead to questions of the character and quality of life in the United States. Ronald Neal analyzes issues of race and democracy in the historic and contemporary South. He concludes by stating our needs in the United States: "There is a great need for telling the truth in American life, especially where American democracy is concerned. There is a need for the kind of politics that will be brutally honest about the condition of the United States in the early twenty-first century."[1] He continues, [D]emocracy is a socially engineered ideal that has to be cultivated in human beings. . . .Democracy is a constructive value."[2]

Analyzing and working to undo the intersection that race, politics, and religion constructs points us toward an idea of community that is engineered around human rights at local levels that are grounded in truth telling. Turning to the words of Grace Lee Boggs, we have already begun to think of new ways of truth telling and activism for social justice:

> Just as we need to reinvent democracy, now is the time for us to reimagine work and reimagine life. The new paradigm we must establish is about creating systems that bring out the best in each of us, instead of trying to harness the greed and selfishness of which we are capable. It is about a new balance of individual, family, community, work, and play that makes us better humans.[3]

Bringing out the best in each of us entails learning new ways of being human together in the United States.

I have argued that human rights are new/continued bases for American community building. Yet I am aware that this is difficult. A saying from Latino/Latina cultures is "*Cada cabeza es un mundo.*" This might be translated as "to each his or her own," a seeming call to relativism. Instead, I am drawing the literal translation: "Each head/mind is a world." And that is the start of the complexity of human rights from below.

Iris Marion Young emphasized that our social differences are in fact resources within a democracy. She stressed that inclusion makes political communication more difficult. Social problems would seemingly be solved quickly and seemingly much more efficiently by keeping "a process under tight and exclusive control. . . . A primary goal of democratic discussion and decision-making ought to be to promote justice in solving problems . . . even as it creates complexity and reveals conflicts of interest that can only be resolved by changing structural relations."[4]

Boaventura de Sousa Santos coined a term that sheds some light on a human rights direction through the social differences in democracy: "interculturality." He states that there are "three principles of social regulation of Western modernity . . . the state, the market, and the community."[5] Because the state and the market have been in pitched contention for control, the community has been able to develop in its own ways. What he finds most significant for community development are stories, the stories we tell each other that cross what should be hardened barriers—interculturality. Further, he contends that this crossing of barriers can "strengthen the legitimacy of both a worldwide and a place-based politics of human rights and . . . radicalize the struggles that can be undertaken in its name. The notion of interculturality is meant to convey the idea that the focus of intercultural exchanges is interpretation, the production and sharing of meaning."[6]

HUMAN RIGHTS FROM BELOW

Throughout this book, I have shared some of the meanings and ideas of American people from different races and cultures, both positive and negative, across different time periods. I have been fortunate to discuss the ideas I encountered with conversation partners, some of whom corrected my thinking. This pattern of looking at the past in order to understand the present while remaining in conversation with people across classes and races is important to undoing the race-religion-politics divides in the United States.

I advocate for human rights from below within the United States. To do so brings human rights into our national consciousness as it applies to ourselves. Let me be clear: human rights are not panaceas, but paths. The problems outlined in American communities in the previous chapters, as different people's identities conflict with their own or other's humanity, can sometimes be resolved by politics or addressed by religions. However, to effect long-term change is beyond either; the race-politics-religion intersection can kick in as groups of people determine that *their* identity is more important than that of others. Race can be used on behalf of or against other people, even while constructing Others. Religion can determine that one group's way is the best and no one may dissent from their beliefs, or they are considered heretical. Politics can set in structural supports for one group over all others, using logical arguments to suggest their solution is most reasonable and fair. None of these inherently holds a human right perspective, no matter how liberal they seem.

To effect change, I do not advocate wishful thinking, such as,

- If only race concepts had not been ingrained in ideologies that denied humanness;
- If only religions had not constructed and defended narrow definitions of holiness and goodness that were related to racist ideology;
- If only race concepts had not been structured by governmental policy and embedded into social mores;
- If only governmental structures had not politically aimed for a social good that was based on an ethics derived from religions that saw god in colors of white.

Human rights from below does not mean ignoring international human rights efforts and ideas. The United Nations Human Rights Council is not the enemy of human rights, but has been unable to refine local responses. One reason is that it often attempts only the political, legalistic solution that is within their charter, reasonable and, yes, efficient. Another reason is that its work sometimes ignores religions.

At the same time, human rights from below does not mean ignoring national efforts and international issues. The growth of white nationalist groups' membership, especially among young American people, tells a story of failure to give grounded history; the lack of thoughtful approaches to our own stories; and the need of some people to create identities because of fear and anger. Yet, even in the midst of these negative experiences, human possibilities expand.

In chapter 1, I told of Ossie Davis's contention that human rights, beyond civil rights, needs the focus of activism. I personally took that contention as a challenge and, here, years later, my understanding of the race-politics-religion intersection has grown. Human rights expand our humanity. Yet I believe that it is in working for human rights at the local (not a theoretical) level that the intersection is pulled apart.

So, I return to questions that I asked in the introduction: How can we recognize our shared humanity? How do we honor our rights as humans?

Can we agree to be human together?

NOTES

1. Ronald B. Neal, *Democracy in the Twenty-First Century: Race, Class, Religion, and Region* (Macon, GA: Mercer University Press, 2012), 121.

2. Neal, *Democracy in the Twenty-First Century*, 123.

3. Grace Lee Boggs, *The Next American Revolution: Sustainable Activism for the Twenty-First Century* (Berkeley: University of California Press, 2012), xxi.

4. Iris Marion Young, *Inclusion and Democracy* (New York: Oxford University Press, 2000), 119.

5. Boaventura de Sousa Santos, *If God Were a Human Rights Activist* (Stanford, CA: Stanford University Press, 2015), 74.

6. De Sousa Santos, *If God Were a Human Rights Activist*, 77–78.

Appendix A: The Universal Declaration of Human Rights

United Nations
This Declaration was proclaimed by the United Nations General Assembly in Paris on 10 December 1948 (General Assembly resolution 217 A) as a common standard of achievements for all peoples and all nations.

PREAMBLE

Whereas recognition of the inherent dignity and of the equal and inalienable rights of all members of the human family is the foundation of freedom, justice and peace in the world,

Whereas disregard and contempt for human rights have resulted in barbarous acts which have outraged the conscience of mankind, and the advent of a world in which human beings shall enjoy freedom of speech and belief and freedom from fear and want has been proclaimed as the highest aspiration of the common people,

Whereas it is essential, if man is not to be compelled to have recourse, as a last resort, to rebellion against tyranny and oppression, that human rights should be protected by the rule of law,

Whereas it is essential to promote the development of friendly relations between nations,

Whereas the peoples of the United Nations have in the Charter reaffirmed their faith in fundamental human rights, in the dignity and worth of the human person and in the equal rights of men and women and have determined to promote social progress and better standards of life in larger freedom,

Whereas Member States have pledged themselves to achieve, in co-operation with the United Nations, the promotion of universal respect for and observance of human rights and fundamental freedoms,

Whereas a common understanding of these rights and freedoms is of the greatest importance for the full realization of this pledge,

Now, Therefore THE GENERAL ASSEMBLY proclaims THIS UNIVERSAL DECLARATION OF HUMAN RIGHTS as a common standard of achievement for all peoples and all nations, to the end that every individual and every organ of society, keeping this Declaration constantly in mind, shall strive by teaching and education to promote respect for these rights and freedoms and by progressive measures, national and international, to secure their universal and effective recognition and observance, both among the peoples of Member States themselves and among the peoples of territories under their jurisdiction.

ARTICLE 1.

All human beings are born free and equal in dignity and rights. They are endowed with reason and conscience and should act towards one another in a spirit of brotherhood.

ARTICLE 2.

Everyone is entitled to all the rights and freedoms set forth in this Declaration, without distinction of any kind, such as race, colour, sex, language, religion, political or other opinion, national or social origin, property, birth or other status. Furthermore, no distinction shall be made on the basis of the political, jurisdictional or international status of the country or territory to which a person belongs, whether it be independent, trust, non-self-governing or under any other limitation of sovereignty.

ARTICLE 3.

Everyone has the right to life, liberty and security of person.

ARTICLE 4.

No one shall be held in slavery or servitude; slavery and the slave trade shall be prohibited in all their forms.

ARTICLE 5.

No one shall be subjected to torture or to cruel, inhuman or degrading treatment or punishment.

ARTICLE 6.

Everyone has the right to recognition everywhere as a person before the law.

ARTICLE 7.

All are equal before the law and are entitled without any discrimination to equal protection of the law. All are entitled to equal protection against any discrimination in violation of this Declaration and against any incitement to such discrimination.

ARTICLE 8.

Everyone has the right to an effective remedy by the competent national tribunals for acts violating the fundamental rights granted him by the constitution or by law.

ARTICLE 9.

No one shall be subjected to arbitrary arrest, detention or exile.

ARTICLE 10.

Everyone is entitled in full equality to a fair and public hearing by an independent and impartial tribunal, in the determination of his rights and obligations and of any criminal charge against him.

ARTICLE 11.

(1) Everyone charged with a penal offence has the right to be presumed innocent until proved guilty according to law in a public trial at which he has had all the guarantees necessary for his defence.
(2) No one shall be held guilty of any penal offence on account of any act or omission which did not constitute a penal offence, under national or international law, at the time when it was committed. Nor shall a heavier penalty be

imposed than the one that was applicable at the time the penal offence was committed.

ARTICLE 12.

No one shall be subjected to arbitrary interference with his privacy, family, home or correspondence, nor to attacks upon his honour and reputation. Everyone has the right to the protection of the law against such interference or attacks.

ARTICLE 13.

(1) Everyone has the right to freedom of movement and residence within the borders of each state.
(2) Everyone has the right to leave any country, including his own, and to return to his country.

ARTICLE 14.

(1) Everyone has the right to seek and to enjoy in other countries asylum from persecution.
(2) This right may not be invoked in the case of prosecutions genuinely arising from non-political crimes or from acts contrary to the purposes and principles of the United Nations.

ARTICLE 15.

(1) Everyone has the right to a nationality.
(2) No one shall be arbitrarily deprived of his nationality nor denied the right to change his nationality.

ARTICLE 16.

(1) Men and women of full age, without any limitation due to race, nationality or religion, have the right to marry and to found a family. They are entitled to equal rights as to marriage, during marriage and at its dissolution.
(2) Marriage shall be entered into only with the free and full consent of the intending spouses.
(3) The family is the natural and fundamental group unit of society and is entitled to protection by society and the State.

ARTICLE 17.

(1) Everyone has the right to own property alone as well as in association with others.
(2) No one shall be arbitrarily deprived of his property.

ARTICLE 18.

Everyone has the right to freedom of thought, conscience and religion; this right includes freedom to change his religion or belief, and freedom, either alone or in community with others and in public or private, to manifest his religion or belief in teaching, practice, worship and observance.

ARTICLE 19.

Everyone has the right to freedom of opinion and expression; this right includes freedom to hold opinions without interference and to seek, receive and impart information and ideas through any media and regardless of frontiers.

ARTICLE 20.

(1) Everyone has the right to freedom of peaceful assembly and association.
(2) No one may be compelled to belong to an association.

ARTICLE 21.

(1) Everyone has the right to take part in the government of his country, directly or through freely chosen representatives.
(2) Everyone has the right of equal access to public service in his country.
(3) The will of the people shall be the basis of the authority of government; this will shall be expressed in periodic and genuine elections which shall be by universal and equal suffrage and shall be held by secret vote or by equivalent free voting procedures.

ARTICLE 22.

Everyone, as a member of society, has the right to social security and is entitled to realization, through national effort and international co-operation and in accordance with the organization and resources of each State, of the economic, social and cultural rights indispensable for his dignity and the free development of his personality.

ARTICLE 23.

(1) Everyone has the right to work, to free choice of employment, to just and favourable conditions of work and to protection against unemployment.

(2) Everyone, without any discrimination, has the right to equal pay for equal work.

(3) Everyone who works has the right to just and favourable remuneration ensuring for himself and his family an existence worthy of human dignity, and supplemented, if necessary, by other means of social protection.

(4) Everyone has the right to form and to join trade unions for the protection of his interests.

ARTICLE 24.

Everyone has the right to rest and leisure, including reasonable limitation of working hours and periodic holidays with pay.

ARTICLE 25.

(1) Everyone has the right to a standard of living adequate for the health and well-being of himself and of his family, including food, clothing, housing and medical care and necessary social services, and the right to security in the event of unemployment, sickness, disability, widowhood, old age or other lack of livelihood in circumstances beyond his control.

(2) Motherhood and childhood are entitled to special care and assistance. All children, whether born in or out of wedlock, shall enjoy the same social protection.

ARTICLE 26.

(1) Everyone has the right to education. Education shall be free, at least in the elementary and fundamental stages. Elementary education shall be compulsory. Technical and professional education shall be made generally available and higher education shall be equally accessible to all on the basis of merit.

(2) Education shall be directed to the full development of the human personality and to the strengthening of respect for human rights and fundamental freedoms. It shall promote understanding, tolerance and friendship among all

nations, racial or religious groups, and shall further the activities of the United Nations for the maintenance of peace.

(3) Parents have a prior right to choose the kind of education that shall be given to their children.

ARTICLE 27.

(1) Everyone has the right freely to participate in the cultural life of the community, to enjoy the arts and to share in scientific advancement and its benefits.

(2) Everyone has the right to the protection of the moral and material interests resulting from any scientific, literary or artistic production of which he is the author.

ARTICLE 28.

Everyone is entitled to a social and international order in which the rights and freedoms set forth in this Declaration can be fully realized.

ARTICLE 29.

(1) Everyone has duties to the community in which alone the free and full development of his personality is possible.

(2) In the exercise of his rights and freedoms, everyone shall be subject only to such limitations as are determined by law solely for the purpose of securing due recognition and respect for the rights and freedoms of others and of meeting the just requirements of morality, public order and the general welfare in a democratic society.

(3) These rights and freedoms may in no case be exercised contrary to the purposes and principles of the United Nations.

ARTICLE 30.

Nothing in this Declaration may be interpreted as implying for any State, group or person any right to engage in any activity or to perform any act aimed at the destruction of any of the rights and freedoms set forth herein.

Source: http://www.un.org/en/universal-declaration-human-rights/

Appendix B: Commentary and Excerpts of Related United Nations Documents and Concepts

The United Nations' statements toward human rights do not often connect on the ground in the United States. While I have outlined some of the reasons for the disconnection or denial in chapter 1, this appendix is recognition of the importance of existing U.N. statements. Some U.N. documents were discussed in previous chapters, but there have been many others, perhaps alluded to, perhaps not mentioned. Therefore, some brief excerpts of and commentary on the documents related to religious freedom, ending racism (including the results of a visit to the United States), and the rights of indigenous peoples follow. That the documents and accompanying organizations have been developed indicate the United Nations' continuing work for human rights on their level. Human rights from below can depend on these statements for some vision even as we consider how to apply them to our home grounds.

RELIGIOUS FREEDOM

The U.N. Declaration on the Elimination of All Forms of Intolerance and of Discrimination Based on Religion or Belief (1981) was the first explicit statement that defined aspects of the Universal Declaration on Human Rights regarding religion. The broad emphasis of this document is religious freedom, including thought and conscience, and opposed to religious discrimination. The entire document follows.

DECLARATION ON THE ELIMINATION OF ALL FORMS OF INTOLERANCE AND OF DISCRIMINATION BASED ON RELIGION OR BELIEF[1]

November 25, 1981

The General Assembly,

Considering that one of the basic principles of the Charter of the United Nations is that of the dignity and equality inherent in all human beings, and that all Member States have pledged themselves to take joint and separate action in co-operation with the Organization to promote and encourage universal respect for and observance of human rights and fundamental freedoms for all, without distinction as to race, sex, language or religion,

Considering that the Universal Declaration of Human Rights and the International Covenants on Human Rights proclaim the principles of non-discrimination and equality before the law and the right to freedom of thought, conscience, religion and belief,

Considering that the disregard and infringement of human rights and fundamental freedoms, in particular of the right to freedom of thought, conscience, religion or whatever belief, have brought, directly or indirectly, wars and great suffering to mankind, especially where they serve as a means of foreign interference in the internal affairs of other States and amount to kindling hatred between peoples and nations,

Considering that religion or belief, for anyone who professes either, is one of the fundamental elements in his conception of life and that freedom of religion or belief should be fully respected and guaranteed,

Considering that it is essential to promote understanding, tolerance and respect in matters relating to freedom of religion and belief and to ensure that the use of religion or belief for ends inconsistent with the Charter of the United Nations, other relevant instruments of the United Nations and the purposes and principles of the present Declaration is inadmissible,

Convinced that freedom of religion and belief should also contribute to the attainment of the goals of world peace, social justice and friendship among peoples and to the elimination of ideologies or practices of colonialism and racial discrimination,

Noting with satisfaction the adoption of several, and the coming into force of some, conventions, under the aegis of the United Nations and of the specialized agencies, for the elimination of various forms of discrimination,

Concerned by manifestations of intolerance and by the existence of discrimination in matters of religion or belief still in evidence in some areas of the world,

Resolved to adopt all necessary measures for the speedy elimination of such intolerance in all its forms and manifestations and to prevent and combat discrimination on the ground of religion or belief,

Proclaims this Declaration on the Elimination of All Forms of Intolerance and of Discrimination Based on Religion or Belief:

Article 1

1. Everyone shall have the right to freedom of thought, conscience and religion. This right shall include freedom to have a religion or whatever belief of his choice, and freedom, either individually or in community with others and in public or private, to manifest his religion or belief in worship, observance, practice and teaching.

2. No one shall be subject to coercion which would impair his freedom to have a religion or belief of his choice.

3. Freedom to manifest one's religion or beliefs may be subject only to such limitations as are prescribed by law and are necessary to protect public safety, order, health or morals or the fundamental rights and freedoms of others.

Article 2

1. No one shall be subject to discrimination by any State, institution, group of persons, or person on grounds of religion or other beliefs.

2. For the purposes of the present Declaration, the expression "intolerance and discrimination based on religion or belief" means any distinction, exclusion, restriction or preference based on religion or belief and having as its purpose or as its effect nullification or impairment of the recognition, enjoyment or exercise of human rights and fundamental freedoms on an equal basis.

Article 3

Discrimination between human beings on grounds of religion or belief constitutes an affront to human dignity and a disavowal of the principles of the Charter of the United Nations, and shall be condemned as a violation of the human rights and fundamental freedoms proclaimed in the Universal Declaration of Human Rights and enunciated in detail in the International Covenants on Human Rights, and as an obstacle to friendly and peaceful relations between nations.

Article 4

1. All States shall take effective measures to prevent and eliminate discrimination on the grounds of religion or belief in the recognition, exercise and enjoyment of human rights and fundamental freedoms in all fields of civil, economic, political, social and cultural life.

2. All States shall make all efforts to enact or rescind legislation where necessary to prohibit any such discrimination, and to take all appropriate measures to combat intolerance on the grounds of religion or other beliefs in this matter.

Article 5

1. The parents or, as the case may be, the legal guardians of the child have the right to organize the life within the family in accordance with their

religion or belief and bearing in mind the moral education in which they believe the child should be brought up.

2. Every child shall enjoy the right to have access to education in the matter of religion or belief in accordance with the wishes of his parents or, as the case may be, legal guardians, and shall not be compelled to receive teaching on religion or belief against the wishes of his parents or legal guardians, the best interests of the child being the guiding principle.

3. The child shall be protected from any form of discrimination on the ground of religion or belief. He shall be brought up in a spirit of understanding, tolerance, friendship among peoples, peace and universal brotherhood, respect for freedom of religion or belief of others, and in full consciousness that his energy and talents should be devoted to the service of his fellow men.

4. In the case of a child who is not under the care either of his parents or of legal guardians, due account shall be taken of their expressed wishes or of any other proof of their wishes in the matter of religion or belief, the best interests of the child being the guiding principle.

5. Practices of a religion or beliefs in which a child is brought up must not be injurious to his physical or mental health or to his full development, taking into account article 1, paragraph 3, of the present Declaration.

Article 6

In accordance with article 1 of the present Declaration, and subject to the provisions of article 1, paragraph 3, the right to freedom of thought, conscience, religion or belief shall include, *inter alia*, the following freedoms:

(a) To worship or assemble in connexion with a religion or belief, and to establish and maintain places for these purposes;

(b) To establish and maintain appropriate charitable or humanitarian institutions;

(c) To make, acquire and use to an adequate extent the necessary articles and materials related to the rites or customs of a religion or belief;

(d) To write, issue and disseminate relevant publications in these areas;

(e) To teach a religion or belief in places suitable for these purposes;

(f) To solicit and receive voluntary financial and other contributions from individuals and institutions;

(g) To train, appoint, elect or designate by succession appropriate leaders called for by the requirements and standards of any religion or belief;

(h) To observe days of rest and to celebrate holidays and ceremonies in accordance with the precepts of one's religion or belief;

(i) To establish and maintain communications with individuals and communities in matters of religion and belief at the national and international levels.

Article 7

The rights and freedoms set forth in the present Declaration shall be accorded in national legislation in such a manner that everyone shall be able to avail himself of such rights and freedoms in practice.

Article 8
Nothing in the present Declaration shall be construed as restricting or derogating from any right defined in the Universal Declaration of Human Rights and the International Covenants on Human Rights.

Greater sophistication in approaching religion and religious freedom are evident in another document, created by international religious and peace-building organizations. The international advisory committee was drawn from a wide variety of religious leaders and experts in genocide studies. The document is intended to assist religious leaders to prevent and counteract incitement that could lead to violence and hate crimes. Religious actors are viewed as key to preventing genocide. The following excerpt is from the much longer document.

PLAN OF ACTION FOR RELIGIOUS LEADERS AND ACTORS TO PREVENT INCITEMENT TO VIOLENCE THAT COULD LEAD TO ATROCITY CRIMES

United Nations Office on Genocide Prevention and the Responsibility to Protect, July 2017.
The Plan of Action for Religious Leaders and Actors to Prevent Incitement to Violence that Could Lead to Atrocity Crimes ("the Plan of Action") . . . integrates respect for and promotion of international human rights standards, in particular the right to freedom of expression and opinion, freedom of religion or belief and peaceful assembly. [2]
The Plan of Action consists of nine groups of thematic recommendations which are organized into three main clusters.

Prevent

1. Specific actions to prevent and counter incitement to violence
2. Prevent incitement to violent extremism
3. Prevent incitement to gender-based violence

Strengthen

4. Enhance education and capacity building
5. Foster interfaith and intra-faith dialogue
6. Strengthen collaboration with traditional and new media
7. Strengthen engagement with regional and international partners

Build

8. Build peaceful, inclusive and just societies through respecting, protecting and promoting human rights
9. Establish networks of religious leaders[3]

(*Under the objectives for each of the nine categories, bullet points of possible actions are listed, directed at specific target audiences. The following is an example from the first category, "Prevent," and drawing from the first subheading, for "Specific actions to prevent and counter incitement to violence." Partial suggestions for only two of the targeted audiences, religious leaders and local communities, are excerpted here.*)

Specific actions to prevent and counter incitement to violence

Target I: Religious leaders and actors

- React to incitement as soon as it occurs to prevent tensions from escalating;
- Learn how to differentiate between speech that merely causes offence and speech that could constitute incitement to violence.[4]

Target II: Local communities

- Build robust multi-faith social action campaigns to prevent and curb incitement to violence. Ensure campaign leaders are diverse faith actors (women, young people, people of different professions);
- Organise community level initiatives such as "flash mobs" and form rapid response networks. Disseminate messages in various forms, including through press conferences, press statements, blogs, op-eds, videos, films, music and visual art.[5]

AGAINST RACISM, DISCRIMINATION, AND INTOLERANCE:

In 2001, following a conference in Durban, South Africa, the United Nations' members released a document against all forms of racism. The United States and Israel were the only two nations who refused to sign the document. The entire document includes articles that address the sources and causes of racism, victims of racism, and ideas for prevention and education as well as a program of action. A brief excerpt, of the Articles of the General Principles, follows.

WORLD CONFERENCE AGAINST RACISM, RACIAL DISCRIMINATION, XENOPHOBIA AND RELATED INTOLERANCE: DECLARATION, SEPTEMBER 2001[6]

General issues

1. We declare that for the purpose of the present Declaration and Programme of Action, the victims of racism, racial discrimination, xenophobia and related intolerance are individuals or groups of individuals who are or have been negatively affected by, subjected to, or targets of these scourges;

2. We recognize that racism, racial discrimination, xenophobia and related intolerance occur on the grounds of race, colour, descent or national or ethnic origin and that victims can suffer multiple or aggravated forms of discrimination based on other related grounds such as sex, language, religion, political or other opinion, social origin, property, birth or other status;

3. We recognize and affirm that, at the outset of the third millennium, a global fight against racism, racial discrimination, xenophobia and related intolerance and all their abhorrent and evolving forms and manifestations is a matter of priority for the international community, and that this Conference offers a unique and historic opportunity for assessing and identifying all dimensions of those devastating evils of humanity with a view to their total elimination through, *inter alia*, the initiation of innovative and holistic approaches and the strengthening and enhancement of practical and effective measures at the national, regional and international levels;

4. We express our solidarity with the people of Africa in their continuing struggle against racism, racial discrimination, xenophobia and related intolerance and recognize the sacrifices made by them, as well as their efforts in raising international public awareness of these inhuman tragedies;

5. We also affirm the great importance we attach to the values of solidarity, respect, tolerance and multiculturalism, which constitute the moral ground and inspiration for our worldwide struggle against racism, racial discrimination, xenophobia and related intolerance, inhuman tragedies which have affected people throughout the world, especially in Africa, for too long;

6. We further affirm that all peoples and individuals constitute one human family, rich in diversity. They have contributed to the progress of civilizations and cultures that form the common heritage of humanity. Preservation and promotion of tolerance, pluralism and respect for diversity can produce more inclusive societies;

7. We declare that all human beings are born free, equal in dignity and rights and have the potential to contribute constructively to the development and well-being of their societies. Any doctrine of racial superiority is scientifically false, morally condemnable, socially unjust and dangerous, and must be

rejected along with theories which attempt to determine the existence of separate human races;

8. We recognize that religion, spirituality and belief play a central role in the lives of millions of women and men, and in the way they live and treat other persons. Religion, spirituality and belief may and can contribute to the promotion of the inherent dignity and worth of the human person and to the eradication of racism, racial discrimination, xenophobia and related intolerance;

9. We note with concern that racism, racial discrimination, xenophobia and related intolerance may be aggravated by, *inter alia*, inequitable distribution of wealth, marginalization and social exclusion;

10. We reaffirm that everyone is entitled to a social and international order in which all human rights can be fully realized for all, without any discrimination;

11. We note that the process of globalization constitutes a powerful and dynamic force which should be harnessed for the benefit, development and prosperity of all countries, without exclusion. We recognize that developing countries face special difficulties in responding to this central challenge. While globalization offers great opportunities, at present its benefits are very unevenly shared, while its costs are unevenly distributed. We thus express our determination to prevent and mitigate the negative effects of globalization. These effects could aggravate, *inter alia*, poverty, underdevelopment, marginalization, social exclusion, cultural homogenization and economic disparities which may occur along racial lines, within and between States, and have an adverse impact. We further express our determination to maximize the benefits of globalization through, *inter alia*, the strengthening and enhancement of international cooperation to increase equality of opportunities for trade, economic growth and sustainable development, global communications through the use of new technologies and increased intercultural exchange through the preservation and promotion of cultural diversity, which can contribute to the eradication of racism, racial discrimination, xenophobia and related intolerance. Only through broad and sustained efforts to create a shared future based upon our common humanity, and all its diversity, can globalization be made fully inclusive and equitable;

12. We recognize that interregional and intraregional migration has increased as a result of globalization, in particular from the South to the North, and stress that policies towards migration should not be based on racism, racial discrimination, xenophobia and related intolerance.

The rights of indigenous peoples were directly addressed by the United Nations. Excerpts of the initial affirming principles and a few of the Articles follow.

UNITED NATIONS DECLARATION ON THE RIGHTS OF INDIGENOUS PEOPLES (2008)[7]

Affirming that indigenous peoples are equal to all other peoples, while recognizing the right of all peoples to be different, to consider themselves different, and to be respected as such,

Affirming also that all peoples contribute to the diversity and richness of civilizations and cultures, which constitute the common heritage of humankind,

Affirming further that all doctrines, policies and practices based on or advocating superiority of peoples or individuals on the basis of national origin or racial, religious, ethnic or cultural differences are racist, scientifically false, legally invalid, morally condemnable and socially unjust, . . .[8]

Article 1

Indigenous peoples have the right to the full enjoyment, as a collective or as individuals, of all human rights and fundamental freedoms as recognized in the Charter of the United Nations, the Universal Declaration of Human Rights [Resolution 217 A (III)] and international human rights law.

Article 2

Indigenous peoples and individuals are free and equal to all other peoples and individuals and have the right to be free from any kind of discrimination, in the exercise of their rights, in particular that based on their indigenous origin or identity.

Article 3

Indigenous peoples have the right to self-determination. By virtue of that right they freely determine their political status and freely pursue their economic, social and cultural development.

Article 4

Indigenous peoples, in exercising their right to self-determination, have the right to autonomy or self-government in matters relating to their internal and local affairs, as well as ways and means for financing their autonomous functions.

Article 5

Indigenous peoples have the right to maintain and strengthen their distinct political, legal, economic, social and cultural institutions, while retaining their right to participate fully, if they so choose, in the political, economic, social and cultural life of the State.

Article 6

Every indigenous individual has the right to a nationality.

Article 7

1. Indigenous individuals have the rights to life, physical and mental integrity, liberty and security of person.

2. Indigenous peoples have the collective right to live in freedom, peace and security as distinct peoples and shall not be subjected to any act of genocide or any other act of violence, including forcibly removing children of the group to another group.[9]

Beyond these basic documents, the United Nations and Office for Human Rights,[10] have continued to develop documents and reports that are substantive and important. But the possibilities of the reports' making an impact in Americans' lives is uneven, at best; many of them remain good ideas that are never actualized. The Working Group of Experts on People of African Descent visited the United States in 2016. The international experts began the final report with an historical overview and legal steps taken to assure human rights of people of African descent. They noted advances that had been achieved. However, they listed current manifestations of racial discrimination including unequal treatment through the criminal justice system; barriers to voting and political participation; and health, housing, and educational disparities. The first of their list of recommendations ties resolutions to injustices firmly to support of human rights.

REPORT OF THE WORKING GROUP OF EXPERTS ON PEOPLE OF AFRICAN DESCENT, VISIT TO THE UNITED STATES, 2016: EXCERPT

88. The Working Group reiterates the recommendation that it made after its visit to the United States of America in 2010 to establish a national human rights commission in accordance with the principles relating to the status of national institutions for the promotion and protection of human rights (Paris Principles). The Government should establish within this body a specific division to monitor the human rights of African Americans.
89. In addition to the above, the Working Group urges the Government of the United States of America to consider the ratification of the core international human rights treaties to which the United States is still not a party, with a view to removing any gaps in the protection and full enjoyment of rights therein. It also encourages the United States to ratify regional human rights treaties and to review the reservations related to the treaties that it has signed or ratified.[11]

NOTES

1. "Declaration on the Elimination of All Forms of Intolerance and of Discrimination Based on Religion or Belief," November 25, 1981, http://www.un.org/documents/ga/res/36/a36r055.htm.

2. "Plan of Action for Religious Leaders and Actors to Prevent Incitement to Violence that Could Lead to Atrocity Crimes," United Nations Office on Genocide Prevention and the Responsibility to Protect, July 2017, 5, https://www.un.org/en/genocideprevention/documents/Plan%20of%20Action%20Advanced%20Copy.pdf.

3. "Plan of Action for Religious Leaders and Actors," 6.

4. "Plan of Action for Religious Leaders and Actors," 7.

5. "Plan of Action for Religious Leaders and Actors," 8.

6. "World Conference against Racism, Racial Discrimination, Xenophobia and Related Intolerance: Declaration," Durban, South Africa, September 2001, http://www.un.org/WCAR/durban.pdf.

7. "United Nations Declaration on the Rights of Indigenous Peoples," March 2008, http://www.un.org/esa/socdev/unpfii/documents/DRIPS_en.pdf.

8. "United Nations Declaration on the Rights of Indigenous Peoples," 2–3.

9. "United Nations Declaration on the Rights of Indigenous Peoples," 4–5.

10. United Nations Human Rights, Office of the High Commissioner, http://www.ohchr.org/EN/Pages/Home.aspx.

11. United Nations Human Rights Council, Report of the Working Group of Experts on People of African Descent on Its Mission to the United States of America, 2016, 18, http://www.ushrnetwork.org/sites/ushrnetwork.org/files/unwgepad_us_visit_final_report_9_15_16.pdf.

Selected Bibliography

Abimbola, Wande. "Religion, World Order and Peace: An Indigenous African Perspective." *Crosscurrents* 60, no. 3 (September 2010): 307–9.

Abramsky, Sasha. "Caravan against Fear." *The Nation* 305, no. 3 (July 31/August 7, 2017): 15–17, 21.

Achenback, Joel. "Life Expectancy Improves for Blacks, and the Racial Gap Is Closing, CDC Reports." *Washington Post*, May 2, 2017. https://www.washingtonpost.com/news/to-your-health/wp/2017/05/02/cdc-life-expectancy-up-for-blacks-and-the-racial-gap-is-closing/?utm_term=.d899e809ac01.

Aguilar, Louis. "Estate of Vincent Chin Seeks Millions from His Killer." *Detroit News*, June 24, 2017. http://www.detroitnews.com/story/news/local/oakland-county/2017/06/24/vincent-chin-th-anniversary/103167672/.

Alcindor, Yamiche. "Ben Carson Calls Poverty a 'State of Mind,' Igniting a Backlash." *New York Times*, May 25, 2017. https://www.nytimes.com/2017/05/25/us/politics/ben-carson-poverty-hud-state-of-mind.html?_r=0.

Alexander, Michelle. *The New Jim Crow: Mass Incarceration in the Age of Colorblindness.* New York: The New Press, 2012.

American Anthropological Association, "Understanding Race." http://www.understandingrace.org/resources/glossary.html.

An, Sohyun. "AsianCrit Perspective on Social Studies." *The Journal of Social Studies Research* 41, no. 2 (2017): 131–39.

Anderson, Carol. *The Unspoken Truth of Our Racial Divide.* New York: Bloomsbury, 2016.

Association of Theological Schools. "2015 Annual Report." 2015. http://www.ats.edu/uploads/resources/publications-presentations/documents/2015-annual-report%20FINAL.pdf.

Backer, Larry Catá. "Not a Zookeeper's Culture; LatCrit Theory and the Search for Latino/a Authenticity in the U.S." *Texas Hispanic Journal of Law and Policy* 4, no. 7 (1998): 7–27.

Baker, Houston A. *Betrayal: How Black Intellectuals Have Abandoned the Ideals of the Civil Rights Era.* New York: Columbia University Press, 2008.

Baldwin, James. "The White Man's Guilt." In *Collected* Essays, 722–27. New York: Library of America, 1998.

Barber, William J., II. *The Third Reconstruction: How a Moral Movement Is Overcoming the Politics of Division and Fear.* Boston: Beacon Press 2016.

Barber, William, and Jonathan Wilson-Hartgrove. "The Strange Career of James Crow, Esquire." *The Atlantic*, February 4, 2016. https://www.theatlantic.com/politics/archive/2016/02/jim-crows-new-legal-career/459879/.

Barzegar, Abbas. "Discourse, Identity, and Community: Problems and Prospects in the Study of Islam in America." *The Muslim World* 101, no. 3 (July 2011): 511–38.

Bebout, Lee. *Whiteness on the Border: The U.S. Racial Imagination in Brown and White.* New York: NYU Press, 2016.

Belt, David D. "Anti-Islam Discourse in the United States in the Decade after 9/11: The Role of Social Conservatives and Cultural Politics." *Journal of Ecumenical Studies* 51, no. 1 (Spring 2016): 210–23.

Bernasconi, Robert. "Crossed Lines in the Racialization Process: Race as a Border Concept." *Research in Phenomenology* 42, no. 2 (2012): 206–28.

Bey, Marquis, and Theodora Sakellarides. "When We Enter: The Blackness of Rachel Dolezal." *The Black Scholar* 46, no. 4 (2016): 33–48.

Boggs, Grace Lee. *The Next American Revolution: Sustainable Activism for the Twenty-First Century.* Berkeley: University of California Press, 2012.

Boschma, Janie. "Black Consumers Have 'Unprecedented Impact' in 2015." *The Atlantic*, February 2, 2016. https://www.theatlantic.com/politics/archive/2016/02/black-consumers-have-unprecedented-impact-in-2015/433725/.

Boston Collaborative Encyclopedia of Western Theology. "World Parliament of Religions (1893)." http://people.bu.edu/wwildman/bce/worldparliamentofreligions1893.htm.

Bromwich, Jonah Engel. "Lawyers Mobilize at Nation's Airports after Trump's Order." *New York Times*, January 29, 2017. https://www.nytimes.com/2017/01/29/us/lawyers-trump-muslim-ban-immigration.html?mcubz=0&_r=0.

Burbaugh, Bradley, Megan Seibel, and Thomas Archibald. "Using a Participatory Approach to Investigate a Leadership Program's Theory of Change." *Journal of Leadership Education* 16, no. 1 (January 2017): 192–204.

Burton, Tara Isabella. "How One Strain of Macho Theology Leads to a Church Choir Singing 'Make America Great Again.'" *Vox*, July 4, 2017. https://www.vox.com/identities/2017/7/4/15913590/muscular-christianity-make-america-great-again-trump-hymn.

Camarota, Steven A. "Immigrants from the Middle East: A Profile of the Foreign-born Population from Pakistan to Morocco." Center for Immigration Studies, August 1, 2002. https://cis.org/Immigrants-Middle-East.

Canlas, Melissa, Amy Argenal, and Monisha Bajaj. "Teaching Human Rights from Below: Towards Solidarity, Resistance and Social Justice." *Radical Teacher* 103 (Fall 2015): 38–46.

Cannon, Katie Geneva. *Katie's Canon: Womanism and the Soul of the Black Community.* New York: Continuum, 1995.

———. "Structured Academic Amnesia: As If This Womanist Story Never Happened." In *Deeper Shades of Purple*, edited by Stacey Floyd-Thomas, 19–28. New York: NYU Press, 2006.

Cave, Damien. "Officer Darren Wilson's Grand Jury Testimony in Ferguson, Mo., Shooting." *New York Times.* November 25, 2016. https://www.nytimes.com/interactive/2014/11/25/us/darren-wilson-testimony-ferguson-shooting.html?_r=0.

Champagne, Duane. "First Treaty Signed at Fort Pitt with Delaware for Trade and Alliance." *Indian Country Media Network*, February 15, 2014. https://indiancountrymedianetwork.com/history/events/first-treaty-signed-at-fort-pitt-with-delaware-for-trade-and-alliance/.

Chokshi, Niraj. "'Taco Trucks on Every Corner': Trump Supporter's Anti-Immigration Warning." *New York Times*, September 2, 2016. http://www.nytimes.com/2016/09/03/us/politics/taco-trucks-on-every-corner-trump-supporters-anti-immigration-warning.html?_r=0.

Clarke, Simon, and Steve Garner. *White Identities: A Critical Sociological Approach.* London: Pluto Press, 2009.

Clifford, James. Introduction to *Writing Culture: The Poetics and Politics of Ethnography*, edited by James Clifford and George E. Marcus, 1–26. Berkeley: University of California Press, 1986.

Coates, Ta-Nehisi. "My President Was Black." *The Atlantic*, January/February 2017. https://www.theatlantic.com/magazine/archive/2017/01/my-president-was-black/508793/.

Colson, Derek. "Transcript of New Orleans Mayor Landrieu's Address on Confederate Monuments." *The Pulse*, May 19, 2017. http://pulsegulfcoast.com/2017/05/transcript-of-new-orleans-mayor-landrieus-address-on-confederate-monuments.

Cone, James. *Black Power and Black Theology.* New York: Seabury Press, 1969.

———. *God of the Oppressed.* New York: Seabury Press, 1975.

———. *Risks of Faith: The Emergence of a Black Theology of Liberation, 1968–1998.* Boston: Beacon Press, 1999.

Coontz, Stephanie. *The Way We Never Were: American Families and the Nostalgia Trap.* Rev. and updated ed. New York: Basic Books, 2016.

Covert, Bryce. "Donald Trump's Imaginary Inner Cities." *The Nation,* November 7, 2016. https://www.thenation.com/article/donald-trumps-imaginary-inner-cities/.

Cox, Daniel, and Robert T Jones. "Nearly Half of Americans Worried That They or Their Family Will Be a Victim of Terrorism." Public Religion Research Institute (PRRI). December 10, 2015. https://www.prri.org/research/survey-nearly-half-of-americans-worried-that-they-or-their-family-will-be-a-victim-of-terrorism/.

Curtis IV, Edward E. *Muslims in America: A Short History.* New York: Oxford University Press 2009.

Davis, Angela Y. *Freedom Is a Constant Struggle: Ferguson, Palestine, and the Foundations of a Movement.* Chicago: Haymarket Books, 2016.

———. *Women, Race and Class.* New York: Random House, Vintage Books edition, 1983.

DeGruy, Joy. *Post Traumatic Slave Syndrome: American's Legacy of Enduring Injury and Healing.* Portland, OR: Uptone Press, 2005.

De La Torre, Miguel A., and Edwin David Aponte. *Introducing Latino/a Theologies.* New York: Orbis Books, 2001.

de Landa, Friar Diego. *Yucatan: Before and after the Conquest.* Translated, with notes, by William Gates. 1566 manuscript. New York: Dover Publications, 1978.

de Sousa Santos, Boaventura. *If God Were a Human Rights Activist.* Stanford, CA: Stanford University Press, 2015.

Deloria, Vine, Jr. *Red Earth, White Lies: Native Americans and the Myth of Scientific Fact.* New York: Scribner, 1995.

DiAngelo, Robin. "White Fragility." *International Journal of Critical Pedagogy* 3, no. 3 (2011): 54–70.

Dorrien, Gary. *Social Ethics in the Making: Interpreting an American Tradition.* Malden, MA: Wiley-Blackwell, 2009.

Douglas, Kelly Brown. *Stand Your Ground: Black Bodies and the Justice of God.* Maryknoll, NY: Orbis Books, 2015.

Douglass, Frederick. "What to the Slave Is the Fourth of July?" July 5, 1852. Reprinted in *The Nation,* July 4, 2012. https://www.thenation.com/article/what-slave-fourth-july-frederick-douglass/.

Du Bois, W. E. B. *Black Reconstruction in America 1860–1880.* New York: Atheneum, 1975.

Durst, Dennis L. *Eugenics and Protestant Social Reform: Hereditary Science and Religion in America, 1860–1940.* Eugene, OR: Pickwick Publications, 2017.

El Museo. "History." http://www.elmuseo.org/history-mission/.

Eligon, John, Yamiche Alcindor, and Agustin Armendariz. "Program to Spur Low-Income Housing Is Keeping Cities Segregated." *New York Times,* July 2, 2017. https://www.nytimes.com/2017/07/02/us/federal-housing-assistance-urban-racial-divides.html.

Elizondo, Virgil. *Guadalupe: Mother of the New Creation.* Maryknoll, NY: Orbis Books, 1997.

Environmental Justice / Environmental Racism. "The Principles of Environmental Justice." October 1991. http://www.ejnet.org/ej/principles.pdf.

Epstein, Kayla. "The Disturbing History of Vandalizing Jewish Cemeteries." *Washington Post,* February 21, 2017. https://www.washingtonpost.com/news/acts-of-faith/wp/2017/02/21/the-disturbing-history-of-vandalizing-jewish-cemeteries/?utm_term=.2ee3d3c02716 .

Epstein, Marc J., and Kristi Yuthas. *Measuring and Improving Social Impacts: A Guide to Nonprofits, Companies, and Impact Investors.* San Francisco: BK Publishers 2014.

Ernst, Carl W., ed. *Islamophobia in America.* New York: Palgrave Macmillan, 2013.

Esaki, Brett J. *Enfolding Silence: The Transformation of Japanese American Religion and Art under Oppression.* New York: Oxford University Press, 2016.

Ezinna, Wes. "Crude Awakenings." *Mother Jones,* January/February 2017. http://www.motherjones.com/environment/2016/12/dakota-access-pipeline-standing-rock-oil-water-protest/.

Felton, Emmanuel. "The Secession Movement in Education." *The Nation* 305, no. 7 (September 25/October 2, 2017): 12–24.

Finn, Rachel L. "Surveillant Staring: Race and the Everyday Surveillance of South Asian Women after 9/11." *Surveillance & Society* 8, no. 4 (2011): 413–26.

Flores, Henry. *Latinos and the Voting Rights Act: The Search for Racial Purpose.* Lanham, MD: Lexington Books, 2015.

Frum, David. "America's Immigration Challenge." *The Atlantic*, December 11, 2015. https://www.theatlantic.com/politics/archive/2015/12/refugees/419976.

Galeano, Eduardo. *Open Veins of Latin America: Five Centuries of the Pillage of a Continent.* 1973. Reprint, New York: Monthly Review Press, 1997.

Galonnier, Juliette. "The Racialization of Muslims in France and the United States: Some Insights from White Converts to Islam." *Social Compass* 62, no. 4 (2015): 570–83.

García, J. L. A. "Is Being Hispanic an Identity?" In *Debating Race, Ethnicity, and Latino Identity: Jorge J. E. Gracia and His Critics*, edited by Ivan Jaksic. New York: Columbia University Press, 2015.

Gaventa, John, and Jethro Pettit. "Invisible Power." *Powercube.* Institute of Development Studies. University of Sussex, UK. 2011. https://www.powercube.net/analyse-power/forms-of-power/invisible-power/.

Gikorea. "Attacks on Korean Shop Owners Featured Heavily in Smithsonian Documentary about the 1992 LA Riots." ROK Drop: Korea from North to South. May 10, 2017. http://www.rokdrop.net/2017/05/attacks-on-korean-shop-owners-featured-heavily-in-smithsonian-documentary-about-the-1992-la-riots/.

Gilkes, Cheryl Townsend. "A Conscious Connection to All That Is: *The Color Purple* as Subversive and Critical Ethnography." In *Personal Knowledge and Beyond: Reshaping the Ethnography of Religion*, edited by James V. Spickard, J. Shawn Landres, and Meredith B. McGuire, 175–91. New York: NYU Press, 2002.

Gilman, Sander L. "The Racial Nose." In *The Body Reader: Essential Social and Cultural Readings*, edited by Lisa Jean Moore and Mary Kosut, 201–27. New York: NYU Press, 2010.

Giroux, Henry. *America's Addiction to Terrorism.* New York: Monthly Review Press, 2016.

Gonzalez, Juan. *Harvest of Empire: A History of Latinos in America.* New York: Penguin Press, 2000.

Gonzalez, Mike. "We Don't Need a National Latino Museum." *Washington Post*, September 23, 2016. https://www.washingtonpost.com/opinions/we-dont-need-a-national-latino-museum/2016/09/23/7f5a0308-7f59-11e6-9070-5c4905bf40dc_story.html?utm_term=.7d86b527708c.

Graham, David A. "Steve King's Improbable Ascendance." *The Atlantic*, March 13, 2017. https://www.theatlantic.com/politics/archive/2017/03/steve-king-nearer-the-throne/519336/.

Grounds, Richard A., George E. Tinker, and David E. Wilkins, eds. *Native Voices: American Indian Identity and Resistance.* Lawrence: University Press of Kansas, 2003.

Guinier, Lani, and Gerald Torres. *The Miner's Canary: Enlisting Race, Resisting Power, Transforming Democracy.* Cambridge, MA: Harvard University Press, 2002.

Gutterman, David S., and Andrew R. Murphy. *Political Religion and Religious Politics: Navigating Identities in the United States.* New York: Routledge, 2016.

Hacking, Amany R. "A New Dawn for Muslims: Asserting Their Civil Rights in Post-9/11 America." *Saint Louis University Law Journal* 54 (2010): 917–41.

Hale, Grace Elizabeth. *Making Whiteness: The Culture of Segregation in the South, 1890–1940.* New York: Vintage Books, 1998.

Hall, Gwendolyn Midlo. *Slavery and African Ethnicities in the Americas: Restoring the Links.* Chapel Hill: University of North Carolina Press, 2005.

Hall, Ronald E. "Anti-Racist Racism as a Judicial Decree: Racism in the Twenty-First Century." *Journal of African American Studies* 19 (2015): 319–28.

Hannah-Jones, Nikole. "Segregation Now . . . " *The Atlantic*, May 2014. https://www.theatlantic.com/magazine/archive/2014/05/segregation-now/359813/.

Harjo, Suzan Shown. "Trail of Broken Treaties: A 30th Anniversary Memory." *Indian Country Today*, November 7, 2002. https://indiancountrymedianetwork.com/news/trail-of-broken-treaties-a-30th-anniversary-memory/.

Hauslohner, Abigail. "In Mississippi, Aging Muslim Community Worries about Its Future." *Washington Post*, July 19, 2017. https://www.washingtonpost.com/national/in-mississippi-aging-muslim-community-worries-about-its-future/2017/07/19/9b609662-6346-11e7-8adc-fea80e32bf47_story.html?utm_term=.5f8e0bf71e1.

Henkin, Louis. "Panel #1 Presentation." In *The United Nations and the World's Religions, Prospects for a Global Ethic, Proceedings of a Conference held October 7, 1994*, edited by Boston Research Center. Cambridge, MA: Boston Research Center for the 21st Century 1995.

Hog Hammock Public Library, "Bilali Muhammad: An American Story, Sapelo Island, GA," http://sapelobilali.blogspot.com/2013/04/sapelo-islands-bilali-muhammad.html.

hooks, bell. *Teaching to Transgress: Education as the Practice of Freedom*. New York: Routledge 1994.

Hsu, Hua. "The End of White America?" *The Atlantic*, January/February 2009, 46–55.

Hurston, Zora Neale. "How It Feels to Be Colored Me." In *I Love Myself When I Am Laughing and Then Again When I Am Looking Mean and Impressive*, edited by Alice Walker, 152–55. New York: Feminist Press, 1979.

———. *The Sanctified Church*. Berkeley, CA: Turtle Island, 1981.

Ikle, Fred. "Semantic Infiltration." *American Spectator*, July 10, 2010. https://spectator.org/39311_semantic-infiltration/

International Monetary Fund. "The IMF at a Glance." April 19, 2018. http://www.imf.org/en/About/Factsheets/IMF-at-a-Glance

Isasi-Diaz, Ada María. *En La Lucha / In the Struggle: A Hispanic Women's Liberation Theology*. Minneapolis: Fortress Press, 1993.

———. *Mujerista Theology: A Theology for the Twenty-First Century*. Maryknoll, NY: Orbis Books, 1996.

Jackson, Sherman A. *Islam and the Blackamerican*. New York: Oxford University Press 2005.

Jacobsen, Douglas, and Rhonda Hustedt Jacobsen. *No Longer Invisible: Religion in University Education*. New York: Oxford University Press, 2012.

Joh, Wohnee Anne. *Heart of the Cross: A Postcolonial Christology*. Louisville, KY: Westminster John Knox Press, 2006.

Johansen, Bruce, ed. *Enduring Legacies: Native American Treaties and Contemporary Controversies*. Westport, CT: Praeger, 2004.

Jones, Robert P. *The End of White Christian America*. New York: Simon and Schuster, 2016.

Jordan, Miriam. "Trump Administration Ends Temporary Protection for Haitians." *New York Times*, November 20, 2017. https://www.nytimes.com/2017/11/20/us/haitians-temporary-status.html?action=click&contentCollection=U.S.&module=RelatedCoverage&region=Marginalia&pgtype=article.

———. "Trump Administration Says That Nearly 200,000 Salvadorans Must Leave." *New York Times*, January 8, 2018. https://www.nytimes.com/2018/01/08/us/salvadorans-tps-end.html.

Jun, Jungmi. "Why Are Asian Americans Silent? Asian Americans' Negotiation Strategies for Communicative Discriminations." *Journal of International and Intercultural Communication* 5, no. 4 (November, 2012): 329–48.

Kalt, Joseph P., and Joseph William Singer. "Myths and Realities of Tribal Sovereignty: The Law and Economics of Indian Self-Rule." Faculty Research Working Papers Series, Harvard University, John F. Kennedy School of Government. March, 2004.

Kammer, Jerry. "The Hart-Celler Immigration Act of 1965." Center for Immigration Studies. September 30, 2015. https://cis.org/HartCeller-Immigration-Act-1965.

Kang, Jay Caspian. "What a Fraternity Hazing Death Revealed about the Painful Search for an Asian-American Identity." *New York Times Magazine*. August 9, 2017.

Kang, K. Connie. "Yuji Ichioka, 66: Led Way in Studying Lives of Asian Americans." Obituary, *Los Angeles Times*, September 7, 2002. http://articles.latimes.com/2002/sep/07/local/

me-yuji7. Kean, Thomas H., ed. *The 9/11 Commission Report*. National Commission on Terrorist Attacks Upon the United States. August 2004. https://9-11commission.gov/report/.

Khabeer, Su'ad Abdul. *Muslim Cool: Race, Religion, and Hip Hop in the United States*. New York: NYU Press, 2016.

Khan, Zeba. "American Muslims Have a Race Problem." *Al Jazeera America*, June 16, 2015. http://america.aljazeera.com/opinions/2015/6/american-muslims-have-a-race-problem.html.

Kiang, Peter N. "Understanding Our Perceptions of Asian Americans." Asian Society, Center for Global Education. http://asiasociety.org/education/understanding-our-perceptions-asian-Americans.

Kidwell, Clara Sue. "Ethnoastronomy as the Key to Human Intellectual Development and Social Organization." In *Native Voices: American Indian Identity and Resistance*, edited by Richard A Grounds, George E. Tinker, and David E. Wilkins, 5–19. Lawrence: University Press of Kansas, 2003.

Kim, Jung Ha. "Spiritual Buffet: The Changing Diet of America." In *Off the Menu: Asia and Asian North American Women's Religion and Theology*, edited by Rita Nakashima Brock, Jung Ha Kim, Kwok Pui-Lan, and Seung Ai Yang, 69–86. Louisville, KY: Westminster John Knox Press, 2007.

Kim, Nami. "The 'Indigestible' Asian: The Unifying Term 'Asian' in Theological Discourse." In *Off the Menu: Asia and Asian North American Women's Religion and Theology*, edited by Rita Nakashima Brock, Jung Ha Kim, Kwok Pui-Lan, and Seung Ai Yang, 23–44. Louisville, KY: Westminster John Knox Press, 2007.

King, Martin Luther, Jr. *Where Do We Go from Here: Chaos or Community?* 1968. Reprint, Boston: Beacon Press, 2010.

Klein, Christopher. "New Study Refutes Theory of How Humans Populated North America." *History*. August 10, 2016. http://www.history.com/news/new-study-refutes-theory-of-how-humans-populated-north-america.

Kulberg, Kelly Monroe. "How Should Christians Think about Immigration Amnesty?" Christianity.com. http://www.christianity.com/christian-life/political-and-social-issues/how-should-christians-think-about-immigration-amnesty.html.

Lawson, Michael L. *Dammed Indians: The Pick-Sloan Plan and the Missouri River Sioux, 1944–1980*. Norman: University of Oklahoma Press, 1982.

Lean, Nathan. *The Islamophobia Industry: How the Right Manufactures Fear of Muslims*. London: Pluto Press, 2012.

Leong, Nancy, and Erwin Chemerinsky, "Don't Use Asian Americans to Justify Anti-Affirmative Action Politics." *Washington Post*, August 3, 2017. https://www.washingtonpost.com/news/posteverything/wp/2017/08/03/dont-use-asian-americans-to-justify-anti-affirmative-action-politics/.

Levine, Dan. "Six Dreamers Sue Trump Administration over DACA Decision." *Reuters*, September 20, 2017. https://www.reuters.com/article/legal-us-usa-immigration-lawsuit/six-dreamers-sue-trump-administration-over-daca-decision-idUSKCN1BT18H.

Levy, Dan, Colleen Pero, Shawn Sanford, and Agustin Arbulu. *The Flint Water Crisis: Systemic Racism through the Lens of Flint*. Michigan Civil Rights Commission. February 17, 2017. http://www.michigan.gov/documents/mdcr/VFlintCrisisRep-F-Edited3-13-17_554317_7.pdf.

Lincoln, C. Eric. "The Muslim Mission in the Context of American Social History." In *African American Religious Studies: An Interdisciplinary Anthology*, edited by Gayraud Wilmore, 340–56. Durham, NC: Duke University Press, 1989.

Lipsitz, George. *How Racism Takes Place*. Philadelphia: Temple University Press, 2011.

———. "Walleye Warriors and White Identities: Native Americans' Treaty Rights, Composite Identities and Social Movements." *Ethnic and Racial Studies* 31, no. 1 (January 2008): 101–22.

Liu, Michael, Tracy A. M. Lai, and Kim Geron. *The Snake Dance of Asian American Activism: Community, Vision, and Power*. Lanham, MD: Lexington Books, 2008.

Livingston, Gretchen. "Today's Multiracial Babies Reflect America's Changing Demographics." Pew Research Center, *Fact Tank*, June 24, 2015. http://www.pewresearch.org/fact-tank/2015/06/24/todays-multiracial-babies-reflect-americas-changing-demographics/.

Long, Charles H. *Significations: Signs, Symbols, and Images in the Interpretation of Religion.* Milwaukee: Fortress Press, 1995.

Long, Tony. "August 3, 1492: Columbus Sets Out to Discover . . . a Trade Route." *Wired*, August 3, 2011. https://www.wired.com/2011/08/0803columbus-sets-sail-trade-route/.

Maillard, Kevin Noble. "The Pocahontas Exception of American Indian Ancestry from Racial Purity Law." *Michigan Journal of Race & Law* 12, no. 2 (2007): 351–86.

Mangum, Maurice. "Black Churches and Black Voter Suppression in Florida and Ohio." In *From Every Mountainside: Black Churches and the Broad Terrain of Civil Rights*, edited by R. Drew Smith, 189–202. Albany: State University of New York Press, 2013.

———. "Explaining Political Trust among African Americans." *Journal of Public Management and Social Policy* 23, no. 2 (Fall 2016): 84–100.

Manne, Kate. "Humanism: A Critique." *Social Theory and Practice* 42, no. 2 (April 2016): 398–415.

Martinez, Sofia. "The Second National People of Color Environmental Leadership Summit: What Next?" Southwest Research and Information Center. http://www.sric.org/voices/2003/v4n1/summit.php.

Mathis-Lilley, Ben. "The Long List of Killings Committed by White Extremists since the Oklahoma City Bombing." *Slate*, August 14, 2017. http://www.slate.com/blogs/the_slatest/2015/06/18/white_extremist_murders_killed_at_least_60_in_u_s_since_1995.html?cq_ck=1486485587473.

Mayer, Ann Elizabeth. *Islam and Human Rights: Tradition and Politics.* Boulder, CO: Westview Press, 2013.

Mbunga, Muoki. "Malcolm X and Christianity: Engaging the Criticisms and Moving towards an African-Centred Christianity That Can Advance Pan-Africanism in the 21st Century." *Journal of Intercultural Disciplines* 13 (Fall 2013): 9–22.

McClain, Dani. "What It's Like to Be Black and Pregnant When You Know How Dangerous That Can Be." *The Nation*, March 6, 2017. https://www.thenation.com/article/what-its-like-to-be-black-and-pregnant-when-you-know-how-dangerous-that-can-be/.

McCutcheon, Russell T. *Critics Not Caretakers: Redescribing the Public Study of Religion.* Albany: SUNY Press, 2001.

McWhorter, Ladelle. *Racism and Sexual Oppression in Anglo-America: A Genealogy.* Bloomington: Indiana University Press, 2009.

Meyer, Robinson. "The Standing Rock Sioux Claim 'Victory and Vindication' in Court." *The Atlantic*, June 2017. https://www.theatlantic.com/science/archive/2017/06/dakota-access-standing-rock-sioux-victory-court/530427/.

Mitchem, Stephanie Y. *Name It and Claim It? Prosperity Preaching in the Black Church.* Cleveland: Pilgrim Press, 2007.

Miyares, Ines M. "Creating Contemporary Ethnic Geographies: A Review of Immigration Law." In *Contemporary Ethnic Geographies in America*, 2nd ed., edited by Christopher A. Airriess, 31–57. Lanham, MD: Rowman & Littlefield, 2016.

Monbiot, George. "Neoliberalism—the Ideology at the Root of All Our Problems." *The Guardian*, April 15, 2016. https://www.theguardian.com/books/2016/apr/15/neoliberalism-ideology-problem-george-monbiot.

Moyers, Bill D. "What a Real President Was Like." *Washington Post*, November 13, 1988. https://www.washingtonpost.com/archive/opinions/1988/11/13/what-a-real-president-was-like/d483c1be-d0da-43b7-bde6-04e10106ff6c/?utm_term=.d547517f3504.

National Council of American Indians. *Tribal Nations and the United States: An Introduction.* Washington, DC: Embassy of Tribal Nations, 2015. http://www.ncai.org/tribalnations/introduction/Tribal_Nations_and_the_United_States_An_Introduction-web-.pdf.

Neal, Ronald B. *Democracy in the Twenty-First Century: Race, Class, Religion, and Region.* Macon, GA: Mercer University Press, 2012.

Nevaer, Louis E. V. "'Hispanic' versus 'Latino' versus "Latin.'" Hispanic Economics. http://hispaniceconomics.com/overviewofushispanics/hispaniclatinolatin.html.

Newkirk, Vann R. "The Fight for Health Care Has Always Been about Civil Rights." *The Atlantic*, June 27, 2017. https://www.theatlantic.com/politics/archive/2017/06/the-fight-for-health-care-is-really-all-about-civil-rights/531855/.

Ngai, Mae M. "The Architecture of Race in American Immigration Law: A Reexamination of the Immigration Act of 1924." *The Journal of American History* 86, no. 1 (June 1999): 67–92.

Nixon, Ron. "About 2,500 Nicaraguans to Lose Special Permission to Live in the U.S." *New York Times*, November 6, 2017. https://www.nytimes.com/2017/11/06/us/politics/immigrants-temporary-protected-status-central-americans-haitians.html?action=click&contentCollection=U.S.&module=RelatedCoverage&region=Marginalia&pgtype=article.

NoiseCat, Julian Brave. "Thirteen Issues Facing Native People beyond Mascots and Casinos." *Huffington Post*, July 30, 2015, updated August 31, 2015. http://www.huffingtonpost.com/entry/13-native-American-issues_us_55b7d801e4b0074ba5a6869c#.

Nowatzki, Mike. "Standing Rock Chairman Asks U.N. Commission to Oppose Dakota Access Pipeline." *Bismarck Tribune*, September 20, 2016. http://bismarcktribune.com/news/state-and-regional/standing-rock-chairman-asks-u-n-commission-to-oppose-dakota/article_421a94ad-d90d-5223-a1ab-fe466860d295.html.

Oliff, Helen. "Treaties Made, Treaties Broken." *Partnership with Native Americans*, March 3, 2011. http://blog.nativepartnership.org/treaties-made-treaties-broken/.

Orfield, Myron, and Thomas F. Luce. "America's Racially Diverse Suburbs: Opportunities and Challenges." Institute on Metropolitan Opportunity, Minneapolis: University of Minnesota Law School. July 20, 2012. https://www.law.umn.edu/sites/law.umn.edu/files/metro-files/diverse_suburbs_final.pdf.

Pac, Teresa. "The English-Only Movement in the US and the World in the Twenty-First Century." *Perspectives on Global Development and Technology* 2, no. 1 (2012): 192–210. http://booksandjournals.brillonline.com/content/journals/10.1163/156914912x620833.

Painter, Nell Irvin. *The History of White People.* New York: W. W. Norton, 2010.

Parliament of World's Religions. "Chicago, 1893." https://parliamentofreligions.org/parliament/new-chicago-1893/new-chicago-1893.

———. "Declaration toward a Global Ethic." September 4, 1993. https://parliamentofreligions.org/pwr_resources/_includes/FCKcontent/File/TowardsAGlobalEthic.pdf.

———. "Faith against Hate." https://parliamentofreligions.org/parliament/faith-against-hate/faith-against-hate.

Parvini, Sarah, and Victoria Kim. "25 Years after Racial Tensions Erupted, Black and Korean Communities Reflect on L.A. Riots." *Los Angeles Times*, April 29, 2017. http://www.latimes.com/local/lanow/la-me-ln-la-riots-unity-meeting-20170429-story.html.

Passel, Jeffrey, and Paul Taylor. "Who's Hispanic?" Pew Hispanic Center. May 28, 2009. http://www.pewhispanic.org/2009/05/28/whos-hispanic/.

Payne, Alan. "Redefining 'Atheism' in America: What the United States Could Learn from Europe's Protection of Atheists." *Emory International Law Review* 27 (2013): 663–701.

Perkinson, James W. *White Theology: Outing Supremacy in Modernity.* New York: Palgrave Macmillan, 2004.

Pew Research Center. "America's Changing Religious Landscape." May 12, 2015. http://www.pewforum.org/2015/05/12/americas-changing-religious-landscape/.

———. "Members of the New Age Movement." Religious Landscape Study, 2014. http://www.pewforum.org/religious-landscape-study/religious-family/new-age/.

Phillips, Kristine. "'Nobody Dies Because They Don't have Access to Health Care,' GOP Lawmaker Says. He got booed." *Washington Post*, May 7, 2017. https://www.washingtonpost.com/news/powerpost/wp/2017/05/06/nobody-dies-because-they-dont-have-access-to-health-care-gop-lawmaker-says-he-got-booed/?utm_term=.b64a387d5b56.

Pilkington, Ed. "Hookworm, a Disease of Extreme Poverty, Is Thriving in the US South. Why?" *The Guardian*, September 5, 2017. https://www.theguardian.com/us-news/2017/sep/05/hookworm-lowndes-county-alabama-water-waste-treatment-poverty.

Pirsig, Robert M. *Zen and the Art of Motorcycle Maintenance.* New York: Bantam Books, 1975.

Potok, Mark. "The Year in Hate and Extremism." The Southern Poverty Law Center. February 15, 2017. https://www.splcenter.org/fighting-hate/intelligence-report/2017/year-hate-and-extremism.

Purcell, Richard. "Trayvon, Postblackness, and the Postrace Dilemma." *Boundary 2* 40, no. 3 (2013): 139–61.

Rankine, Patrice. "'The World Is a Ghetto:' Post-Racial America(s) and the Apocalypse." In *The Trouble with Post-Blackness*, edited by Houston A. Baker and K. Merrida Simone, 162–87. New York: Columbia University Press, 2015.

Rauf, Feisal Abdul. "There Is Everything Right with Being an American Muslim," *Vital Speeches of the Day* 76, no. 11 (November 2010): 482–85.

Roediger, David R. *The Wages of Whiteness: Race and the Making of the American Working Class.* London: Verso, 1991.

Rojas, Rick. "4 Plead Guilty in Baruch College Student's Hazing Death." *New York Times*, May 15, 2017. https://www.nytimes.com/2017/05/15/nyregion/baruch-college-hazing-death-pi-delta-psi.html?_r=0.

Romero, Augustine F. and Martin Sean Arce. "Culture as a Resource: Critically Compassionate Intellectualism and Its Struggle against Racism, Fascism, and Intellectual Apartheid in Arizona." *Journal of Public Law and Policy* 31 no. 1 (2009): 179–217.

Ryo, Emily. "On Normative Effects of Immigration Law." *Stanford Journal of Civil Rights and Civil Liberties* 13, no. 1 (2017): 95–135.

Sablich, Liz. "7 Findings That Illustrate Racial Disparities in Education." Brookings, Brown Center Chalkboard, June 6, 2016. https://www.brookings.edu/blog/brown-center-chalkboard/2016/06/06/7-findings-that-illustrate-racial-disparities-in-education/.

Said, Edward. *Orientalism.* New York: Vintage Books, 1978.

Sanchez, Ray. "After ICE Arrests, Fear Spreads among Undocumented Immigrants." CNN, February 2017. http://www.cnn.com/2017/02/11/politics/immigration-roundups-community-fear/.

Sanders, Laura, Ramiro Martinez, Margaret Harner, Melanie Hamer, Pilar Homer, and Jorge Delva. "Grassroots Responsiveness to Human Rights Abuse: History of the Washtenaw Interfaith Coalition for Immigrant Rights." *Social Work* 58, no. 3 (April 2013): 117–25.

Sandstrom, Aleksandra. "Faith on the Hill: The Religious Composition of the 115th Congress." Pew Research Center. January 3, 2017. http://www.pewforum.org/2017/01/03/faith-on-the-hill-115/.

Sarsour, Linda. "Islamophobes Are Attacking Me Because I'm Their Worst Nightmare." *Washington Post*, July 9, 2017. https://www.washingtonpost.com/opinions/linda-sarsour-no-i-did-not-call-for-violence-against-trump-heres-what-jihad-means-to-me/2017/07/09/c2acb086-64b6-11e7-9928-22d00a47778f_story.html?hpid=hp_no-name_opinion-card-f%3Ahomepage%2Fstory&utm_term=.3e8970ae007c.

Schilling, Vincent. "The Story of Pocahontas: Historical Myths versus Sad Reality." *Indian Country Today*, March 21, 2017. https://indiancountrymedianetwork.com/history/genealogy/true-story-pocahontas-historical-myths-versus-sad-reality/.

Schmidt-Leukel, Perry. "Buddhism and the Idea of Human Rights: Resonances and Dissonances." In *Buddhist Approaches to Human Rights*, edited by Carmen Meinert and Hans-Bernd Zollner. New Brunswick, NJ: Transaction Publisher, 2010.

Scott, Mia. "Nielsen 2016 Report: Black Millennials Close the Digital Divide." *Nielsen*, October 17, 2016. http://www.nielsen.com/us/en/press-room/2016/nielsen-2016-report-black-millennials-close-the-digital-divide.html.

SCOTUSblog. "Dollar General Corporation v. Mississippi Band of Choctaw Indians." June 23, 2016. http://www.scotusblog.com/case-files/cases/dollar-general-corporation-v-mississippi-band-of-choctaw-indians/.

———. "Fisher v. University of Texas at Austin." June 23, 2016. http://www.scotusblog.com/case-files/cases/fisher-v-university-of-texas-at-austin-2/.

Shanmugasundaram, Swathi. "Anti-Sharia Law Bills in the United States." Southern Poverty Law Center. August 8, 2017. https://www.splcenter.org/hatewatch/2017/08/08/anti-sharia-law-bills-united-states.

Shellnutt, Kate. "Evangelical Experts Oppose Trump's Refugee Ban." *Christianity Today*. January 25, 2017. http://www.christianitytoday.com/news/2017/january/evangelical-experts-oppose-trump-plan-to-ban-refugees-syria.html.

Singer, Peter. *The Most Good You Can Do: How Effective Altruism Is Changing Ideas about Living Ethically.* New Haven, CT: Yale University Press, 2015.

Slessarev-Jamir, Helene. *Prophetic Activism: Progressive Religious Justice Movements in Contemporary America.* New York: NYU Press, 2011.

Smith, Gregory A., and Alan Cooperman. "The Factors Driving the Growth of the Religious 'Nones' in the U.S." Pew Research Center, *Fact Tank*, September 14, 2016. http://www.pewresearch.org/fact-tank/2016/09/14/the-factors-driving-the-growth-of-religious-nones-in-the-u-s/.

Sorkin, Amy Davidson. "Steve King and the Case of the Cantaloupe Calves." *New Yorker*, July 25, 2013. http://www.newyorker.com/news/amy-davidson/steve-king-and-the-case-of-the-cantaloupe-calves.

Spickard, James V. "On the Epistemology of Post-Colonial Ethnography." In *Personal Knowledge and Beyond: Reshaping the Ethnography of Religion*, edited by James V. Spickard, J. Shawn Landres, and Meredith B. McGuire, 237–52. New York: NYU Press, 2002.

Spivak, Gayatri Chakravorty. *Other Asias.* Malden, MA: Blackwell Publishing 2003.

State of Missouri v. Darren Wilson. Grand Jury Volume V, September 16, 2014. https://www.documentcloud.org/documents/1371222-wilson-testimony.html.

Stephens, Alexander H. "'Corner Stone' Speech: Savannah, Georgia. March 21, 1861." Teaching American History. http://teachingamericanhistory.org/library/document/cornerstone-speech/.

Stout, David. "A Nation Challenged: The First Lady; Mrs. Bush Cites Women's Plight under Taliban." *New York Times*, November 18, 2001. http://www.nytimes.com/2001/11/18/us/a-nation-challenged-the-first-lady-mrs-bush-cites-women-s-plight-under-taliban.html?mcubz=0.

Stratton, Stephen P. "Mindfulness and Contemplation: Secular and Religious Traditions in Western Context." *Counseling and Values* 60, no. 1 (April 2015): 100–118.

Stringfellow, Thornton. "A Scriptural View of Slavery." In *Slavery Defended, Views of the Old South*, edited by Eric L. McKittrick, 86–98. Englewood Cliffs, NJ: Prentice-Hall, 1963.

Sugrue, Thomas J. *The Origins of the Urban Crisis: Race and Inequality in Postwar Detroit.* Princeton, NJ: Princeton University Press, 1996.

Sullivan, Shannon. *Good White People: The Problem with Middle-Class White Anti-Racism.* Albany: SUNY Press, 2014.

Swarns, Rachel L., "272 Slaves Were Sold to Save Georgetown. What Does It Owe Their Descendants?" *New York Times*, April 16, 2016. http://www.nytimes.com/2016/04/17/us/georgetown-university-search-for-slave-descendants.html?_r=0.

Tan, Jonathan Y. "Dynamics of Interfaith Collaborations in Postcolonial Asia: Prospects and Opportunities." In *Postcolonial Practice of Ministry: Leadership, Liturgy, and Interfaith Engagement*, edited by Kwok Pui-lan and Stephen Burns, 167–82. Lanham, MD: Lexington Books, 2016.

Taylor, Dorceta. *Toxic Communities: Environmental Racism, Industrial Pollution, and Residential Mobility.* New York: NYU Press, 2014.

Taylor, Michael. *Contesting Constructed Indian-ness: The Intersection of the Frontier, Masculinity, and Whiteness in Native American Mascot Representations.* New York: Lexington Books, 2015.

Taylor, Paul, ed. *The Rise of Asian Americans.* Pew Research Center. April 4, 2013. http://www.pewsocialtrends.org/files/2013/04/Asian-Americans-new-full-report-04-2013.pdf.

Tidwell, Jordan. "FBI Investigates Graffiti Vandalism at Two Mosques, Suspects Wanted." 5News KFSM, October 20, 2016. http://5newsonline.com/2016/10/20/fbi-investigates-graffiti-vandalism-at-two-fort-smith-mosques-suspects-wanted/.

Tinker, George E. *Spirit and Resistance: Political Theology and American Indian Liberation.* Minneapolis: Fortress Press, 2004.

Townes, Carimah. "Cop Justifies Repeated Shooting of Unarmed Black Man with the 'Zombie' Defense." *Think Progress*, August 6, 2015. https://thinkprogress.org/cop-justifies-repeated-shooting-of-unarmed-black-man-with-the-zombie-defense-3fb6b17b86ba.

Tran, Alisia G. T. T., and Richard M. Lee. "You Speak English Well! Asian Americans' Reactions to an Exceptionalizing Stereotype." *Journal of Counseling Psychology* 61, no. 1 (2014): 484–90.

Trinh T. Min-ha. *Woman, Native, Other: Writing, Postcoloniality, and Feminism.* Bloomington: Indiana University Press, 1989.

Ummel, Deborah. "Dream or Nightmare? The Impact of American Eugenics, Past and Present." *Cross Currents* 66, no. 3 (September 2016): 389–98.

Unidos US. "We Are Unidos US." https://www.unidosus.org/about-us/.

United States Commission on International Religious Freedom. "USCIRF Releases 2017 Annual Report." April 26, 2017. http://www.uscirf.gov/news-room/press-releases/uscirf-releases-2017-annual-report.

United States Department of Justice, The. "Fair Housing Act." August 6, 2015. https://www.justice.gov/crt/fair-housing-act-2.

U.S. Equal Employment Opportunity Commission. "What You Should Know: EEOC's Fiscal Year 2016 Highlights." https://www.eeoc.gov/eeoc/newsroom/wysk/2016_highlights.cfm.

Vongkiatkajorn, Kanyakrit. "Here Are the Churches Fighting Back against Trump's Immigration Crackdown." *Mother Jones*, February 21, 2017. http://www.motherjones.com/politics/2017/02/sanctuary-church-movement-trump-deportation/.

Wallis, Jim. *America's Original Sin: Racism, White Privilege, and the Bridge to a New America.* Grand Rapids, MI: Brazos Press, 2016.

———. *The Soul of Politics: Beyond "Religious Right" and "Secular Left."* San Diego: Harvest Book, 1995.

Ware, Lawrence. "Why I'm Leaving the Southern Baptist Convention." *New York Times*, July 17, 2017. https://www.nytimes.com/2017/07/17/opinion/why-im-leaving-the-southern-baptist-convention.html?src=me&_r=0.

Ware, Rudolph T., III. *The Walking Qur'an: Islamic Education, Embodied Knowledge, and History in West Africa.* Chapel Hill: University of North Carolina Press, 2014.

Warikoo, Niraj. "Vincent Chin Murder 35 Years Later: History Repeating Itself." *Detroit Free Press*, June 23, 2017. http://www.freep.com/story/news/2017/06/24/murder-vincent-chin-35-years-ago-remembered-asian-americans/420354001/.

Weheliye, Alexander G. *Habeas Viscus: Racializing Assemblages, Biopolitics, and Black Feminist Theories of the Human.* Durham, NC: Duke University Press, 2014.

Welch, Sharon D. *Real Peace, Real Security: The Challenges of Global Citizenship.* Minneapolis: Fortress Press, 2008.

White, Abbey. "A Major Global Foundation Just Pledged $1 Million to the Standing Rock Sioux." *The Nation*, June 19, 2017. https://www.thenation.com/article/a-major-global-foundation-just-pledged-1-million-to-the-standing-rock-sioux/.

White, Charles. "An Account of the Regular Gradation in Man, and in Different Animals and Vegetables, and from the Former to the Latter." Read to the Literary and Philosophical Society of Manchester at different meetings, in the year 1795. https://archive.org/details/b24924507.

Whitford, David. "A Calvinist Heritage to the 'Curse of Ham': Assessing the Accuracy of a Claim about Racial Subordination." *Church History and Religious Culture* 90, no. 1 (2010): 25–45.

Williams, Timothy. "Quietly, Indians Reshape Cities and Reservations." *New York Times*, April 13, 2013. http://www.nytimes.com/2013/04/14/us/as-american-indians-move-to-cities-old-and-new-challenges-follow.html.

Wilmore, Gayraud S. *Black Religion and Black Radicalism: An Interpretation of the Religious History of Afro-American People.* 2nd ed. Maryknoll, NY: Orbis Books, 1983.

Wilson, Valerie. "People of Color Will Be a Majority of the American Working Class in 2032." Economic Policy Institute. June 9, 2016. http://www.epi.org/publication/the-changing-demographics-of-americas-working-class/.

Winant, Howard. *Racial Conditions.* Minneapolis: University of Minnesota Press, 1994.

———. *The World Is a Ghetto: Race and Democracy since World War II.* New York: Perseus Books, 2001.

Winter, Jana, and Sharon Weinberger, "The FBI's New U.S. Terrorist Threat: 'Black Identity Extremists.'" *Foreign Policy*, October 6, 2017. http://foreignpolicy.com/2017/10/06/the-fbi-has-identified-a-new-domestic-terrorist-threat-and-its-black-identity-extremists/.

Woods, Ashley. "Nancy Kaffer Wins 2015 Scripps Howard Award." *Detroit Free Press*, March 8, 2016. http://www.freep.com/story/opinion/columnists/nancy-kaffer/2016/03/08/columnist-nancy-kaffer-wins-2015-scripps-howard-award/81499558/.

Working Group on Slavery, Memory, and Reconciliation, *Slavery, Memory, and Reconciliation*. Washington, DC: Georgetown University, Summer 2016. https://www.documentcloud.org/documents/3038068-Georgetown-University-Working-Group-on-Slavery.html.

World Bank. "History." http://www.worldbank.org/en/about/history.

Wu, Ellen D. *The Color of Success: Asian Americans and the Origins of the Model Minority*. Princeton, NJ: Princeton University Press, 2013.

Wu, Frank H. "Embracing Mistaken Identity: How the Vincent Chin Case Unified Asian Americans." *Harvard Journal of Asian American Policy Review* 19 (2010): 17–22.

Young, Iris Marion. *Inclusion and Democracy*. New York: Oxford University Press, 2000.

———. *Justice and the Politics of Difference*. Princeton, NJ: Princeton University Press, 1990.

Zeiny, Esmaeil, and Noraini Md Yusof. "The Said and Not-Said: New Grammar of Visual Representation." *GEMA Online® Journal of Language Studies* 16, no. 1 (February 2016): 125–41.

Zhang, Qin. "The Mitigating Effects of Intergroup Contact on Negative Stereotypes, Perceived Threats, and Harmful Discriminatory Behavior toward Asian Americans." *Communication Research Reports* 33, no. 1(January–March 2016): 1–8.

Zimring, Carl A. *Clean and White: A History of Environmental Racism in the United States*. New York: NYU Press, 2015.

Zirin, Dave. "A Majority-Immigrant Church Vandalized with 'Trump Nation/Whites Only,' Becomes a Site of Resistance." *The Nation*, November 21, 2016. https://www.thenation.com/article/a-majority-immigrant-church-vandalized-with-trump-nationwhites-only-becomes-a-site-of-resistance/.

UNITED NATIONS DOCUMENTS

"Declaration on the Elimination of All Forms of Intolerance and of Discrimination Based on Religion or Belief." November 25, 1981. http://www.un.org/documents/ga/res/36/a36r055.htm.

"International Covenant on Civil and Political Rights," United Nations, Treaty Series, No. 14668, Article 14, no. 3 (a), (c) and no. 4. December 1966. https://treaties.un.org/doc/publication/unts/volume%20999/volume-999-i-14668-english.pdf.

"Report of the Working Group of Experts on People of African Descent on Its Mission to the United States of America." August 18, 2016. http://www.ushrnetwork.org/sites/ushrnetwork.org/files/unwgepad_us_visit_final_report_9_15_16.pdf.

"United Nations Declaration on the Rights of Indigenous Peoples." March 2008. http://www.un.org/esa/socdev/unpfii/documents/DRIPS_en.pdf

WEBSITES

American Humanist Association, https://americanhumanist.org/what-is-humanism/.

Black Lives Matter. http://blacklivesmatter.com/about/.

"The Boston Declaration." November 20, 2017. https://thebostondeclaration.com/.

Colon Free Trade Zone. http://www.colonfreetradezone.com/freezone-colon.html.

Dakota Access Pipeline Facts. https://daplpipelinefacts.com/.

Define American. https://defineamerican.com/.

Indivisible. https://www.indivisible.org/act-locally/.

Poor People's Campaign: A National Call for Moral Revival. https://poorpeoplescampaign.org/

Reparations.me. http://www.reparations.me/about.

Sanctuary Movement. http://www.sanctuarynotdeportation.org/.

Society for Race, Ethnicity, and Religion. https://www.sorer.org/.

State Civil Rights Offices. http://civilrights.findlaw.com/enforcing-your-civil-rights/state-civil-rights-offices.html.

Moorish Science Temple web page. https://www.msta1928.org/.

United States Commission on International Religious Freedom. http://www.uscirf.gov/about-uscirf.

Index

Religion in the Modern World

Series Advisors
Kwok Pui-lan, Episcopal Divinity School
Joerg Rieger, Southern Methodist University

This series explores how various religious traditions wrestle with the dynamic and changing role of religion in the modern world and examines how past changes reflect on today's critical issues. Accessibly and engagingly written, books in this series will look at secularization, global society, gender, race, class, and sexuality and their relation to religious life and religious movements.

Titles in Series

Not God's People: Insiders and Outsiders in the Biblical World by Lawrence M. Wills
The Food and Feasts of Jesus: The Original Mediterranean Diet, with Menus and Recipes by Douglas E. Neel and Joel A. Pugh
Occupy Religion: Theology of the Multitude by Joerg Rieger and Kwok Pui-lan
The Politics of Jesús: A Hispanic Political Theology by Miguel A. De La Torre

CPSIA information can be obtained
at www.ICGtesting.com
Printed in the USA
FFHW021350270219
50749995-56150FF